SYNTAX AND GRAMMAR

Frag. Fragmentary sentence
D.M. Dangling modifier pp.
M.M. Misplaced modifier pp. 302–303
Agr. Agreement of subject and verb pp. 290–293
Ref. Reference of pronoun and antecedent p. 311
R.O. Run-on (fused) sentence pp. 311–312
// ism Faulty parallelism pp. 303–305
C.S. Comma splice pp. 294–296

SPELLING

Sp. General Discussion pp. 312–316
Sp: ie i before e rule p. 315
Sp: cons. Double consonant rule p. 315
Sp: wds. Troublesome words p. 316

PUNCTUATION

⌃ Comma pp. 306–307
⌃ Semicolon pp. 305–306
⌃ Dash p. 308
⌄ Quotation marks pp. 309–310
cap. Capitals pp. 293–294
! Exclamation point p. 311
⌃ Period p. 305
⌃ Colon pp. 308–309
⌄ Apostrophe p. 316
( ) Parentheses p. 308
[ ] Brackets p. 293
? Question mark p. 311
No. Numbers p. 303

NEATNESS AND CONVENTIONS IN MANUSCRIPT FORM

Accept. Form Paper acceptable for type and size, legibility, title centered, one inch margin frame around all four edges of paper, erasures barely discernible, pages numbered. p. 262

College Writing

College Writing SECOND EDITION

Harry H. Crosby
BOSTON UNIVERSITY

George F. Estey
BOSTON UNIVERSITY

HARPER & ROW, Publishers
New York, Evanston, San Francisco, London

Sponsoring Editor: *George A. Middendorf*
Project Editor: *Karla B. Philip*
Designer: *Frances Torbert Tilley*
Production Supervisor: *Will C. Jomarrón*

COLLEGE WRITING, Second Edition

Library of Congress Cataloging in Publication Data

Crosby, Harry H.
  College writing.

  Includes bibliographical references and index.
  1. English language—Rhetoric. I. Estey, George F.,
joint author. II. Title.
PE1408.C717   1975   808'.042   74-17696
ISBN 0-06-041439-1

Acknowledgments

American Heritage Publishing Company, Inc., definition of "speed." Copyright ©
1969, 1970, 1971, 1973 by American Heritage Publishing Company, Inc. Reprinted by permission from the *American Heritage Dictionary of the English
Language*.

Jacques Barzun, "In Favor of Capital Punishment." Reprinted from *The American
Scholar*, Volume 31, Number 2 (Spring 1962). Copyright © 1962 by the
United Chapters of Phi Beta Kappa. By permission of the publishers.

Peter L. Berger and Brigette Berger, "The Blueing of America." Reprinted by
permission of *The New Republic*, © 1971 Harrison-Blaine of New Jersey, Inc.

Max Black, "Principles of Really Sound Thinking." Reprinted from *Scientific
Monthly*, Volume 66 (March 1949), pp. 232–234.

Stokely Carmichael, "Toward a Black Liberation." Copyright © 1966 by the
Student Non-Violent Coordinating Committee. Reprinted from the *Massachusetts Review*, September 1966.

"The Enlisted Man." From "The Talk of the Town;" © 1973, The New Yorker
Magazine, Inc.

E. M. Forster, "India Again" in *Two Cheers for Democracy*. Reprinted by permission of Harcourt Brace Jovanovich, Inc.

Leonard Freeman, "Superstar Shines." *Episcopalian,* January 1971. Reprinted with permission.

FUNKY WINKERBEAN cartoon by Tom Batiuk. *Boston Sunday Globe,* September 29, 1974. Copyright by Field Enterprises, Inc. Courtesy of Publishers-Hall Syndicate.

Howard Mumford Jones, "Patriotism—But How?" *The Atlantic Monthly,* November 1938. Copyright © 1938, renewed 1966, by The Atlantic Monthly Company, Boston, Mass. Reprinted with permission.

Kevin Kelly, "Interview of Lloyd Corbin." *The Boston Globe,* March 12, 1972. Courtesy of *The Boston Globe.*

Jonathan Landau, "Review of Bessie Smith Re-release." *The Boston Phoenix,* August 1, 1970. Reprinted by permission of the author.

MISS PEACH cartoons by Mell Lazarus. Reprinted by permission of Publishers-Hall Syndicate.

Max Lerner, *America As a Civilization.* Copyright 1957 by Simon & Schuster, Inc. Reprinted by permission.

James A. Michener, *The Quality of Life.* Copyright © 1970 by J. B. Lippincott Company. Reprinted by permission.

Robert Nemiroff, *To Be Young, Gifted and Black: Lorraine Hansberry in Her Own Words.* Reprinted by permission of the William Morris Agency, Inc. Copyright © 1960 by Robert Nemiroff and Robert Nemiroff as Executor of the estate of Lorraine Hansberry.

George Orwell, "Shooting an Elephant" in *Shooting an Elephant and Other Essays.* Copyright 1945, 1946, 1949, 1950 by Sonia Brownell Orwell. Reprinted by permission of Harcourt Brace Jovanovich, Inc.

J. L. Simmons and Barry Winograd, "The Hang-Loose Ethic." Reprinted from J. L. Simmons and Barry Winograd, *It's Happening: A Portrait of the Youth Scene Today,* by permission of McNally & Loftin, Publishers.

THE SMALL SOCIETY cartoons by Brickman. Reprinted by permission of the Washington Star Syndicate, Inc.

"Sweet Tooth, Sour Facts," from "Wonderful World of Words." Reprinted by permission from *Time,* The Weekly Newsmagazine; Copyright Time, Inc.

Roul Tunley, "America's Unhealthy Children." *Harper's Magazine,* May 1966. Copyright © 1966 by Minneapolis Star and Tribune Co., Inc. Reprinted by permission of the author.

"A Visit to La Cantina." Excerpted from the column "The Fat and the Lean," *The Boston Phoenix,* March 6, 1973. Reprinted with permission.

E. B. White, "This Is New York." Abridged from *Here Is New York* by E. B. White. Copyright 1949 by E. B. White. Reprinted by permission of Harper & Row, Publishers.

David B. Wilson, editorial column of May 21, 1973. Courtesy of *The Boston Globe.*

Preface

Students who realize that they are using a second edition of a textbook may wonder what they will be expected to do and learn that was different for students who worked with the first edition. For those students who are concerned, we have provided a brief summary of both the similarities and the changes that have been made in this edition.

The second edition is similar to the first in that it attempts, at every opportunity, to stress the writing *process* rather than the writing *product*. Students need to be able to recognize good writing; hence samples of excellent writing of the past and present are included. More importantly, students need to know how excellent writing is developed; accordingly, you will find numerous case histories of how a student's ideas generated an outline, a rough draft, a fair copy, and how an "almost-submitted" paper underwent rigorous last-minute revision.

This brings up a problem and an opportunity for us to state our policy. What should be done with student papers? Should they be edited by text-book authors? In this edition we have decided that in all respects, student papers would be published as we received them. Our theory is that discussion of papers for which there is still something to be desired can be valuable. Since all of these papers have room for improvement, and some are even replete with spelling and grammatical errors, we have identified these papers as "Uncorrected Drafts." You will see many student papers, warts and all.

Secondly, this edition is similar to its predecessor in that in every instance we have tried to demonstrate the rationale behind any suggestions we have made. We know of the prescriptive-descriptive controversy. In the former case the student is told, "Do this because it is right." In the latter case the student is told, "Do this because it is done by effective writers." We have tried to go beyond both of these. We tell the student, "Try this because we think it will, in certain ways, help you achieve *your* objective."

What we refer to as the "rhetorical imperative" is a case in point. Organization can, in part, be taught by familiarizing a student with the standard patterns of development. Beyond this, students can be helped by becoming sensitive to how they create questions in the minds of their readers when they make controversial or provocative statements. When the student writes, "That politician deserves his shady reputation," the student *ought* to know that the reader will wonder, "What reputation? What has he done to deserve it?" With this sensitivity, student writers know the issues they must face and the structure of writing needed for the subject. Organization grows out of such awareness, as well as out of a familiarity with cause-and-effect structure.

Finally, this edition is similar in that we firmly believe that writing is infinitely more than just the application of certain principles and knowledge about the language. If writing is anything, it is a social event. For that reason, we continue to stress the psychology and sociology of rhetoric. Writers must know themselves—and the effect their temperaments and authority will have on the message and the reader. Writers must know a reader will react to the writer, the message, and the situation.

Although every chapter has had some revision of text, illustrations, and exercises, the major changes can be explained as follows:

It is healthy for a student to have some early triumphs. We know that while few educators are comfortable with the concept of relevance, most students prefer to do what seems to have some immediate worth. For this reason we have given more emphasis to the writing of précis and journals. Most students accept their role as students, and they know that writing careful condensations of their reading and study materials is very useful. They quickly produce good products. Most students also realize that they are living in an important time, not only in their personal lives, but also in the development of our country and our civilization. If they give their journals a college try, they will create valuable contributions to social history. The instructor enjoys reading them, and the students know that their work will be a significant personal record in a very few weeks. This early sense of triumph is a sweet association with the writing process.

Secondly, we question the method of instruction employed when a body of knowledge is "covered." Students *do* forget, but this is not crucial if during the "coverage" certain attitudes and sensitivities have been strengthened. In the first section there is much discussion about writing, which we hope will help the students go forward in their training. But the real function of the section on "Pre-Writing" is to help students feel at home in the world of communication. We have come more and more to accept Jerome Bruner's concept of the process of education that suggests that the student should meet a concept under one set of circumstances and then meet it again under a different set. In Part I, students will be introduced to ideas of organization, development, and style; in Parts II, III, and IV they are exposed to them again—more deeply, more analytically. Students do not learn to organize in one lesson; they must work on improvement one step at a time. The ebb and flow of consideration—the repetition, if you wish—which is a new characteristic of the second edition of *College Writing* is based on this precept.

Third, two chapters that appeared in the first edition have been dropped. They were included in the first edition because we think that college students should have as part of their liberal education a store of information about how people think and how the English language developed. Many courses in freshman composition are of one semester's duration, while others are part of a composition-literature course, neither of which leaves time for the in-depth study of logic and language provided in the first edition. We still maintain that this information is important—in fact, we hope to make it available in a separate book—but we want this to be a specialized book, focused entirely on the process of writing.

Finally, to demonstrate our increasing conviction that students have important ideas to express, the "Library Paper" has become "The Research Paper." Students are encouraged to support their library investigations with reports from their own experiences, interviews, questionnaires, observations, and statistical compilations—in short, to engage in primary, original, and creative research.

As we worked on this revision, we became more concerned with the sources of our ideas. This conscious concern for theory and philosophy made us more aware of what Aristotle told us about structure, Bacon and Mill about cause and effect, Jerome Bruner and Robert Zollner about learning theory and the process of education, Martin Buber about impersonality, Chaim Perelmen and Northrup Frye about the sociology of rhetoric, and Daniel Fogarty, Martin Steinman, and Edward Corbett about classical roots for rhetoric. We list these names not so much to thank them as to identify the underpinning of the instruction contained in this textbook.

In our first edition we acknowledged our debt and gratitude to various teachers, associates, and scholars. We thank them again; however, after the many responses we received from users of the first edition, we will not list names because we may unintentionally miss an important contribution. We do give special thanks to Louise Rorabacher, Roger Wilcox, and Angela Peckenpaugh who so helpfully critiqued a draft of this edition.

In four books we have thanked Horatio LaFauci for his support. Now that he is no longer our Dean, no longer—figuratively speaking—signing our paychecks, we reiterate our respect for a man about whom a student once said, "There goes class."

Finally, we wish to reaffirm our affection and appreciation to our wives, Barbara Estey and Jean Crosby, for their cooperation and encouragement.

H.H.C.
G.F.E.

Contents

Part ☐ Pre-Writing

Chapter 1 A Brief Introduction

If you wish to converse with me, define your terms.—*Voltaire*

What is Rhetoric?

Before we go far in this college study, we should understand and agree upon what we are doing.

Rhetoric is not a study of grammar, spelling, and punctuation. It is not a study of linguistics. It is not a study of a style book filled with rules about what to do and not to do. These may all be part of rhetoric, but it is more than any one of them.

Primitive human beings make noise or scratch marks on the walls of caves. Many years go by before the noise and marks mean more than "This territory occupied. Keep out." Men and animals get the message, but only men go beyond that form of communication. Man develops a complex language.

Words, by themselves, may not mean much. An outburst of words may serve only to make you feel better. You may use words for *self-expression* and have no *communication*. Communication is the act of transmitting thoughts, attitudes, and/or opinions. Self-expression can be obscure; communication must not be. If it is not clear, it is not communication.

Rhetoric is more than communication.

```
       RHETORIC
          ↑
    COMMUNICATION
          ↑
   SELF-EXPRESSION
          ↑
  NOISE, SCRATCHES
```

Rhetoric is the use of words in a way that will cause a reader or listener to *want* to understand or agree with you and to do so. Communication requires language and logic. Rhetoric requires language and logic—plus psychology and sociology. Rhetoric does not take place with you alone in a forest. Rhetoric involves you, your reader, your message, and the time and circumstances in which you are writing. You must consider them all.

At its best, rhetoric goes far beyond communication. In the spring of the year 430 B.C., at the funeral of a friend, Pericles gave an oration before the citizens of Athens. His message was simple: he wanted Athenians to continue the Peloponnesian War. His message was successful, because he appealed to the individual pride and social values of his audience. He described Athens as an ideal state—where free and intelligent citizens obeyed a just code of laws, where men of merit found their way to leadership, where political efficiency existed but did not strangle commerce, education, and art. Athens was all of that, and Athenians were part of it.

In a high-pitched voice an unpopular president, speaking at a cemetery in Pennsylvania on November 19, 1863, showed that a battle just finished was part of one of man's noblest experiments. Abraham Lincoln's Gettysburg Address was high rhetoric.

In 1927, in a Massachusetts jail, an Italian shoe factory worker named Sacco wrote a letter that pointed wonderingly at the twist of fate which made his impending death an important cause. His appeal to individual sympathy and national pride went beyond the simple fact that he was saying good-bye. When Martin Luther King said, "I have a dream," his audience felt that each step forward in the civil rights march was a personal and social reward.

When you write home, "Dad, I need ten dollars," you are communicating. He will get the message. But if you tell the whole, vivid story—that you are depressed and need an evening out, that after a pleasant weekend you will be able to dedicate yourself once again to your education—you will appeal to his sympathy and social conviction. He may be more likely to reach for his checkbook.

To move from Pericles, Lincoln, Sacco, and Martin Luther King to your father's checkbook is to plunge from the sublime to something less, but each is an instance of rhetoric at work. Each is communication plus psychology and sociology.

And that is what rhetoric is all about.

The Psychology of Rhetoric

As you sit at your desk, faced with the problem of writing for a vast, unseen audience, you should realize that your reader can have almost any state of mind.

1. How knowledgeable is he on the subject? Is he
   ignorant?
   uninformed?
   slightly informed?
   well informed?
2. Does he accept new ideas easily? Is he
   radical?
   liberal?
   neutral?
   conservative?
   reactionary?
3. At the moment, how does he stand about your subject and opinion?
   Is he antagonistic?
   Is he doubtful?
   Is he neutral?
   Are his feelings favorable?
   Does he agree with you?
4. What does your reader think of you as an authority? Does he
   distrust you?
   suspect you?
   feel neutral toward you?
   accept you?
   respect you?
5. What is the effect of your personality, temperament, and presentation on your reader?
   Is she antagonized?
   Does she question you?
   Is she attracted to you?
   Does she find you absolutely charismatic?

Because you must ask these questions as you write, because you try to get into the mind of your reader, and because you are going beyond problems of language, you are dealing in psychology.

The Sociology
of Rhetoric

Your reader and you are only two aspects of the total rhetoric system. Your message is a third. The three—you, your audience, and the message —do not exist in a vacuum. There is a fourth aspect—the *situation* at the time you write.

There are times when people are interested in new ideas; there are times when you could not sell a new idea for love or money. There are times when your audience might buy your idea if they were not preoccupied with more intense problems or if their money were not being soaked up elsewhere.

What we are talking about is sociology. What are the current problems which influence the hope of your getting your audience to say, "I understand" or "I agree"?

A college student had a great idea. He devised a simple system for mounting numbers and street names on a panel. He was sure he could make a fortune selling the address plates to homeowners.

In the first town where he tried to sell his product, he had a rough time. The citizens were unfriendly and did not care whether people could find their houses. In the second town everything went wrong. A factory had just closed, people were out of work, and money was scarce. The police enforced the so-called Green River law, which prohibited peddling by out-of-town agents, and he spent a few hours in jail before he was summarily carried in a police car to a bus station. In a third town he found a neighborhood where people needed and wanted address numbers for their sparkling new homes—and he did (almost) make his fortune.

Sociologically, in the first and second towns the situations were wrong. In the third the situation was just right; he hardly had to give a sales talk. In the first town if he could demonstrate how clear, valuable, and useful his signs were, he could sell enough to make it worth his time. In the second town no sales talk would have had any effect. He had to deal with sociology.

Obviously, a person can deliberately confuse people by using dishonest psychology and by taking advantage of a social situation. When a writer appeals only to the emotions and has no substance to his message, he is misusing rhetoric. When he takes advantage of a situation, as Hitler did when he used the poverty and humiliation of a nation to turn Germany into a fascist state, he is practicing demagoguery.

Since rhetoric can be misused, the process often falls into disrepute. In this course we hope to teach you to avoid being the victim of bad rhetoric and to use rhetoric wisely.

A Complete Definition

From all of this it should be clear that rhetoric is complex. It is a college subject. It is the study and practice of the skill by which a speaker or writer, aware of the situation in which he is writing, makes the best use of his own authority and personality to transmit a message that causes the reader, affected by attitude, awareness, and inclination, to say, "I understand" or "I agree."

Project

For the first pages of the notes you have taken for your other subjects, define and, in the method used in this chapter, describe each course you are enrolled in. Your definition should tell what the course is and what it is not. Contrast it only to courses with which it might be confused. Is economics, for instance, part of sociology? The first word in the title "Western Civilization" reveals that the course is not what? Tell what the goals or objectives of the course are. If you are not certain what one of your courses deals with, resolve to find out.

Chapter 2

Getting Some Early Positive Reinforcement with Précis and Journals

Two Early Triumphs
Projects—Précis
Projects—Journals

This book has been written to help you become a more effective writer. Before we can hope for success, you must answer the question, "Do you really want to improve?"

Your answer is all-important.

Abraham Lincoln desired so strongly to write well that with a piece of chalk on the back of a shovel he wrote lines from Shakespeare in his own words. Benjamin Franklin wanted so badly to be a good writer that he copied and recopied the works of Addison and Steele. The black martyr, Malcolm X, decided in jail that wherever he wanted to go, he could get there faster if he could write very well—which he proceeded to learn to do.

Are you that ambitious to improve your writing?

Is there anyone who cannot profit from being an effective writer? Ahead of you are all kinds of writing: essay examinations, term papers, that letter home asking for just ten more dollars this month, a letter to a friend, a letter to an editor or a congressman, a report to the police court that your stereo or bike has been stolen, a job application or an application to graduate school—reams of letters, reports, position papers, memos, and even published articles and books. They are waiting for you. Will you be able to do them well? Will you be better off if you can?

Writing may be the single best means of discovering what you really think. As Francis Bacon wrote, "Reading maketh a full man; conference a ready man; and writing an exact man." What you write you will scrutinize. You will ask yourself if that is really what you believe. If you would know yourself, write.

As a student, you may know that writing is important, yet when you sit down to write, you suddenly get an abiding yen for something to eat. You suddenly have to go to the toilet. You turn on the stereo. You scratch your ear and notice you have a rough fingernail. Your desk is a mess; you must take a moment or a half hour to straighten it out.

Who wants to work on that theme anyway? Every theme you ever wrote came back dripping with red ink and ringing with impolite comments.

Many professional writers have the same problem. Herman Melville had his housekeeper lock him in his study and keep him there until he had written so many lines. Nathaniel Hawthorne wrote in his journals about his "hated pen." Anthony Trollope kept a rotten apple in his desk because he liked the smell and it added at least one pleasant aspect to his tedious task. Most writers find it almost impossible to keep themselves at their desks. They lash themselves there by keeping charts of the hours they work or by keeping a record of the pages they finish.

It may be some consolation to reflect that this very difficulty of keeping to the job of writing holds one of writing's important lessons: to write takes a tremendous amount of willpower. Once developed, self-discipline is invaluable. In the nineteenth century the English began to notice that an inordinate number of effective people—brigadier generals, admirals, members of Parliament, poets, novelists, inventors, industrialists—came from a then little-known prep school. When people visited the school, they found crusty old Tom Arnold in charge as headmaster.

"What do you teach them, Mr. Arnold?"

The old man scowled. "Anything. Just so they hate it."

The message is clear: if you can master a task that you detest, you can master almost any job.

Water skiing, jogging, and photography are fun from the very first, because you do not have to be highly skilled to enjoy them. Skiing is a thrill the first weekend. In contrast, tennis, squash, oil painting, chess, and cabinet making take time; you have to work at them awhile before they become a pleasure.

You must do the same with writing. At first you endure some dismal results. You look at a paragraph and know it is jumbled. You must go on to the next. Think of what headmaster Tom Arnold's son, Matthew, said: "Do what you think is right; eventually habit and skill will make it a pleasure." This advice applies to writing. When you become fairly good at it, it will yield an immense sense of accomplishment.

That sounds very good indeed, but it would be helpful if you could get a sense of accomplishment as soon as possible.

Two Early Triumphs

It is therefore important that you do some writing that almost guarantees immediate success, that is, develop some immediate rewards which will spur you on. You must exploit the principle of positive reinforcement. There are two kinds of writing that are immediately fulfilling.

POSITIVE REINFORCEMENT 1: THE PRÉCIS

When the late President John Kennedy was a student, he was not a dedicated one. His father frequently scolded him for spending too much time on fun and too little on books. Nevertheless, he got high grades. When his roommate, a future congressman, asked him how he got such high grades, Kennedy responded, "I do not study any more than you do, but I always write down a summary of what I have just read." Learning theorists know what he had discovered; they say, "there is no learning without verbalization."

You are a student, and you will have much studying to do. You will learn more if you write down a condensation of what you are studying. You can kill two birds—you know the expression—when you write précis, because at the same time you will be improving your writing.

There are many names for what you are writing—*abstract, summary, synopsis, digest, abridgement,* and even *epitome*—but we use the word *précis* (its plural is spelled the same) in the English university sense. The other words refer only to the act of condensation; they are shorter versions of longer works of writing. They can be written roughly, even in snatches of sentences. A précis follows the order of the original and should be written smoothly and engagingly. Now to tell why you will profit from writing the précis.

One reason that beginning writing is unimpressive is that it is dull and insignificant. Unskilled writers have often not yet learned what they can write about that is interesting and important. It's there, but they have not found it. The guitar student has it easier. He has only to master the instrument; he does not have to write the tune and the words. If, as a writer, you follow someone else's tune and words, you will have to think only of your instrument, which is language. The analogy is becoming complex, but our point is that when you select some interesting and important originals to condense, your précis will be interesting and important. You can concentrate on your method of expression.

As a writing student, you will profit in two ways.

First, you will develop a tighter style. Beginning writers almost inevitably are wordy. They use too many words to say too little. If you are trying to reduce a 3,000-word chapter to 150 words, you will find the exact single word to express a whole sentence.

For example, one original source contained a list of works by Norman Mailer joined with these words: "He has written the novels . . . , the plays . . . , several television plays including . . . , a drama . . . , some poems with . . . having attracted the most notice, a series of magazine and newspaper articles, one of which covered the Democratic convention and even an oratorio. . . ."

The sentence in précis became: "Norman Mailer's publications include. . . ." or even, simply, "Norman Mailer has written. . . ."

Writing a précis helps you discover how to make general words, like *publication,* cover more specific ones, like *novel, poem, magazine,* and *newspaper article.*

Second, you will increase your vocabulary. If you are studying a chapter or book on philosophy and you write a précis of it, you automatically soak up its terminology. In your précis you may wish to define a word, and you can do it briefly. The following is a brief précis of the 176-page book *Situation Ethics* by Joseph Fletcher:

> *Situation Ethics* is neither legalistic (based on absolute laws) nor antinomian (subjective and spontaneous). It is pragmatic, relative, personal, and positive. One's moral code should be based on *agape,* brotherly love tempered by reason. Since such love is "distributed," that is, aimed at all people, it guarantees justice. The tests of right conduct are: (1) What is its purpose, or end? (2) What is the means, the manner of achieving the end? (3) What is the motive? What is the drive behind the act? (4) What are the foreseeable consequences? *Situation Ethics* is the basis of "The New Morality."

Remember: a précis contains thoughts, not topics. The following paragraph is *not* a précis; if anything, it is a table of contents.

In his 176-page book *Situation Ethics,* Professor Joseph Fletcher discusses the new morality. He lists the characteristics of situation ethics and shows what questions must be asked of moral conduct.

Projects—Précis

1. You will not be the only person writing précis. The *Reader's Digest* contains précis of articles of general interest; the *Intellectual Digest,* now defunct, was a collection of précis about science, education, literature, philosophy, and other demanding subjects. Almost every college discipline has its own publication of abstracts (for instance, *English Abstracts*), which contains condensed articles on literary criticism. Your college library will have many of them. Find a précis that interests you and compare it to its original. See what has been kept, what retained. Note how the language of the précis contrasts to that of the longer version. (The editors of *Reader's Digest* are sometimes criticized for changing the meaning of the original. Watch for such possible alterations as you compare your précis, or condensation, with the original.)

2. Write at least one précis a day of something you have read, perhaps a chapter in one of your textbooks or an article from a newspaper or a magazine.

POSITIVE REINFORCEMENT 2: THE JOURNAL

Some writers of the past go in and out of favor, but Henry David Thoreau goes on forever. He became the patron saint of the protest movement of the 1960s because of his "Essay on Civil Disobedience." He is now *in* favor because he is the ideal Romantic and naturalist, the enemy of the Establishment, the darling of the ecologist.

If you would know Henry David Thoreau, read his *Journals.* He puts first things first. He wrote, "In the beginning I did not read books. I hoed beans." He carried his distaste for civilization so far that he blamed it for the spread of weeds. "Ticks, burrs, and similar weeds," he wrote, "do not stick to bare skin. Savages, going naked, do not disperse them as much as civilized man."

He was amused when he chanced across a law passed in 1695 requiring every unmarried man to kill six blackbirds or three crows before he could be given a marriage license. Noticing many blackbirds around his house, Thoreau concluded, "Either many men were not married, or many blackbirds were!"

Our point? Simply that you should consider keeping a journal.

You may be wondering why the journal is "rewarding," why it is "positive reinforcement." The answer lies in part in the aphorism (quite widely accepted) that every person can write one interesting novel. This belief is based on the fact that everyone should be able to write about his own life, and that life is bound to be interesting. *Catcher in the Rye* by J. D. Salinger is about adolescence; *Of Human Bondage* by Somerset Maugham is about a college student. You might think that their heroes, Holden Caulfield and Philip Carey, are rather dull people; nevertheless, their lives are fascinating. So is yours. Your life is as significant as those described in *The Bell Jar* by Sylvia Plath, *Strawberry Statement* by James C. Kumen, and *Johnny Got His Gun* by Dalton Trumbo—all about young people.

If you write about your daily life, you will see some interesting and memorable writing unfolding before you. Do not write *that* you ate; write *what* you ate. A few decades ago college students ate hamburgers; then they switched to pizza and subs or heroes. That is valuable sociological information. Are students eating organic foods now? In the mid-sixties girls suddenly got very candid and openly discussed their sex lives, even masturbation; now they seem more discreet. What do young people talk about today? What do young people do at parties? Not "have fun," that's too vague. Do they talk about politics? What candidates? Do they drink? What? In the fifties girls drank screwdrivers and gimlets. The drinks did not taste much like alcohol; they were learner's drinks, like the Tom Collins their mothers drank when they were in college in the thirties. Is alcohol returning to favor in the light fruit wines? Are these also learner's drinks? What has happened to smoking tobacco or pot? Or is it grass or hash or marijuana?

What films are you seeing? Are you attending church or temple? What books are you reading? Do you read the funny papers in your newspaper? Are they amusing or serious? What clothes do you wear to school? To parties? To travel in?

What do you think is happening in newspaper headlines? Who are your favorite entertainers? What happened to magicians? What is the favorite sport of your friends? What appears most often in your school newspaper? All of these questions, answered with anecdotes, names, conversations, and examples, are what history is made of. If you give your journal a try and work at it, eventually you will catch the thrill of recording your times. Observing and writing about your life will help you enjoy it more.

If you leaf through magazines, you surely will perceive the dozens of articles written by and about people your age. Adults are fascinated by what it is like to be young, and you are one of the world's greatest authorities about the subject. Try it.

If you write enough and if you experiment with enough subjects, you will find what you can handle interestingly. You may find that you are effective when you write about sports. You may in the future become a sports writer. You may find that you discuss your parents feelingly and interestingly. Are you a budding psychologist? What do you cover best? Science? Travel? Parties? You will be learning a great deal about yourself—as well as improving your writing. The success feels good.

Projects—Journals

Since one of the values of journals is self-discovery, which comes best from self-direction, we give instructions with caution. We suggest that entries will be most pleasing to you if they are exact, pictorial, detailed. We suggest that you write them with the thought that they may be useful to you some twenty-five years from now when you are sending a son, daughter, niece, or young friend off to college, and you want to remember exactly what it is like to go off to school. What are the sights, the sounds, the smells, the fears, the chills, the quiet, happy moments of being young?

1. You may wish to begin by just writing down random thoughts. This will give you a chance to decide what you really think about something. In the following entry, for instance, the student wrote his thoughts about his father.

Wednesday, September 28. Now that I have come to college I find that we talk a great deal about our parents, and I have decided that my father has some weird ideas. Before I got here I was used to them, but now, in contrast to other fathers, I don't know. My first name is Mark, and that is all right. My middle name is Seven. Yes, that's right, Mark Seven. In World War II my father was a fighter pilot, and he flew the P-51 Mark Seven, and that is where he got my name. Maybe I should be glad I have him as a father instead of another father I have heard about. He named his first daughter April, because he wanted her boy friends to remember her birthday. That wasn't so bad, but the second daughter he calls "Toby." Yes, you guessed it, her name is "October."

---

2. We suggest that variety will be one of your earliest pleasures. Try for different kinds of entries almost every week. To help you, we have suggested a number of different topics. You may wish to check this list every week, or when you begin to run dry, to obtain some new ideas.

    a. Did you meet a new person? What did you think of him? Do more than describe him. Tell why you thought him impossible, for instance. In several years you will be able to see just what your standards were. One girl wrote, "I saw this fellow sitting there, and I liked him instantly. He seemed so very, very alone."

b. Did you read an interesting article or see an interesting television program? Summarize it, perhaps copy down the phrases you like, and then tell how, had you found the article earlier, you would have acted differently some time in your life. Here is an example of what one student wrote:

Wednesday, March 14. Last night (Tuesday) I was fortunate enough to be able to watch a television special by Alistair Cooke entitled <u>America.</u> It was an hour-long film essay on the immigrant at the turn of the century. Alistair Cooke is shown walking through the old immigration station on Ellis Island, now a burned-out skeleton, which was once a veritable human stockyard. He showed actual films of the thousands of people who passed through the buildings on their way to a new life.

There were old people, some who had to be carried through the lines that seemed never to end. Mr. Cooke gave a brilliant commentary on how some people even ended up with new names after passing through the registration lines due to an Irish inspector trying to get information out of an old Romanian who spoke no English. This really rang close to home for me because it was a situation such as that where I got my original surname. As the story goes, my grandfather came over from Russia and spoke very little English. When the inspector asked for the last name, he didn't understand and gave his wife's maiden name which was Gervitz. The inspector wrote Horwitz. Until I was three years old my name was Horwitz. At that time my mother, who hated the name, convinced my father to have it changed to Lande, which was close to what it was supposed to be, Landen.

---

c. Did you have a happy weekend? Describe it exactly. Jot down the jokes your friends used, the topics they discussed, the opinions they stated, and then ask yourself why you were glad you were with them —and answer the question.

d. Did you see a film which was a little out of the ordinary? Write a brief précis of it, being sure to list the title, names of the leading actors, and the name of the director. Then comment on what the film was trying to say. What did it say about life? Did it touch *your* life?

e. Are you particularly caught up in some of the work in one of your classes? Describe it and your reaction, as one student has in the following entry.

Tuesday, November 20. I'm becoming extremely involved in my psychology project. I've picked a topic that Prof. Mac-Intyre called a "Taboo Topic." My paper will be an in-depth report of the American Perspective of Death. I'm finding that most of the people who hear of my topic say things like, "Why would you want to talk about such a morbid subject," or "I don't want to talk about it, change the subject." The more comments I hear like this, the more intensely occupied I become with the research. It is with these attitudes that I am concerned. We Americans seem to have a very unrealistic and irrational attitude about death. We are almost totally lacking in any "death education," and as adults, we refuse to acknowledge it. I can't tell what I'll be writing but I plan to raise questions about aging, retirement, heaven, hell, wills, and what we think about them all. My professor tells me that I am writing about <u>eschatology.</u> For some reason it amuses and flatters me to be writing about something with such a name.

f. Did you read a book or see something on television that impressed you or distressed you? Did you think it was well written? That it was an accurate statement of how people think? An unfair attack on your friends? Write a careful—and fair—précis and then give your reaction. Do not be content just to dash off a generalization—"It stinks!" Instead, thoughtfully tell why it disturbs you, as in the following example:

Monday, March 19. I would like to get something off my chest. I am sick and tired of watching television advertisements that treat the listening public as if we were all elementary school children. Now I know that most of the commercials that I watch are not directed at me, and I realize also, that competition in advertising is fierce, but there is no ex-cuse for some of the simple-minded trash that is being viewed.

Let me set the stage. It is 11:45 P.M., certainly late enough so that Junior is in bed, but early enough on a week-end that a large, mildly intelligent audience will be watch-ing. The color cartoon scene opens with a large yellow dog, ears standing straight up, tail wagging freely, watching television. Sitting next to "Rover" (how original!) is a

larger than life, grey and white cat that is also intently
watching TV. Sitting on a chair to the right of the TV is a
little boy, with blond hair and blue eyes. Now the plot
thickens; the little television that the two animals and
the young lad are so engrossed in is also showing a commercial
about vitamins. After watching the little screen, the dog
turns to the cat and says, "I sure wish someone would invent a vitamin just for us animals." At this the cat replies,
"Why haven't you heard, there is a vitamin and it's just for
us pets, it's made by—" End of commercial.

Now let's analyze what has happened. The advertising agency needed a gimmick to get people to watch the commercial.
The first rule of selling something is to get their attention. In this case instead of having an animal expert, or a
pet owner telling us of the need of vitamins in our pets'
lives, we get it straight from the "cat's mouth." How clever!

---

3. In your journal write a précis of this comment by Austin Warren, a
professor from the University of Michigan, and tell what you think of it.

> Throughout my adult life, I have understood and sympathized with the
> young, have either taken their side or attempted to mediate between it
> and the administration, the powerful elders. I still instinctively feel for the
> critical and rebellious young; but the present situation is difficult for me to
> face. The tension between the establishments and their young critics is
> more extreme than any I have known. I try hard to sympathize with the
> young; but they seem to me so unlovely, so intolerant, so opinionated, so
> ungenerous. I dislike their limited vocabulary, their designed or feigned
> inarticulateness. I dislike their economic dependence on the very parents
> whom they despise. I find them inimical to any culture save their own
> limited and provincial sub- and counter-culture, and arrogant in their
> ignorance of history. Undoubtedly what irritates me most in the current
> young is their sense of uniqueness and their pride in it.—AUSTIN WARREN,
> from *The Search for the Sacred,* edited by Michael B. Blory, Jr.

Here is one student's journal entry:

Wednesday, January 21. After reading and re-reading the
paragraphs by Austin Warren, I must say that in some respects
I couldn't agree with him more. His observations concerning
the intolerant, opinionated youth are accurate. I must say
that even though he is correct in his statement about economic dependence on the parents they despise, he is over-
looking one point. It is my belief that this very dependence

is one of the factors that causes the "friction" between
youth and their elders. Parents nowadays have a very subtle
way of sheltering their offspring to the point that they
(children) don't know, or can't find the way to freedom. The
youth of today [are] searching desperately for identity,
and blaming their elders for not preparing them for the
task.

I agree with his findings that youth of today [are] inimi-
cal to any culture save their own, but I can understand why,
and not be so hard. Today's youth [have] grown up and had to
live with all the mistakes that the "wise" elders made before
them. It is this distrust, and differences of values that
has kept the young from becoming involved in cultures other
than their own. They are proud of their uniqueness because
"they" didn't create this unloving, war-minded culture.

In summary, I would like to point out that I am not so much
defending the youth as I am explaining them. It is the elder
generation that has created the mistrust, the un-caring, and
the laziness of the modern youth. I do believe that the trend
is changing, in that young people are starting to realize that
if they do indeed want changes they must bring them about.
In order to change a system, you must first understand it.
Many of my younger friends seem to have a very healthy appetite for knowledge, and it's no surprise to hear a group
of young people discussing a play or a novel. As far as love
of man, well, I don't think this country has ever had a period
in its history when more social change has taken place due
to the actions of our young. Mr. Warren does have some good
points, but I think they are already a little outdated.

---

4. In this textbook we are trying not to ask you to write anything that is
frivolous or irrelevant. We ask you to do only the kind of writing that you
may someday decide to do on your own. In that vein, you will find you are
not alone in writing journals. Others are doing it, and someday their journals or yours may be important.

The library has many published diaries and journals which might interest
you. Go to the biography section of your library, and you will see dozens of
journals. Read them and you will find some that speak directly to you. For
instance, Anne Morrow Lindbergh's *Bring Me a Unicorn* tells, day by day,
what it is to go to college, to feel pressure from parents, to realize that an

older sister is more intelligent and more accomplished. You will see her meeting her future husband—a famous aviator—and see him more interested in the older sister. You will travel with her, learn to fly. You may wish to read her husband's *Journal of the War Years* to see what he, Charles Augustus Lindbergh, came to think of her. In his college journal, *A Darkening Green*, Peter Prescott questions all the old myths about campus publications, interscholastic sports, and sexual practices.

Chapter 3 Observation: The Source of Description and Narration

Not long ago, in an *Esquire* article, Tom Wolfe, author of *The Electric Kool-Aid Acid Test,* wrote with wonderment about what happened to him when, very young, he arrived in New York. "I couldn't believe the scene I saw spread out before me. . . . What really amazed me as a writer was that I had it practically all to myself." What he saw, and what he became famous for writing about, was "hip-huggers . . . minis, the boots and the bells and the love beads," what young people were wearing and saying. He and his friends in new journalism wrote about new politics, sports, the counter-culture, music, films, and so on. They wrote about what the young were doing.

It has always been the same. Young people do not have a monopoly on what is worth writing about, but they have a chunk of it.

What we suggest here is that if you describe well what you are seeing, hearing, and even smelling, you may produce very interesting, perhaps exciting, writing. If you tell the story of your life, or part of it, you may be your generation's Tom Wolfe.

You: The World's
Greatest Authority On . . .

Categorically, we can say that somewhere there is someone interested in what you are experiencing. Your parents, if they have not seen it, would like a description of your room. Your best friend would like an account of the evening you spent with your new girl- or boyfriend. Thirty years ago dormitory life seemed ideal on college and university campuses, and hundreds of dormitories were built. Now many students prefer an apartment, no matter how small and drab. Adults simply cannot understand why these lovely clean dormitories, with all that good fun offered by the resident advisers, do not attract you. Perhaps you may write answers to some of the questions your generation is asked. The more vividly you describe or narrate, the more interesting and valuable your writing will be.

The Psychology
of Description and Narration

Earlier in this textbook we noted that rhetoric is more than communication, because it is more than language and logic. It includes psychology. We therefore suggest that you consider the feelings of your reader. You should avoid making judgments for your reader. If you use words like *great, beautiful, fun, lovely, ugly, humorous, nice, cute, neat, unfortunate, awful,* or *terrible,* you are making up your reader's mind for him. If you describe or narrate exactly what you saw or what happened, your reader may come to the same conclusions that you do. Since he is a human being, he will appreciate your respect for his ability to make up his own mind. On a person-to-person basis, you will have scored, and you will have enhanced your goodwill. Your next point will come easier.

Another psychological factor that you must consider when describing or narrating is that your reader must have a reason for wanting to turn the page. A motorist will listen to a description of the road up ahead if it takes him to where he wants to go. A friend will listen to a narration if there is a punch line at the end or if he is rewarded by a chance to chuckle. Rarely do description or narration occur by themselves. They usually have a purpose.

The Key:
Your Power of Observation

If you are to describe and narrate vividly and interestingly, you must observe carefully. Use every sense and record every essential detail. You can refine your powers of observation by filling your notebooks with word snapshots and verbal motion pictures.

Think of yourself as the scenario writer for a documentary film. When you complete your writing, you will hand it to a film director. He must transfer your words into settings and action. He must place a chair exactly there, a two-year-old baby boy with a smelly diaper over there. He must know when to have a crash of thunder make the baby cry.

Then you have effective description and narration.

Description

We suggest that in addition to observing carefully to avoid shutting out those details that make up the truth, you apply these principles.

POINT OF VIEW

Your reader should know from what perspective you are describing. Are you in front or behind or on the side? Up in a tree? Looking out a window or through the rear-view mirror? If it matters, your reader should know your bias. Are you shorter than the person you describe? Jealous of him? Angry?

THE ORGANIZING PRINCIPLE OF DESCRIPTION: SPATIAL

For the reader to follow you, you must clarify the sequence of the details you present. If a drama critic wants to describe a stage setting, an architect wants to talk about the façade of a building, a football coach wants to explain a defensive lineup, or a student wants to describe the layout of his college campus, the pattern of organization is almost inevitably *spatial*. The stage description may move from front to back. The building description may proceed from floor to floor, perhaps from the foundation upward. The description of the defensive lineup may move from the left side to the right side of the line and into the backfield. The student may move from the outskirts to the center of the campus.

You must indicate to your reader which way his head should turn, where his eyes would focus. Suppose you are describing a parking lot. First you should give your reader some idea of how big it is. Select an accepted unit of measure. Rural people know what an acre is; most people know how large a football field is. Actually, they are just about the same size, the gridiron being just a bit larger. Then indicate that you are moving from left to right, from north to south, from front to back, or "along the Vesey Street side." You have now given your reader a frame of reference.

You may wish to establish this perspective by comparing your subject to something familiar, as in the following examples.

> They used to say that Oskaloosa is one "H" of a town. It grew along two parallel railroads with one highway joining them so that on the map it looked like the first letter in the word *hell*.

> The battlefield, unfortunately, was shaped like a funnel.

> Even after Red was too old for major league baseball he still thought like a ball player. He bought a 200 acre stretch of good Missouri bottom land and told me what he did with it. "Where home plate would be I put the house. Out in left field I put some of the best corn you ever saw. Center and right field are in wheat which I alternate with alfalfa. My wife has a garden near first base, and my tool sheds and barns string along the other base lines. I like to think of it as the biggest diamond I played on."

USE OF SENSES

Use the senses of sight, smell, hearing, touch, and perhaps even taste. When you tell what you see, tell it in technicolor. Did you move away from the man because of his garlic breath? Is the noise of the airplane overhead part of the scene in front of you? How often do you hear the wail of an ambulance siren? Did the urchin clutch a thin coat across his chest? Could you see his breath? Did the girl hasten past the drugstore to avoid smart remarks from boys? What were their comments? Did she hurry past the unshaven, smelly, old man sitting on the curb? Is it silent in your room? When the chair squeaks do you jump? Did you and your friends bump into each other in the car? Was the boy at your side hard and all elbows and the girl soft and all curves, or the reverse?

THE LANGUAGE OF DESCRIPTION

When you write description, you have an opportunity to learn about nouns, the name words. The general rule is to select the noun that most vividly re-creates what you saw. Look for the specific word instead of the general, the concrete instead of the abstract. *Car* is a poor word for a description; *Volkswagen bug* or *finned 1958 Cadillac* are more exact and pictorial. Try to spare your reader's time by selecting the noun that tells it all in one word. For *small house* try *cottage, hut, cabin,* or *shack*. You may learn to make general descriptive words (in this case adjectives) unnecessary.

Projects—Description

1. Which principle of description does this selection demonstrate?

> I first met Rip in Phoenix, Arizona, at a plastic motel near the airport. The lobby was something out of Alphaville, with red plastic imitation naugahyde,

a mannequin for a desk clerk, veneered walls, and two huge, imposing vending machines with everything from 25-cent prophylactics to $1.50 phylacteries. Outside was a swimming pool which smelled heavily of chlorine. It was surrounded by a hundred rooms with colorfully painted doors, each with a plaque bearing the name of a movie star. There was John Wayne, Bob Hope, Elizabeth Taylor, Paul Newman. I think we found Rip inside Bette Davis.—CRAIG PYES, "Rip Torn: The Case of the Hollywood I," *Ramparts*

2. Describe your room, having in mind some one reader to whom you are addressing your description. If the reader is one of your parents, stress where you have placed items they have given you or know about. If the reader is your writing instructor, stress whether you have good studying facilities. If the reader is your best friend, tell it all.

3. Take a walk for at least a half hour; then write a description of the most interesting view you found. In the description try to show (not tell) what caught your fancy. Stress the surprises. The pretty parts. The thoughts your walk generated, such as "I had forgotten how noisy a forest is."

4. Describe a person whom you dislike or like, disdain or admire, that is, for whom you have a definite feeling. Show what he or she does that brings out this feeling. Does his appearance contribute to this feeling? Be sure to include such details.

Narration

Narration, unlike static description, covers action. Narration tells a story. Since the first caveman gathered his fellow hunters around the fire and told of his kill mankind has been engrossed in accounts of the events of life. We all hear children report excitedly about the day's events: "Then I said, and then she did, and then Johnny hit me, and then the teacher came, and then she said, and then I did, and then Bobby came over, and then . . . and then . . . and hit Johnny. . . ." The "and then," stated or implied, identifies narration and its characteristic organization.

THE ORGANIZING PRINCIPLE: CHRONOLOGY

Whenever a writer's topic involves the passage of time, he will probably use *chronological* order. He will break his narration into steps or events, describing each event in the order in which it occurred. This is one of the simplest forms of organization and presents few problems.

Whenever someone gives directions, whether it be how to get to a filling station or on how to uncover information from the Dead Sea Scrolls, he senses that sequential order may be most appropriate. Whenever a writer wishes to tell what has happened in the past or what should happen in the future, he will consider using chronological order. He may decide to jump ahead in the story and then flash back to an earlier incident, but he will not let his reader lose sight of how each part of his narrative is related to the others. The main point, always, is to be consistent and clear.

THE LANGUAGE OF NARRATION

Since narrative is action, it demands action words, that is, strong verbs. Description helps you develop your skill with nouns; narrative helps with verbs. Verbs must show vivid, exact pictures. When the action is in progress, you will rarely find passive voice or a form of "be."

Projects—Narration

1. Consider the following narrative, which demonstrates both the chronological structure of narration and the use of verbs. Do its structure and language suggest scenes for a film? In particular note the verbs, which are italicized, and note which ones move the action along most graphically. How would you improve the narration?

A VISIT TO LA CANTINA

A few months ago . . . I *decided* to *take* some very special out-of-town friends to La Cantina, which at that point I *had misconceived* as a cozy Italian bistro. When we *walked* in, we *were surprised* to find ourselves in a small, brightly lit room with varnished wooden tables and chairs, somewhat like the inside of a high school library. We secretly *applauded* this lack of pretension and *sat* down to order from a menu which *had* no Italian dishes on it. Surprised once again, we secretly *applauded* this lack of ethnicity and one of us *ordered* broiled chicken with cranberry sauce and the rest of us *ordered* corned beef hash, a decision I *have* since *been puzzling* over since none of us *had* ever *ordered* corned beef hash anywhere before.

I *was* already a little uncomfortable because this place *wasn't* at all what it *was cracked* up to be and I *could see* my out-of-town friends *were* disappointed.

Suddenly we *heard* two women *yelling* quite loudly behind us. We *turned*. They *were sitting* two feet away from each other.

"Jerry *said*," one of them *screamed*, "that he *wouldn't be able to pick* Helen up. He *has* to *go* to the supermarket."

"What?" the other *shrieked*, inclining her head.

"TO THE SUPERMARKET," she *repeated*.

"Oh," the other *replied*, nodding.

It *was* that kind of thing and it *went* on for a while but we *were* the only table that paid any attention to it because everyone else *was* pretty old himself and *was* probably accustomed to it. It *would be* fair to say that except for the waitress and the restaurant's owner, we *were* the only people there under sixty-five. We secretly *applauded* the way this restaurant *hadn't fallen* for the counterculture.

The food *came* in small portions, just like a hospital meal and we *couldn't contain* our amusement and sadness. It *was* the kind of food you *serve* to people who *aren't* healthy enough to eat. We *were* pretty sure we *were* in a hospital by now or at least near one. It *looked* like the last supper for a lot of the clientele.

"It's predigested," one of my guests *joked,* holding up a forkful of hash.

"That's not funny," *said* another, holding up a forkful of hash.

"*Wait* till dessert," the first *came back.* "You *get* a choice of bread pudding or ten minutes in an oxygen tent."

"That's enough," the other *said* because the waitress and the owner *were looking* in our direction. My out-of-town guests *weren't* too happy and even after we *had gone* to *get* cherry cheese cake at the Midget they still *weren't* talking to me. I *think* the moral of the story *is* that old age sometimes *seems* silly to the young, but old people *don't* even *notice* it.

2. Try to recall the most amusing anecdote you have heard and write it down, either for your journal or to be submitted in class. Try to pace the story so the laugh will come suddenly at the end.

3. Recall and write down an incident that taught you something, perhaps one that showed you who your friend really was or that taught you when to keep your mouth closed. At the end state the lesson learned.

4. When you go home for vacation, what you are likely to do? Recount the action in detail, and then ask yourself whether your account shows your reader what you wanted it to. If not, rewrite the narrative, trying to point up the importance of what you do. Then look at your verbs. Try to make each one say as much as possible as briefly as possible. Change *walk* to *saunter, stroll, skip, meander,* or *lunge,* for instance. Avoid words made up of a *general* verb plus a preposition. Delete, for instance, *look at* and substitute *view, inspect,* or *stare*; for *appeal to* try *beg, implore,* or *address.*

Chapter 4 Paragraphs As Muted Conversation

Did you ever wonder what happened to "Yes" or "No?"

On a television talk show, the interviewer asks, "Do you agree with the president that . . . ?"

The answer could be "yes" or "no," but it rarely works out that way. A nod or shake of the head is too simple; the reply takes ten minutes. Even when your instructor confronts you with an essay question, you could often answer with "yes" or "no," but obviously that would never do. Thus we have extended communication.

Definitive Assertions

To be sure, some ideas are not complex. They can be expressed simply, definitely and clearly:

"My name is Janet Fox."

"This watch has a leather strap."

"When I was twelve, I joined the Boy Scouts."

These statements might start a conversation. The response might be, "How odd. I knew Janet Fox once," or "How can you stand a leather strap? When I wear one, I perspire, and the strap begins to smell," or "Me, too. Did you have as much fun as I did?" A conversation might result, but it would develop from the special interests of the speaker and listener.

Normally, such assertions, which we call *definitive*, do not start conversations. They are complete in themselves. Your reader thinks to himself, "Oh?" and that's that. But some assertions do raise questions.

We are suggesting that communication, if it is anything, is a social event. If communication is serious, if it has any importance at all, it is a conversation. A writer or speaker makes a statement. His audience replies: "I do not fully understand you; I need to know more," or "I do not agree with you. You must say more to convince me." The writer has generated a response. That is what causes paragraphs. That is what causes long articles. That is what causes books.

Operative Assertions

"That dude deserves his shady reputation."

After this statement there would be a conversation, and we can almost predict what the conversation would be about:

"What is his reputation?"
"How did he get it?"

"Several years ago a most remarkable frog grew up in Oxford."

After James Watson wrote this provocative, operative sentence, he correctly assumed that his reader would want to know what was so remarkable about the frog. He answered the question, and that was what his article in *Intellectual Digest* was all about.

More must be said after such sentences, for if a sentence is "a group of words expressing a complete thought," the statement about the man with the reputation or the remarkable frog is not a "sentence." It is incomplete, elliptical. It leads you on. It is a tease.

Characteristically, such a sentence creates questions, and to a great extent we can predict those questions, as in the following examples:

1. *The Sentence:* "John has a bright future."
   The Response: "He has? What makes you think so?"

2. *The Sentence:* "A scientist in Palo Alto, California, has discovered a cure for arthritis."
   The Response: "What's his name? What is the cure? Where can I get some for my grandmother?"
3. *The Sentence:* "Winston Churchill's success began with an early, calamitous mistake."
   The Response: "It did? Success in what? What was the mistake?"
4. *The Sentence:* "There is a way to end war."
   The Response: "You really think so? How?"

These sentences vary in importance, complexity, breadth, and vagueness, but they are alike in that they generate questions that must be answered if they are to be clear and convincing. We say they have *predictive content;* by the way they are expressed, they hint at what must be said to continue the dialogue.

Dialogue As Question and Answer, Statement and Response

One of the most important skills a writer needs is the ability to anticipate the questions he generates and provide the proper information to answer them. To develop that sensitivity, we suggest that you turn your attention to handling dialogue.

One way to start is by reading the *Dialogue* by Plato called "Crito." Socrates is awaiting execution for "impiety and corrupting the young." Crito visits him with a plan for escape, but Socrates, after listening to the plan, rejects it as a violation of his past beliefs and teachings. As he replies to Crito, he demonstrates how the speaker can lead his listener.

Soc: Is the pupil who devotes himself to the practice of gymnastics supposed to attend to the praise and blame and opinion of every man, or of one man only—his physician or trainer, whoever he may be?

Cr: Of one man only.

Soc: And he ought to fear the censure and welcome the praise of that one man only, and not of the many?

Cr: Clearly so.

Soc: And he ought to act, and train, and eat and drink in the way which seems good to his single master who has understanding, rather than according to the opinion of all other men put together?

Cr: True.

Soc: And if he disobeys and disregards the opinion and approval of the one, and regards the opinion of the many who have no understanding, will he not suffer evil?

Cr: Certainly he will. . . .

Soc: Very good; and is this not true, Crito, of other things, which we need not separately enumerate? In questions of just and unjust, fair and foul, good and evil, which are the subjects of our present consultation, ought we to follow the opinion of the many and to fear them; or the opinion of the one man who has understanding? Ought we not to fear and reverence him more than all the rest of the world; and if we desert him shall we not destroy and injure that principle in us which may be assumed to be improved by justice and deteriorated by injustice;—there is such a principle?

CR: Certainly there is, Socrates.

In this conversation Plato is stacking the deck. More often, instead of being as docile as Crito is, listeners ask crucial, troublesome, and even offensive questions, which we will soon call issues. To become aware of the questions people carry around in their heads and the questions you will raise as you talk, try listening to conversations around you.

Does the following dialogue sound like a conversation between a student and professor? As you read, mentally rephrase any words or sentences which seem inappropriate to you.

THE STUDENT, MAYBE YOU: Okay, okay. So you want us to learn dialogue. But I know what will happen. An English teacher asked me to write about my hobby, and I wrote what I thought was a good paper about drag racing. I used words like *cam duration* and *fuel injection* and *hole shot* and the paper came back with red ink around the words, and "Jargon" in the margin.

PROFESSOR: We are talking about two kinds of writing. When you write dialogue, you must be sure your characters use the words natural to them, and put them in quotation marks. When you write as writer, you can still use the words, but—

YOU: (*interrupting*): But how do I make sure my audience knows what the words mean?

PROFESSOR: That's the right question. When you write as writer, you can define the unfamiliar words. When you are writing dialogue you have to make the expressions clear in more subtle ways.

YOU: Okay, okay. I sometimes think that I get all that red ink because English teachers don't like me. What kind of audience should I have in mind when I write?

PROFESSOR: Often you know quite specifically. A professional writer knows to what magazine he is submitting his article, and if the magazine is *Boys' Life*, he uses a different vocabulary than if it is *Motor Homes*. Such magazines as *Time, Playboy, Harper's, The Atlantic Monthly*, and *Psychology Today* assume rather well-educated, sophisticated audiences, and that is what you can do safely when you write papers in college.

YOU: What about history terms for history papers? I have heard it said that teachers like to have you use the terminology of their subject matter.

PROFESSOR: Of course.

YOU: One psychology teacher told me that one of the reasons he assigns papers is to find out if his students can work their way around in terms of the subject. I used terms like *Oedipus complex, misplaced aggressions, role playing, phallic symbol* and got an A on the paper.

PROFESSOR: You must have done something else right in the paper but you are getting the idea.

YOU: I can see that I can use standard vocabulary in all my college themes, perhaps rather higher than in ordinary conversation, but I have to define terms for specialized information—unless it is in the subject matter of my instructor. Okay?

PROFESSOR: Err-r-r, okay.

This imaginary dialogue goes beyond the idea that when you represent the dialogue of a person, you use his exact language. In addition, the exchange shows that when you are acting as a writer, when you have an unseen and perhaps unknown audience out there, you must use language that is clear to a reader you envision. You must use language that is appropriate for the subject. You may occasionally have to define terms.

Dialogue
As Journal Entry

Besides listening to conversations around you, we suggest that you record them, and there is no better place than in your journal. Try to catch the exact words, the exact pronunciations, the flow of question and answer, of statement and response, a flow that is basic to all communication. The following is an example:

> Monday, July 15. I went downtown to try to get my tape recorder repaired, trying not to get a parking ticket while I was at it. I failed in both endeavors.
>
> "This is a pretty old machine," said the man in the service department.
>
> The thing's six years old. If it were a kid it'd be in the first grade. But you're not supposed to have bought a tape recorder that long ago, and if you did, you're not supposed to have kept it.
>
> No, the man couldn't fix the microphone, but he sold me a plug for $1.50. *One dollar and fifty cents.* I would have been able to go to the movies six times for that when I was a kid.
>
> July 15.—The young man walks into a restaurant. "I'll have a cheeseburger," he says. "How much?"
>
> Says the counterman: "That's $8.00 and $1.60 tax makes $9.60."
>
> "How do you sell them so cheap?"
>
> "Volume."
>
> "Well, here's a 500-dollar bill and let's see if I have the 60 cents. Nope, all my change rusted again."—JAMES KUMEN, "Notes from the Journal of a Gentle Revolutionary," *Strawberry Statement*

Paragraphs

Paragraphs are difficult to define. Visually they are apparent enough. On a page you see the left margins of the lines of print occasionally broken by an indentation. The indention is a relief. The page looks less formidable if it has several paragraphs. Most writers indent at least three times per page to avoid frightening their readers. That might be called "paragraphing for visual relief."

In addition, paragraphs occur because communication almost invariably consists of a series of operative assertions followed by the definitive sentences needed to explain or prove them. We have seen that a conversation might go:

"That dude deserves his shady reputation."

"Yeah? What *is* his reputation? How did he get it?"

The writer does not hear the question but he comes to realize when he generates a question. And he knows he must answer it. A paragraph might go:

> That dude deserves his shady reputation. He has smooth talked more chicks than anyone else on the street. He takes a girl out once, promises her the moon, takes what he can get, and then never buzzes her again. The girl thinks she has a date for a flick, and blows an evening when he doesn't show. I know at least ten girls who would like to shoot him. They call him a wolf, a lecher, an operator, a stud.

Or observe this paragraph written by an English essayist, Richard Hoggart:

> A paper by Marshall McLuhan, delivered to a conference called "Vision" at Southern Illinois University, gives a useful pointer. Young people today, says McLuhan, are "data processors" on a large scale. They have to work hard and constantly at (a) processing all the fluid data (offered attitudes and styles) which their technological, electronic, mass-communication, consumers' society throws at them, and (b) matching that against the more ordered, classified, scheduled outlook which the classroom, the older, established environment, offers. So they become bewildered, "baffled because of this extraordinary gap between the two worlds."—RICHARD HOGGART, *On Communication and Culture*

Suppose this were a conversation. Can you hear a listener asking, after the first sentence, "What is that useful pointer?" The development of a paragraph answers a question that never gets asked out loud.

As you can see, the paragraph has two parts: (1) the provocative or operative assertion, often called the topic sentence, and (2) after the assertion which generates the questions, the answer, or development.

Effective writing is predictable. A writer expresses his provocative assertions, and the reader can comfortably expect what is to come, the answers to the questions raised. Good writing has texture, which is a term used for tapestry or rugs to express the variety of high and low points on the patttern. Paragraphs contain this variety, the high points of assertion and the specific, concrete, factual points of the development. That makes for interest.

Paragraphs, then, can be referred to as "muted conversation." The writer, in his imagination, is writing dialogue. He makes an assertion and "hears" a question he knows he has raised. He does not record the question; he mutes it. He leaves it out. But in the development of his paragraph, he certainly answers it.

Projects

1. Is there any hobby or occupation you know so well that you know its special words, its jargon or lingo? Skiing, stamp collecting, foreign cars, football, hockey, chess? Working in a garage, summer camp, theater, sandwich shop? Create a conversation which shows the language used. Try to give the exchange a focus at the end by showing what seems to be important to the people involved.

2. Show a dialogue between two roommates, in which one student is telling why he did badly (or well) at midterm. Then show the same student talking to his parents about it. Go ahead. Use your imagination. To whom might he be more honest? What difference would there be between the interests of the roommate and those of the parents? What suggestion might the roommate make at the end? What promise would the parents request at the end? The dialogue should be a mini-drama, providing a smile or a lesson at the end.

3. How do taxi drivers say, "hello?" Write a paragraph answering the question.

4. How do natives of Oskaloosa, Iowa (or New York City, or Marin County, California, or anywhere else you know) tell how to get to the supermarket? In your neighborhood do they tell you to "turn north" or "bear right"? Write a paragraph on the topic.

Write a dialogue between a stranger seeking direction and a native giving it. Place the scene in a location familiar to you. Try to let your conversation show differences in the two people's language and ideas about what's important. Show the confusion if the native uses a local term like *spa, soft drink parlor,* or *the jug handle turn.*

5. How do professional athletes or rock musicians discuss girls? What do they call the girls? "Foxes?" "Groupies?" How do girls discuss "jocks" and "rocks?" Show either contrast in a conversation.

6. This project should help you feel the two-part nature of a paragraph, as a blend between the provocative topic sentence and the development needed to explain or prove it. Write a paragraph with any one of the following as a topic sentence, and be sure to start out by writing the topic sentence.

    a. I know him (or her) too well.
    b. _____reminds me of my father (or mother).
    c. Even though Hank Aaron holds the home run record, Babe Ruth is the more impressive hitter.
    d. The boys I know do not really understand girls.
    e. _____is an entertaining book (film, play, entertainer).

Chapter 5

The College Theme: A Dialect

The College Dialect

Does anyone know better than a college student that we do not always talk and write in the same way? When a college freshman writes to his grandparents, does he write the same letter he sends to his best friend? He not only writes about different topics, but he also uses a different language: different words, different allusions, different jokes. Perhaps his grandparents even rate a more legible handwriting. He writes differently, not because he is a hypocrite, but because he wishes to make sure he reaches his grandparents. He uses a style they understand.

A student new to college often feels that he is learning several new dialects. Each course introduces its own vocabulary; each dormitory invents its own slang. His new friends and his college teachers seek more than just his opinion; they want to know *why* he thinks *what* he thinks. They require exact expression, but they also want an analysis of the argument. Almost more than anything else, they want evidence. They require him to scrutinize his own thinking and defend it.

Frequently, the college freshman becomes bewildered, hurt, and angry. He feels that he is being asked to change his whole personality as well as his expression. In high school he may have been encouraged to write "creatively," to express his ideas as they came to him without fear of challenge, perhaps in the form of free-style poetry. Now he is not free. People keep asking him, "What do you mean?" Then he is challenged to "prove it." They are as rigid in their expectations as the newspaper reader who wants to learn in the first paragraph "Who? What? Where? When?"

For what may seem a digression but actually is not, we ask you to read the following article by Leonard Freeman, published in the violent 1960s at the height of the student revolution. It defends music, and music set the tone for the revolution; it defends a heretical religious position. *Jesus Christ Superstar* hinted at illicit desire by Mary Magdalene for Jesus; it made Judas Iscariot a sympathetic figure.

SUPERSTAR SHINES

Have you been wondering what all those surreptitious religious ramblings were leading up to in such things as The Beatles' *Let It Be*, Norman Greenbaum's *Spirit in the Sky*, and The Byrds' *Jesus Is Just All Right?* Well this is it.

At this point the author shows why you might be interested.

Jesus Christ Superstar, a double-LP, rock-opera on Decca (DXSA-7206), makes it on all three scores—as rock, opera, and religious rumbling.

Here he makes his point: The opera makes it in three ways.

The musicians, including members past and present of Deep Purple, Joe Cocker's Grease Band, Nucleus, the entire eighty-five piece City of London Ensemble, and the 1970 Moscow Tchaikovsky piano competition winner, are some of Britain's best—rock or otherwise. And some of the cuts, *I Don't Know How to Love Him, Damned for All Time*, and *Herod's Song*, could easily make it on the Top 20, though their controversially religious lyrics may preclude that.

Point 1: This section asserts that the opera is good rock.

As an opera *Jesus Christ Superstar* is a great contribution. Unlike the much vaunted first rock-opera, *Tommy*, by The Who (really a long story told in disjointed vignettes), *Superstar* ought to be stageable with little difficulty.

Point 2: It is good opera.

The form is dramatic with definite acts and climaxes, all the dialogue is handled musically, and the characters are fairly well developed. It's not something your youth group can "put on" some Sunday afternoon, but if some major opera company doesn't put this into production it will be a crime. It cries out to be seen.

Superstar really shines, however, in its treatment of its subject matter: Jesus, Judas, and the Passion narrative. It's been the sad fate of overtly religious themes in our media to degenerate either into schmaltz or cynicism (witness the Hollywood "biblical" epics and much of our church school material). But Tim Rice's lyrics come on with as much integrity and urgency as anything since Matthew, Mark, Luke, and John did the originals. And more to the point, its impact direction is the same. It's a confrontation and it calls for a response.

Point 3: The opera is sound religion.

Jesus Christ, Jesus Christ,
Who are you? What have you sacrificed?
Jesus Christ Superstar
Do you think you're what they say you are?

An answer to those questions can't be spoon-fed either way. But the alternatives are real and must be dealt with. It's the job of the evangelist and the modern Christian apologist to lay it out there, to set up the confrontation with Jesus, and to force the question "Who are you? Are you what they say you are—for me?" In that sense *Jesus Christ Superstar* may well be one of the most evangelistic things to come down the pike since Billy Graham discovered revival meetings.

A real problem for many will be the expectation that the Church is supposed to provide the answers—and more than answers, proof. The fact of the matter is (as the Bible, life, and Bill Cosby's great "Noah" bit all attest) God doesn't work that way. Judas (masterfully portrayed by Murray Head) is a focal "Everyman" who goes to his grave wailing:

Don't you get me wrong
I only want to know

I only want to know, I only want to get it all socked-in and in my control, to get God and all his rules all wrapped up in my back pocket. The Christian thing isn't a matter of knowledge; it's a matter of trust and faith. And as *Superstar* develops it, that's the point of crunch between Jesus and Judas. Neither one of them "knows" what God's up to, but finally Jesus trusts and Judas can't.

You're far too keen on where and how
and not so hot on why

Jesus (Ian Gilliam) tells God in the Garden of Gethsemane, "But you hold every card . . . take me now—before I change my mind."

As powerfully as anything this writer has experienced, *Jesus Christ Superstar* sets up and lays out clearly the decision that everyone makes but which nobody answers except on faith:

In concluding, the author shows why he feels the opera is so important.

Whom do men say that I am?
Whom do you say that I am?

You can be the judge of whether the author was right. If *Superstar* has been forgotten, the critic was wrong. If it is now a classic and still gets produced, he was right. Our point here, however, is that during a time when all kinds of traditions and conventions were under attack, the author used the methods of argument and exposition which are the form of communication customary on the college campus. In a midnight discussion your friend across the room will ask, "But what's your point?" Then he says, "I just do not see it that way." You must respond with your evidence. You learn that you cannot make a point by repeating it in different words.

Our point is also that college writing is a new dialect. Characteristic of the college convention is a blending of assertion with proof or explanation, all expressed in particularly exact language. In the review you just read the assertion is: *"Jesus Christ Superstar* makes it." The statement is slangy; it means that the rock opera is a success. The reader would respond, "Defend your belief," or "Why do you say that?" The critic answers the question with three related sub-opinions: the opera makes it on "three scores—as rock, opera, and religious rumbling." Then, for each, he provides specific information drawn from the rock opera itself. The reader must either accept the original assertion or refute the evidence. To do the last, he must listen to the rock opera to gather his *own* specific evidence.

A Prototype

By now you may have a sense of progression in your writing training. We suggested that you write précis because the précis gives you practice in concise writing without your having to produce the ideas for a theme. We suggested that you write description and narration because these modes permit you to practice writing without spending much time in analytical thought. Furthermore, we noted that in producing journal entries, narratives, and descriptions, you have considerable authority on your subject.

We now take another practical step. Throughout your college career, you will have an audience that your present writing teacher knows very well— your college professors. In the next four years your important writing assignments will be read by other college professors. Furthermore, your writing teacher knows what we have just been discussing; he knows the college habit of communicating by means of balanced assertion and development. He can help you master the kind of writing your other teachers have come to expect.

You will do yourself *and* your professor a favor by using the college theme format we will describe. You do him a favor by working with a format he finds familiar. You free him to work with your ideas rather than your presentation. You do yourself a favor by following the pattern that ensures that you will focus on assertions and provide the necessary development. When you clothe your ideas in this standard dress, you free yourself for more time with your ideas. You can experiment with form later. Great poets mastered the rigidily structured villanelle and sonnet before they attempted free verse; great painters drew bones and muscles before they dared to try the formlessness of modern art.

You have just read, in the review of *Jesus Christ Superstar*, an example of the structure we are recommending. Compare the structure of this review with the structure of reviews of more recent albums; you will see that the form is often used beyond the college campus. Besides, you have undoubtedly heard your secondary school teachers say that you should organize in three parts: introduction, body, conclusion.

The college theme also has these three parts. In the introduction the writer attempts to get his reader's interest; he states his purpose. In the body the writer tries to fulfill this purpose, and in the conclusion he stresses his purpose.

The explanation or evidence in the body, often complicated and long, is divided into subpoints or subtopics, just as Ira referred to in the cartoon is hated for a series of reasons. Presumably, if the conversation in "Miss Peach" were continued, we would receive the concrete evidence that the maligned Ira is indeed a liar, a cheat, and a "worthless, low, sneaking little wretch."

Some defenders of conventional organization and structure contend that civilized, educated persons inherently think in these patterns. Perhaps. What you must realize, however, is that whether customary structures are in-

MISS PEACH   by Mell

herent in logical thought or are the results of education and conditioning, your reader expects such structures, and you can communicate with him more effectively if you work within them.

THE DISTINCTIVE "LOOK"

The five-hundred-word theme has long been the workhorse of college writing courses. Its advantages are apparent: it can be prepared in the time available; it is short enough to provide specific focus, yet long enough to develop an important idea effectively. It can readily be criticized by instructors.

Assume that your paper will be three typed pages. It will have five or six paragraphs, each about a half page in length. The first paragraph may be just under a half page or just a little more. The last paragraph may be shorter. The first paragraph will have its most important sentence at the end; the middle paragraphs will have their most important, or topic, sentences at the beginning. The paper thus is divided into an introduction, a body (the middle paragraphs), and a conclusion.

Your introductory paragraph may be somewhat "upside down" in that it works toward the final sentence. It may begin with a general question leading into background material, for instance, "Should we adopt a no-cut policy of attendance?" At the end of the paragraph you announce your position: "We should establish a no-cut policy." This is the thesis sentence.

Each of the paragraphs in the body of the paper begins with a reason to support your thesis. In their most mechanical rough-draft form, the topic sentences might be:

> *Paragraph* 1: The first reason we should establish a no-cut system is that students have been suffering academically from the unlimited cut system.
> *Paragraph* 2: The second reason we should establish a no-cut system is that classes with all students present accomplish more.
> *Paragraph* 3: The most important reason is that, with compulsory attendance, students learn to meet their obligations and thus profit more from college.

Whether or not you approve the sample topic or the language of the rough draft, try to get a sense of the *form* suggested. In each paragraph within the body of the paper, the writer presents the evidence he can muster in support of the particular reason he has cited.

The concluding paragraph (rarely beginning, "In conclusion . . .") provides the writer with his last opportunity to convince his reader of the position asserted at the beginning. If you defended a no-cut policy, perhaps you would conclude with a brief recapitulation of the major points and a strongly worded final statement. In addition, you might provide a telling anecdote, perhaps a quotation from a former student, who failed because he seldom attended classes, since there was no penalty for cutting.

With the distinctive look we have just described in your memory, read the following student theme. How closely does the writer match what we

---

                           The College Surprise

        If you have been a member of a State Department, UN, or
military family, and have lived in foreign countries more than
you have in the United States, state-side college is bound to
be strange. People who know I have lived in Karachi, Bogota,
Milan, and Guadalajara and have never attended an American school
ask me what it's like on an American campus. Even the editor of
the Reporter, a newspaper published in Guadalajara for the American
colony, asked me to write an article on it. Well, I will tell you
that it is a culture shock. Life at an American college is one
surprise after another.

        First, there are the boys. They will fool you every time.
I am accustomed to the dark-skinned races in which the men come
right out and say what they think. They believe that American
girls practically burn with passion, and they are frank in their
attempts to start the fire. I have had my bottom pinched in Rome,
and a Pakistani Air Force cadet told me he preferred girls who
wear D cups to C. My foreign courtiers have asked me to share a
hotel room with them just after we have shaken hands. With them,
you know where you stand, but with American boys I am always off
balance. I had never heard an American "line" till I got back to
the United States. I did not know the games people play. A boy
told me he loved me, but I found out he told my roommate the same

                                 1

INTRODUCTION
Appeal
Thesis

BODY
Transition and topic sentence for part 1
Development for part 1

2

Topic sentence
for part 2

Transition

BODY

Development
for part 2

story on the same night. I was invited to a party and when I got
there, I was the party--and I was in an apartment with only one boy.
Another boy asked me to teach him Latin dances, but I later learned
that he was practically a professional at it--and at other talents.
I have not learned to play the game yet, and I am looking forward
to meeting one American boy who is what he seems.

My first impressions of American students in general have been
equally deceptive. When my father went to college, he told me, he
practically seceded from society. He had time to party, but school
was the main deal. With my generation, this is not so. At first,
I thought students do very little work. School itself is actually
quite easy. We have a paper, a mid term, and a final examination,
and we are accountable for nothing else. School is a soft life, I
thought. What I have now learned is that every student I know is
doing something outside the ivy walls. The black student who sits
next to me in History is taking two drama courses in another school.
Susan is doing yoga, Bob is converting to Bahai, and Molly is taking
ballet and Italian. Another student audits a course in History of
Revolution. The ones who aren't doing extra studying are tutoring
Puerto Rican kids, working on Headstart, or reading to the elderly
at a convalescent home. Every week a bus loads up forty students
outside my dorm and they go to be aids at a school for the mentally
retarded. I expected young Americans to be hostile or apathetic,
and they are--to the Establishment--but each one seems to be leading
a double life, and a valuable one.

3

Topic sentence for part 3 →

Perhaps my biggest surprise came from the faculty. I had heard
that in an American school, you become an IBM number. I had to
memorize eight numbers to identify myself in various circumstances.

Transition →

My address takes five lines on an envelope. When I walked into my
first class I almost turned right around and got on a plane for
Guadalajara. There were 1100 other students in the class, and the
professor was a metallic voice over the amplifying system. A
graduate student critiques my term paper; a computer "services"
my final exam. The surprise came when I decided to "confer" with

Development for part 3

my professor. I found him in his office on a fifth floor and I
have never seen a person so pathetically eager to be approached. He
has been rebuffed so many times by hostile students that he seems
almost frightened by them. He spent two hours helping me, and he
invited me to dinner with his wife and six other students. This

Extension of thesis beyond personal experience

has been the pattern for all my classes. I have been asked to serve
on faculty-student committees. I have been given free tickets to
plays. Philip Wylie wrote that he thinks most American young people
do not have a single adult friend. I think I have at least three on
the faculty.

We non-American American students write letters, and I have
decided that the scene is much the same at New Haven, Champaign,
Bowling Green, Berkeley and Beloit--and perhaps on all campuses.
College or university is not all good. It is not all bad. But it
is full of surprises.

BODY

CONCLUSION

Summary; restatement of thesis

recommend? Does she provide the specifics you are led to expect? A study of this theme will repay you with a sense of just how specific the writer was in supporting her points.

AN ADMISSION

What we are suggesting is that for a while you deliberately and knowingly use what is very acceptable conventional form for your early college papers. We have called the form a *prototype*. With it you tell your reader, the professor, that you know what clothes to wear in the country you are visiting. You tell your reader something about yourself—that in the interest of clear communication, you will go along for a while with the system. Until you have mastered some unusual and perhaps more creative form, you will follow the introduction-body-conclusion format, and establish the purpose in the introduction and develop the main ideas in each paragraph. In these early papers your professor will know what to expect, and he can help you. Later you will test your own strong wings.

Projects

1. This chapter contains the assertion that members of the college community use a specialized form of English which we call the college dialect. What other dialects have you noted? Take notes in your other courses on the new terminology which is being introduced. How specialized are the usages? Are some seemingly ordinary words given new and narrow meanings, in psychology or sociology, for example? What proportion of terms (words or phrases) in your other courses have this specialized nature? Your quizzes and essay examinations in all courses will gain accuracy and force if you regularly use the language of the individual course. Discuss these observations in class or record them in your journal.

2. Since most people on campus have fairly strong opinions and since strong opinions often differ, acceptable methods of resolving differences long ago were developed. In the dorms, at the cafeteria, and in the local pub, bar, or lounge—or library, for that matter—observe how frequently a statement of opinion will be challenged by someone across the room or on the other side of the table, and how often the first speaker supports his point with as much specific material as he can recall. (You may also discover that some people repeat, this time shouting, their opinion—perhaps you can conclude that these opinion holders have no support for their views.)

3. To help you achieve some early success in writing college themes of the kind discussed in this chapter, we suggest that you write a college theme defending one of your strongest convictions. To help you focus on a single

conviction and to give you the feeling of a living opponent against whose arguments you will need evidence, you may wish to select a controversial statement made by a public figure. This will give you some assurance that you have selected a significant, timely topic. You may either refute or defend the statement, so long as you remember there is sizable opposition to your point of view and that you cannot resort to general statements and assertions without proof.

Here are some possible springboards for your paper:

"In America today women are not really exploited."

"America is still a land of opportunity."

"For institutions in general and for universities in particular, I favor the greatest possible decentralization of authority."—DENNIS HAYES, a Stanford student, campaigning for a position on the Stanford University Board of Trustees

"The Trustees of a university must make certain that the control of a university remains in the hands of the Trustees and of a president who aggressively and forcefully implements their policies."—MASON ELVIN BYLES, who ran opposite Dennis Hayes for election to the Stanford University Board of Trustees

"Public education rarely fulfills its obligations."—CHARLES E. BROWN, former Superintendent of Schools, Newton, Massachusetts

"My high school produces good (or bad) college students (or athletes)."

"Being a member of the Boy Scouts (or other organization) was fun, but (and) the experience means little (or much)."

"I generally approve of the Republican (or Democratic, liberal, conservative, radical) point of view."

"My hometown does not provide equal opportunity for its young people."

If you choose one of these topics, you will probably want to qualify your statement of the thesis to fit your own experiences. For instance, you may qualify the fifth suggestion in this way: "If my friends' experiences are typical, public education does not fulfill its responsibilities." Or you may wish to choose a different topic.

We suggest the following organization:

Paragraph 1: Introduce your belief, perhaps first quoting some recent speaker or writer who holds the opposite view; then showing that the belief is important to you and *briefly* indicating the two or three reasons you will use to support your view.

Paragraph 2: State the first reason for your belief, and support it with specific evidence. (The order in which you present your reasons may not be important, but sometimes you may want to conclude with your strongest reason, or funniest, or something. Think about the order of presentation.)

Paragraph **3**: Give the second reason, supported by specific evidence related to this reason. As with the order in which you present your reasons, think about the order in which you present your evidence. What do you want the reader to see last on this point?

Paragraph **4**: You may discuss another reason, if you want to put one in or if you have several. Otherwise, this will be your concluding paragraph. *You will not be so unsophisticated* as to begin this paragraph, "In conclusion, I wish to restate. . . ." Perhaps you *do* want to summarize your three reasons, but you can do that briefly, and then suggest, perhaps, that the reader should now agree with your view.

If your instructor assigns this theme as an early formal paper, be sure to follow his instructions for preparing the manuscript. And please *proofread* your paper before handing it in. Check everything twice, and then ask your roommate to check it. With a little extra care at this point, you can catch a dozen silly or careless errors that simply crept in while your attention was somewhere else.

4. Ideally, a course in writing should help you translate profound thoughts into good writing. Regrettably, profound thoughts do not come at one's beck and call; nonetheless, college students are often expected to write extemporaneously in class. How, you ask, can I dredge up a significant paper between the opening and closing bells of a single class?

You cannot always do so—although some remarkable papers have been written in such circumstances, and a number of them have been published. A fact you must face, however, is that whether the profound thoughts come or not, you must practice writing, and extemporaneous exercises serve this purpose. To guard against drawing a total blank, you can select ahead of time four or five rather broad topics which interest you and seem important. Possible examples:

Education
Life-styles
Sports
Popular music (or literature)

Your instructor may suggest topics, or he may ask you to draw up a list of topics which you are willing to write about. In choosing a topic, you may say to yourself, "This is something I should know anyway, and I usually read about it in newspapers and magazines." You should mull over your list of topics occasionally. Keep it up to date, and master some thoughts, perhaps keeping notes on names, exact dates, and statistics. Make frequent entries about them in your journal. Then, if at various times in the semester, your instructor asks you to write a pointed, well-organized, fully developed theme on one of your subjects, you will be able to come up with an interesting paper which demonstrates the principles of effective writing.

While you are developing this repertory of subjects, you must think in terms of what your reader might expect or want to know. If your audience is your professor or your classmates, what do you know that they might not?

Part II Writing

Chapter 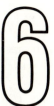 Organization

Good writing, like a good house, is an orderly arrangement of parts. Each major part has a certain amount of independence. . . . It may have an interior structure of its own. But it must also be connected with the other parts—that is, related to them functionally—for otherwise, it could not contribute its share to the intelligibility of the whole.
—*Mortimer Adler,* How to Read a Book

The Need
for Organization

Some ideas are more complex than others. Some may be communicated in one word; others need more than fifty thousand. When a writer deals with ideas that require more than a hundred words or so, the problem of organization arises. He cannot throw all his notions at the reader at once. He must divide his ideas and deliver them in some kind of order. He must devise a route and a set of sign posts by which he can lead the reader through a maze of information to the conclusion he desires. That process is *organization;* it results in *structure.*

At first it might seem that the obvious way to organize would be for the writer to reproduce his ideas in the order in which they came to him. All he would have to do is to describe his experiences, or research, and his thoughts about these as they occurred to him. Since the writer arrived at the conclusion, presumably the reader would do likewise.

Sometimes this method works; sometimes it does not. Usually, the message has a predictive quality that comes to have dynamics of its own. The writer often conceives his idea in stages, and the order of those stages depends largely on chance and circumstance. Once the idea is formed, it has a predictive quality which determines how it should be communicated.

Synthesis: The Writer Getting a Manageable Perspective

Every task of communication necessitates the writer's mastery of the material and his formulation of exactly what he wants to say. Since he can hold only so much in his mind, he must limit his subject. Since he needs a guiding force to tell him what is necessary and what is not, he must phrase his purpose.

NARROWING

A writer must realize the difference between a broad subject and a narrowed topic. A premedical student, given a free assignment, may decide to write about health or hospitals, but he knows he cannot fully cover either subject. He may narrow the broad subject in *time*; that is, he may write about a day in a hospital instead of a year. He may narrow it in *space*; that is, he may write only about the language used in an operating room.

SELECTION OF A CONTROLLING QUESTION

To discipline himself further and make sure that he has clearly forced himself to focus on just one central message, a writer often phrases what is called a *controlling question*. This step, more than any other, will tell exactly what information is relevant and how the paper should be organized. Suppose you are writing a paper on the subject of hospitals and have narrowed the topic to language in the operating room. You realize that if you write "about" the topic, you play only the role of the parrot or the camera. You would be repeating what you heard or describing what you saw. "Where does my brain go to work?" you ask. "What is creative about merely 'covering' a topic?" you wonder. A deeper, more significant paper, and probably a more interesting one, would result from answering the question "Why is there so much jargon in the hospital operating room?" Your answer might be that although some of it is used merely to avoid unpleasantness, much of the special language is used because when doctors and nurses are under tension in the operating room, such language is accurate, hence safe.

This sentence, if you use it as the central message of your paper and then explain or defend it, would be called the *thesis* of the paper. The process of considering all the information you will cover and focusing it to explain or defend one idea is called *synthesis.*

Synthesis is the term for all the mental activity involved in experiencing and observing, research, note taking, head scratching, mumbling, coffee drinking, puzzling, despairing, false starting, writing down, tearing up, putting in, and taking out—the term that covers all the thinking that precedes the moment when you finally and often suddenly perceive what is the central message, the thesis, that you wish to convey.

The process of synthesis continues while you write. For your first draft you may just begin to write, perhaps rather aimlessly. After a paragraph or page or two you will chance upon an idea that gives you a feeling of direction. That sentence may or may not be an answer to the original question or topic you planned to confront, but it does reveal what you want to write.

Now that you know *what* you want to do, you turn your attention to *how* to do it. You say to yourself, "I can't do it all in the first paragraph. What do I do first? What, in order, are the separate steps I must take?" The task of taking your message apart is called *analysis.*

Analysis:
Determining Issues

In some cases the division of your message is relatively easy. If you are describing a process, you may elect to divide it into steps or units of time. The pattern is *chronological* or *sequential.* If you are describing a scene or object, you may elect to divide your description into units of space, for instance, basement, ground floor, and attic. That is easy enough. This pattern is called *spatial.*

Some other common patterns are suggested by a glance at your controlling question or thesis. If your question is "Why did the student body vote to reject ROTC?" you may divide your response into reasons. If your thesis is "Although the students' intent was good, the abolition of ROTC by the student government has had three unfortunate results," obviously your paper would discuss, in turn, the three results. Papers are often organized around causes, effects, classes, kinds, objections, issues, and such parallel concepts. In such cases the pattern is *topical.*

You may at this moment note a subtle change in what is influencing you. During synthesis *you* were the major force. You were deciding or learning what it was you wanted to write, what it was that you could write. Now the message is indicating to you how the paper should or can be structured. You have little choice in some cases. The force of your message is what we are referring to when we say that the message has its own dynamics.

One of the most inescapable patterns arises when you decide you wish to ask someone to do something, whether it is to turn off the headlights, adopt a new form of student government, or vote for a president. The questions that you must answer are so inevitable they are called *stock issues*.

STOCK ISSUES

An issue is a question that must be faced in a discussion. A congressman whose thesis is "America should intercede in the uprising in Montenegro" or the student arguing for the abolition of the grading system must consider the following stock issues:

1. Is there a need for a change in the present situation? (If not, why all the fuss?)
2. What plan is being advocated? (Okay, I'm interested now; can you correct the problems you describe?)
3. Would this plan solve the problem? (Show me.)
4. Is the plan feasible and preferable to another plan? (Can we pay for it? Is there a better plan?)

PROBLEM AND SOLUTION

Frequently, the stock issues are condensed into two major points, problem and solution. For instance, if an editorial recommends a bond issue to provide money for a new junior high school, it discusses first the need and then the proposed solution. Problem plus solution is very often the structure of a paper arguing for an action or policy.

OPERATIVE ASSERTION: SOURCE OF ISSUES

In any extended composition the broadest statement in the paper is its thesis or statement of purpose. The thesis, like any idea, can be classified according to certain types: observation, classification, generalization, judgment, or causal relationship. Each class of idea tends to generate certain questions from the reader. If the writer is aware of what kind of idea he is using, he can anticipate more successfully what questions his readers will ask. Thus he knows how to divide his task and how to organize his paper.

Throughout this book we have stated and restated the idea that assertions start rather than finish a dialogue. In conversation, when a speaker comments that "John has a murky future," he is guided in his next remarks by his companion's response: "He has? What makes you think so?" His original sentence was operative; it caused his friend to ask questions.

Having been started by this sentence, the conversation proceeds alternately between speaker and audience. When the speaker does not make a point clear, he is stopped: "Wait a minute. What do you mean?" If the speaker fails to prove an assertion, his audience may interrupt: "Hold on. I do not agree. I happen to know something to dispute your point." The speaker must then refute his companion's argument and buttress his own point with further evidence.

The writer has no such recourse. He must look out at his unseen audience of one or one million and presuppose what its questions will be. He must decide what assertions need proof, what terms need clarifying. He has no puzzled expression, no smile, no reaction of any sort to guide him. Fortunately, however, he does not always have to guess. Ideas do fit into categories, and by their nature these categories give the writer hints about how he should organize his writing. One of the most important reasons for studying rhetoric is that it will help a writer anticipate the questions his statements will generate, even when the audience is a reader who will not be seen and, perhaps, never even be known.

Observation

The first class of idea might be called no idea at all, since ideas in this category often require little mental activity. An *observation* is simply a statement of what has happened. The writer makes no comment about the source of the observation; he may have derived it from his own sensory perceptions, or he may have learned it from some other source. It may be true or false; if it is true—that is, if it can be verified by some acceptable standard and if people generally agree with it—it is called a fact. The following sentences are observations:

> Abdul Kareem Jabbar played basketball at U.C.L.A. before he became a member of the Milwaukee Bucks.
>
> I burned my finger.
>
> Antoine Lavoisier was admitted to the French Academy of Sciences in 1768.
>
> The amino acid analysis revealed a trace of an amino sugar.

The observation is *definitive*; it is complete in itself. It says all there is to be said. It does not often fall into the class of generative sentences requiring development and organization, but when it does, the structure of what follows is usually suggested by the breadth or vagueness of one of the terms. For instance, "Jim Ryun won the mile run" may not require any development, because we agree that the word *won* means "he came in first." Another sentence containing the same verb, "The Americans won the last Olympics," probably does need developing, because few countries agree on what it means to "win" the Olympics. The issues raised are these:

1. What do the terms of the observation mean?
2. In what respects are the terms justified?

When the Russians talk of "winning" the Olympics, they prefer to consider every sport, since they usually pile up a number of points in such sports as Greco-Roman wrestling, in which the United States is feeble or does not compete at all. Since their women athletes usually excel, Russia also likes to include results for both men and women. The United States prefers to consider only those track and field sports that characterize an American meet. The writer would have to show what he means by *won*, and then he might show why he thinks the term can be used.

Classification

Suppose we say, "John F. Kennedy was a man." What we have said in the technical language of a logician is that "The thing called John F. Kennedy is included in the class of things called man." Suppose we say, "Los Angeles and San Francisco are cities in California." We have placed the two in a class—that is, cities in the state of California.

Whenever we label something, we classify it. When we say, "The car is a classic Pierce-Arrow," we have classified it. If we say, "That crooked politician should be impeached," we have expressed the following classifications:

> That politician is in the class of people called crooked.
> He is a member of the class of people who should be impeached.

Often these labels are matters of opinion or judgment, which will be discussed later; judgments may require considerable explanation, but if the classification does not depend on a personal judgment, it can be communicated with relative ease. All we need do to be understood is to be sure that our audience understands and agrees with the definition of the class. For the preceding sentences our audience must agree with us about the meaning of *John F. Kennedy, man, Los Angeles, San Francisco, cities, California, car, Pierce-Arrow, crooked,* and *impeached.* The total communication required is really only a retracing of the thinking process by which we derived the idea. We decided upon the abstract qualities of the class, and we observed or stated that the specific example fitted the class.

Often when we classify, we do not communicate, because there may be less agreement about the class than we think. Take the simple statement "Pete is an adult." It seems clear enough, but is it? On Friday night Pete goes to the movies. Since he is fourteen, he pays an adult price for his ticket. On Saturday the picture changes, and he goes again. Outside the theater he sees a huge poster with a half-naked girl and an "X-rated, Adults Only" label on it. Confidently, he lays down his adult fee, but the ticket seller stops him.

"Are you eighteen?" she asks.

Pete realizes that on Friday he was an adult, but on Saturday he is not.
This simple example illustrates that when we use a sentence containing
a classification, we have an obligation to define our terms. You can imagine
the responsibility we assume when we use amorphous labels or classes like
liberal, conservative, radical, and so on.

If the writer's thesis is *classification,* two issues immediately suggest
themselves:

1. What are the characteristics of the class?
2. How does the specific instance satisfy the requirements of the class?

If the generative sentence is "Senator Flelps is a right-winger," the issues
are: "What is a right-winger?" and "In what way does Senator Flelps act
like a right-winger?" What issues are suggested by the following sentences?

Hampshire is an open-curriculum college.

Chopin was a romantic.

A Grateful Dead concert is a reunion.

It does not necessarily follow that every written composition whose thesis
is a classification will have a body composed of two equal sections. For instance, in an article based on the third sentence, the writer, Ben Gerson,
spent just a few words describing a reunion as an event "to memorialize,
perhaps relive, a past which never quite existed." Then he spent about five
hundred words demonstrating that in the past the rock group, the Grateful
Dead, participated in concerts, maybe "for free," which were "a wave of
spontaneous love." The old enchanted days were ones where the "good vibe
bands," with "their sheer, manifest pleasure in just playing," felt "equal to,
not above, the audience." Now that the band is "finally, improbably making
money," such good fellowship might not be expected, but a Grateful Dead
concert even now has the old verve. Thus Gerson dealt with the two issues
of his classification, but not at equal length.

Generalization

Whenever we state that some idea is true of a class of things, we are
making a *generalization.*

Newspapers print news.

Americans are imperialistic.

Men are more aggressive sexually than women.

Apples are sweet.

Table salt is a compound of nitrogen and glycerin.

Drugs broaden the mind.

These six statements are generalizations. They also contain certain classifications. Newspapers are included in the class of things that print news. Americans are included in the class of things that are imperialistic and so on. But because the statements assert what is claimed to be true about a group, they are primarily generalizations.

You may have noticed that the fifth statement is unequivocally false. Table salt is a compound of sodium and chloride. The sentence was included to demonstrate that a statement can be either true or false and still be a generalization.

Since no exceptions are mentioned in the sample generalizations, the word *all* is implied at the beginning of each sentence; truly or falsely, the last sentence, for instance, says that all drugs broaden the mind. In the sentence "The water is hot," the definite article *the* indicates that we mean some specific water, the water in a certain tea kettle perhaps. We have made an observation. If we were to say simply, "Water is hot," we would be implying that we mean all water, even though we did not say "all."

We can, in addition, make generalizations about *one* object or phenomenon by making an assertion about its actions or qualities:

John is dependable.

That dog does not bite.

The sun rises in the east.

In these sentences the word *always* is implied; the sentences seem to say that John is *always* dependable, that the dog *never* bites, and—whether it is true or not—that the sun *always* rises in the east. Unless the writer uses a *qualification*, like "some" or "usually," there are no exceptions implied.

When the thesis for a paper is a generalization, the issues that it generates are:

1. What is the meaning of the generalization?
2. What are the instances that yield the generalization?
3. Are the instances sufficient to merit a generalization?

If the thesis is "The French are impolite to tourists," the writer must classify the impoliteness as rudeness by cab drivers, hotel employees, pedestrians, newspapers, and hosts in general. This would be necessary because he could not even suggest that he had been exposed to all Frenchmen, although he may have met all "classes" of French people.

Analyze the following generalizations for the structure they imply:

Boxer dogs slobber.

He has no capacity for business.

Both generalizations have their own natures, in that the issues they generate may require differing amounts of discussion. For the first sentence it would be easy to define *slobber*. It would also be easy to describe several examples of slobbering that the writer has observed. The difficulty would be in dealing with the third issue, that is, proving that this unlovely habit is characteristic of *all* boxer dogs. Usually, the answers on more difficult issues, the crucial ones, take up more space. Very often the issues are telescoped, as would be probable with the statement about the boxer dogs. The writer might describe as many examples as he could, to convince his readers that every time he had ever seen a boxer dog—the combined sum of his specific instances—the dog had drooled all over the area.

For the second sentence the writer would first have to define *capacity for business*. In contrast to the thesis about boxer dogs, which would require almost no space for definition, in this case the simple definition of terms would occupy a large share of the paper.

Judgment

Suppose, as we idly observe two boys mowing lawns, we notice not only that one boy is moving more rapidly than the other, but also that his mowing is neater. We decide that his mower, powered by a small engine, is "better" than the other, pushed by the boy. This thought is a *judgment*, a statement that evaluates or compares goodness or effectiveness.

All judgments demand a standard or a measuring device. In judging the two mowers, we abstracted the quality of goodness and said, perhaps too hastily, that one is better than the other. What we thought of as goodness was based on two standards, speed and neatness. In these two respects, which might add up to the abstraction of effectiveness, the power mower is definitely to be preferred. But for the general judgment of better, we must consider all respects. What about those extra pollutants being thrown into the air? What about cost? What about durability? We know that power mowers, which often cost over a hundred dollars, have a distressing habit of wearing out in about three years; a hand mower will easily last for ten. These convictions are based on observations of some specific incidents. We have seen advertisements in the newspapers that indicated prices of both types of mowers, and we remember the length of time our family mower lasted. To make the broad judgment of better, we must consider all the criteria.

In the sentence "This pan is hot," we can easily understand the relationship between the two concepts. Something included in the class of things called pan is included in the class of things called hot. But what is meant by *pan*? Which pan? What kind of pan? Unless the statement is accompanied by a gesture to indicate *this* pan or *that* pan, the audience will be confused. And what is meant by *hot*? A hot day, hot spices, hot coffee, and a hot pan all suggest quite different temperatures. What we are now talking about is the kind of judgment in which both the process of abstraction and the language can be confusing.

A man asks a waiter if the coffee is hot.

"Yes, sir, it is hot."

The customer puts the cup to his lips, takes a sip, and burns his tongue. "It's not hot," he rages; "it's boiling!" Sitting at a table next to this customer is another customer who is quite mystified. He really likes hot coffee; he finds the coffee just right.

Judgments differ on all kinds of issues. Is this film star beautiful or insipid? Is the Grand Canyon magnificent or useless? (It doesn't grow one ear of corn!) Is that political ideology unacceptable? A person can accept Christianity but question Roman Catholicism. He can call Sally a lovable person and Jim a likable one.

If you become a literary critic (or an English major), you may write, "Ernest Hemingway was America's greatest novelist of the twentieth century." Or you may write, "Ernest Hemingway was highly overrated." Whatever you become, you will make such judgments as "The Plymouth is the best car; I think we should buy one" or "The Plymouth is a terrible car; I would never buy one."

If your thesis is a judgment, the issues that suggest a framework of organization resemble those for classification and generalization. This might be expected, since the boundary between any two kinds of ideas is often indistinct. The issues are:

1. What are the criteria for the judgment?
2. How does my specific instance fit the criteria?

If a writer were to develop the thesis that William Faulkner is a great writer, his organization probably would be suggested by the need for a criterion, perhaps that a "great writer uplifts the human heart" (which was Faulkner's own standard). He then might have to show that Faulkner, in spite of his preoccupation with sodomy, rape, and other aberrant behavior, demonstrated his faith in the family and in human strength and believed that they could triumph even in a doomed society.

For practice, analyze how the following judgments and the issues raised could provide a structure for a theme:

Eudora Welty has more humanity than other contemporary writers.

Willie Mays was the greatest of all center fielders.

Although business contractions make job opportunities scarcer both for experienced workers and for this year's college graduates, the figure of 4 percent unemployment would be considered an "acceptable" rate in the United States.

Causal Relationship

When we say that B is the result of A, we have indicated a *causal relationship*. Touching something hot causes pain, and running into a tree causes a different kind of pain. Clapping your hands makes a noise. Sometimes these relationships can be explained by physical or chemical laws. Heat burns or oxidizes tissue, which irritates nerve endings, which in turn causes a pain response in the brain. Clapping your hands causes violently oscillating sound waves that vibrate your eardrums, which activate nerve ganglia and send messages to the brain, where they are translated into sound.

Other causal relationships are not so easy to explain. A new football coach is hired by your college, and the team starts winning. Is he the cause, or did the school suddenly start getting better material? Or did other schools field poorer teams?

Whenever the thesis indicates a causal relationship, the issues are:

1. Did the consequence occur every time the antecedent was present?
2. Was the antecedent present every time the consequence occurred?
3. Was the antecedent the only possible cause present when the consequence occurred?
4. Is there a natural explanation of why A, the antecedent, causes B, the consequence?

Almost all scientific reports that announce a new discovery are organized around these issues, which, after all, are the heart of the scientific method. Certainly, any account of Louis Pasteur's discoveries would reflect his concern for these issues. Pasteur's theory that germs (the antecedent) cause disease (the consequence) was disputed by many of his contemporaries, who thought that disease, mold, and sourness of milk developed spontaneously. Pasteur disproved the theory of spontaneous generation by boiling the milk and killing all the minute mold-producing organisms (or the antecedent) and demonstrating that mold (or the consequence) did not develop when the bacteria were absent. At another point in his demonstrations, he showed that if a hydrophobic dog bit a man and the saliva from the dog entered the human system, the man got the dog's disease. Whenever he found a person suffering from a disease, Pasteur used his microscope to prove that bacteria were present.

Strategy:
Source of Proportion and Order

Would that life were so simple that if you analyzed your thesis and answered the questions you generate, you would succeed in all your writing. Unfortunately, writing to explain or convince is much more complex than that. One problem is that your assertions are not always one kind of assertion or the other. When you write that apples are sweet, you are classifying —that is, you are saying that apples are in the class of food that is sweet. The statement is also a generalization. Since the questions generated have some similarity, this is no great problem; once you are sensitive to the idea that your assertions generate issues, your common sense will tell you what the issues are.

A more troublesome problem is that after you perceive the issues you will confront, you must decide on a strategy as to how much attention to pay to each issue and the order in which to discuss them.

Once again your emphasis changes. At first you looked at external circumstances. Were you assigned a subject by your instructor? Were you writing for a job? Were you responding angrily to a comment in a newspaper?

Then you shifted to your own interests. What part of the subject (narrowed topic) could *you* handle? What do you know about it? What exactly do you want to say? What could you say that your reader would respect?

Once again a shift, this time to the message. What issues did it generate? What structure did the message, by its very nature, dictate? Now the concern shifts to your reader and the situation at this particular moment.

Sometimes the paper you are writing will be a response, or refutation, to some speech or written document. You may, for instance, begin a letter to an editor: "I read with distress of Senator Jones' plan to vote against the right of newsmen to protect their source of information. You gave his three reasons. I think he is wrong on all three counts."

You might understandably proceed to attack his three reasons in the order in which he provided them. What you have done is to organize your letter by a point-by-point response, because you think that is the best strategy. Your strategy, as you might expect, can vary with different circumstances and with your reader's state of mind.

PROPORTION

The following story shows that organization must vary with circumstance and cannot be based purely on the analysis of a thesis statement; the story also shows that the writer must be flexible and exercise his own judgment, especially when it comes to the relative importance he assigns to each issue and the resulting proportion of space he devotes to each subtopic within his paper.

A debate team in a small college prepared for the subject "Resolved: The United States Congress Should Nationalize the Oil Industry." Taking the affirmative, the members of the team planned to defend the change on the basis of the stock issues. They secured evidence that the oil companies were not serving the country well. The debaters worked out a plan for nationalization, based on what Mexico had done. With Mexico and a number of other countries for comparison, they convinced themselves that the plan would work and solve our oil problems.

To the surprise of the affirmative team, the opponents conceded the first points. Yes, the oil companies were doing a bad job. Yes, nationalization worked in other countries. But—and here the negative team concentrated its efforts—such a plan would be dangerous to the American way of life. When Mussolini took over Italy, when Juan Perón became dictator in Argentina, when Stalin wished to tighten his hold on Russia, their first acts were to destroy private business. When America no longer has private industry, it is no longer America. So went the argument—and the negative team made it stick and won.

By the time of its second debate, our team was ready for this American way of life business. After all, the team members were prepared to argue, America has a history of having the government run some of its business, the Postal Department and the Tennessee Valley Authority, for instance.

Once again, however, they were unprepared for the crucial issue. The negative team agreed with practically every argument the affirmative team advanced.

This negative team argued, however, that a simple plan of regulation would solve the problem. Why bother with such a drastic step? Our team lost again.

The point to this sad story is that although the nature of the message raises the issues, the situation and the reader determine the treatment and order. An argument may be raging in town about a new swimming pool. A newspaper editorialist might waste space by discussing the need for such a facility, when the whole town wants the pool, but its citizens are at each other's throats about its location. The need for the pool is a dead issue; the site is the crucial one. The writer must try to find out which issues are crucial to his reader or readers in a given situation—and he must shape his work accordingly.

The situation and the reader may affect the structure in other ways also. For instance, a certain plan may require special terms, and the writer might insert some definitions, because he suspects his readers will not know the terms. He may have to supply some background information, which he would introduce, although in more specific terms, by a sentence such as "Before the problem can be understood, it is necessary for one to know a great deal about the history of the situation." A writer must learn to anticipate any questions, uncertainties, opposition, or counterplans that might arise in a discussion of his problem, and he must use this awareness to determine the structure of his paper and the relative proportion of space he will devote to each issue and its consequent development. Organization is not mechanical; it requires a great deal of sensitivity and judgment on the part of the writer.

ORDER

When the writer has done the necessary synthesis and analysis and he knows his thesis or purpose, his major points, and the information he will use to develop them, he can go on to the next problem of organization. He must decide what order to present his points in, and he may have to decide whether to present his point of view in the introduction as a statement of purpose, whether to announce his topic, and whether to set up a controlling question.

Here again, you, as a writer, should try to anticipate the audience's state of mind. Take the problem-and-solution structure. If you were trying to convince an apathetic audience to adopt a new plan, you would probably have a better chance of success if, instead of presenting your plan at the outset, you first aroused the audience as to the evils of the present situation.

Suppose you are writing an expository paper with three main sections. Here are some suggestions that may be appropriate.

1. Try putting your most important or most interesting point first to get your audience's attention. Don't, however, trail off, leaving your least interesting or least significant idea for last; put it in the middle and save a dramatic or important idea for the end.
2. If one point depends on another for clarity, you must, of course, cover the explanatory point first.
3. Since psychologists believe that the last point is remembered longest, the first point next longest, and the middle point least, you may wish to put the idea you want your reader to remember most of all as your last point.
4. If you are presenting a controversial topic, you will usually be wise to lead off with those points that will be most readily acceptable to your potentially hostile audience. Get them nodding their heads in agreement; then hit them with the point they will be least likely to accept.

The phrasing of your thesis statement will provide clues as to the order of your points. If your thesis is "An irritating situation in Egypt is caused by the difficulty in getting trained men to work in the villages," you first answer the question "What is the irritating situation?" and then turn to the cause, the difficulty of getting trained men to work in the villages. Your pattern of organization is effect and cause; your phrasing provides the clue as to which topic should be discussed first. Conversely, you might decide to word your statement, "The difficulty of getting trained men to work in the villages has caused a severe problem in Egypt." Here you would discuss the cause before the effect.

Occasionally, your thesis will be a compound or a complex sentence. If it is compound, you will probably have to decide which idea is easily acceptable to your audience or which idea is basic; that idea comes first. If the first clause is not controversial but the other is, begin with the noncontroversial topic. For instance, suppose you have been asked to compare a Volkswagen and a Renault. You might come up with the thesis: "Although the VW is cheaper, the Renault is more comfortable." If the first idea is generally accepted, you may wish to dispose of it first and then lead your audience to your more original and controversial conviction.

As you plan your organization, you may hit upon a pattern that makes very good sense but does not exactly fit your thesis. If you decide that this pattern has greater truth than the one your original thesis would generate, rephrase your thesis until it exactly fits your preferred plan. As you have seen, the analysis of your message, or thesis statement, whether it is observation, classification, generalization, judgment, or causal relationship, determines the basic issues. Analysis of the situation and the reader determines the order of your major points as well as the relative amount of space you will devote to each one. With this strategy mapped out, you can rough in the body of your paper. Then you should turn to making sure the parts all stick together.

Transitions

After you have decided your thesis, your major points, and their order— and after you have written a rough draft of the body of your paper—you may still have to worry about how to weave the parts together. Ideally, the sentences and sections would be so coherent, so logically related that the connections are clear, but this is not always the case. Instead, the points of your final paper may seem to be a series of unrelated sentences, paragraphs, or essays, and if this is the case, your paper will lack strength and coherence. What you may need are *transitions,* to provide a smooth flow in meaning, structure, and sound from one sentence to the next and to reinforce the relationship of each unit to the total message of the composition.

In many cases writers have the logical relationship between sentences and paragraphs quite clearly in mind, but, forgetting that their audience is not composed of mind readers, they fail to insert helpful connections. Note the absence of connectives in the following paragraph:

```
Because my grandfather had to help his family, he had to
leave school after the sixth grade. He worked every day,
read every night, and obtained his bachelor's and master's
degrees from Columbia after he was married.
```

The student who wrote the paragraph obviously knows all about his grandfather, and the relationships are clear in his own mind; but because of the lack of transitions, the reader can only wonder what happened between the time Grandfather left school and the time he obtained his degrees. After the student revised the paragraph, these relationships became clear:

Because my grandfather had to help his family, he had to leave school after the sixth grade. He did not want to give up his education entirely, however. From the day he had to leave school and start working, he read for a couple of hours every night. As a result, he covered the whole high school curriculum on his own and, after he was married, was able to enter Columbia University. In due course, he obtained his bachelor's and master's degrees there.

As you can see, gaps between sentences can be filled either by necessary information or by transitional devices.

Transitions between sentences often present more trouble than transitions between paragraphs. In the following selection, for instance, a student described his automobile. These two sentences occurred fairly early in the paper:

The motor itself is in good condition. Such things as the carburetor, battery, oil filter, brake, and radiator are not always up to par, especially at the most inappropriate times.

An instructor—particularly one unfamiliar with the workings of an automobile engine—might write in the margin, "Illogical. Aren't you contradicting yourself?" An inserted transition (plus a change to compound sentence structure) explains what the student had in mind.

The motor itself is in good condition, but such things as the carburetor, battery, oil filter, brake, and radiator are not always up to par, especially at the most inappropriate times.

There are numerous ways of achieving coherence between sentences. For example, in the second sentence you may repeat a word or phrase that appears in the first sentences:

> A favorite device was to make a *moccasined* person tread in the tracks of the *moccasined* enemy, and thus hide his own trail. Cooper wore out barrels of *moccasins* in working that trick.—MARK TWAIN, "Fenimore Cooper's Literary Offenses"

In the second sentence you may use a synonym for a word in the first sentence:

> When I go home for a vacation, *my kid brother* invariably presents the greatest threat to my peace of mind. *The little pest* thinks nothing of waking me with shouts of glee at six o'clock every morning.

As another device, you may use a pronoun in the second sentence whose antecedent is in the first sentence:

> Very few Americans realize that *Khrushchev* did not change the basic character of *Soviet society*. *He* did not make *it* a revolutionary or even a socialist regime but one of the more conservative and even class-ridden regimes of the western world.—ROBERT F. DRINAN, *Vietnam and Armageddon*

You may also begin two consecutive sentences with the same grammatical construction:

> *On the right* the visitor sees a dark brown, dismal-looking, apparently abandoned cage, with the word *INFORMATION* on it. *On the left* is a wooden table, which, at twelve o'clock, is piled high with various student paraphernalia.

All too often a careless writer uses connectives loosely, forgetting that each one has a specific meaning and a special use. Even an experienced writer can profit from occasionally checking over his supply of transitional words and phrases. Here is a partial list:

and, in addition, moreover, similarly, also, and then, secondly, thirdly (etc.), finally, indeed, in fact	*To introduce a parallel idea*
since, because, so that, for	*To show cause*
for example, for instance, to illustrate	*To introduce an example*
on the other hand, nevertheless, however, still, but	*To introduce a contrasting idea*
therefore, in conclusion, consequently, accordingly, in other words, as a result	*To conclude*

The following paragraph, taken from a student theme about the stereotyped quality of some motion pictures, demonstrates the value of transitions. In variant A transitions between sentences and ideas have been omitted. In variant B they have been supplied. Study the differences between these two versions and determine exactly the relationships between sentences and ideas that are indicated by the italicized words in variant B.

A

The "western" or cowboy movie could use some changes. The cowboy movie opens with two dirty and unshaven cowboys walking along in the desert. They are lost after chasing a no-good outlaw. Their horses are dead, and their canteens are empty. Tex drops to the ground and declares he can't go another step. Idaho drags Tex to some shade and says he'll go for help. He is attacked by Indians, wounded by outlaws, and bitten by rattlesnakes. Idaho makes it to town, has a drink, rides all the way back, shoots his gun to scare all the vultures, and saves Tex's life. A contented vulture sitting on the bones of old Tex would be a better final scene.

B

Another type of movie that could use some changes is the "western." The *cowboy movie* opens with two dirty and unshaven cowboys walking along in the desert. *One's name is Tex, and he comes from (of course) Texas; the other one's name is Idaho, and he comes from Massachusetts.* They *had been* chasing a no-good outlaw and are *now* lost *in the desert. As we join the boys,* their horses are dead, and their canteens are empty. Tex drops to the ground and declares he can't go another step. Idaho drags Tex to some shade and says he'll go on for help. *On the way* he is attacked by Indians, wounded by outlaws, and bitten by a rattlesnake. Idaho, *however,* makes it to town, has a drink, *procures a horse,* rides all the way back, shoots his gun to scare all the vultures, and saves Tex's life. *Just once* I would like to see old Idaho not make it back, *and let the final scene be* a contented vulture sitting on the bones of old Tex.

Once you have the body of the paper structured, written, and stuck together, you need to look at your introduction and conclusion. You may have been fortunate and steamed up enough to have jotted down a beginning and an ending that will stand. Good for you. Even so, you should go back and check to see if polishing is necessary.

The Introduction

While we are discussing how to "finish off" a paper, we suggest some points you should consider about the beginning and endings of extended communication. To give you a basis to test your ideas, we provide some alternative methods.

Consider whether you accept our perception of what an introduction should do:

1. It summarizes the message.

For any number of reasons, including inattention, poor reading ability, or a natural inclination to find what he wants to find instead of what the author intended, the reader needs a precise synopsis of what a writer is trying to say. Without such a synopsis, the message that emerges may be quite different from the one the writer intended.

2. It dictates to the writer what explanation or evidence he must provide.

In any essay the most heavily loaded sentence of all is the thesis statement. If the thesis is "There were many reasons for South Carolina's belligerence before the Civil War," that statement dictates the essay's subsequent content. The writer must state those reasons. The predictive content of a thesis statement tells the writer what information he must provide and what he must avoid.

3. It indicates what structures will be appropriate.

Beyond having predictive content, the thesis statement carries an implication of structure. Besides indicating what content is necessary, it indicates the way that content should be arranged. In the thesis statement just mentioned, "There were many reasons for South Carolina's belligerence before the Civil War," the structure implied is obviously a list of reasons. Had the thesis statement read, "South Carolina had a long history of belligerence before the Civil War," the same reasons might be included, but the structure of the paper would be chronological.

4. It indicates the nature of the language that will be used.

Obviously, if the thesis is a technical one, the language will be equally so. If, however, the paper relates some of last summer's experiences, the language would inevitably be less technical. The introduction, in its statement of purpose, indicates the tone of the paper—and the language may be either humorous or somber. It indicates the degree of conviction—and the language may be either cool and measured or vehement.

5. It indicates whether the essay will be expository or argumentative.

All nonfiction writing can be divided into two classes. The classification is based on whether the writer intends to explain or convince. If a writer wishes to explain cybernetics, the objective correlative, or the quantum theory, he will write exposition. If he wishes to convince his audience that Jean-Paul Sartre is the most important thinker of the twentieth century or that a new school building should be constructed, he will write argumentation. This distinction is extremely important, because it dictates the nature of the development needed in the essay. The development required for expository writing is called exposition; the development required for argumentation is called evidence. Just as development differs for exposition and argumentation, so do the organization and the language that are required.

There are several types of argument, and when the writer indicates his purpose, he also indicates what type of argument he is using—and what evidence, structure, and language are required. A writer may argue for agreement with his thesis. The following theses exemplify *argument for agreement:*

> The counterculture—rock music, the underground film, and the commune —is setting standards of taste today.
>
> Harry S Truman was one of the ten greatest presidents of the United States.
>
> Basketball, not baseball, deserves to be called America's national sport.

Since all these are controversial, to defend them would be to write argumentation. If the writer's argument is successful, the reader responds "I agree" at the end.

Another kind of argument is *argument for action.* The writer not only wants his reader to agree with him; he wants his reader to act. Consider the following theses:

> Noisy motorcycles should be banned.
>
> This dormitory should be coeducational.
>
> The practice of taking attendance in college classes should be abolished.

The writer has succeeded in this type of argument if his reader responds at the end, "I agree; I will *act.*" Since the action does not always come immediately but is intended, this form is sometimes called *argument for policy.*

Technically, all argument, when properly structured, is based on sound reasoning. It follows the rules of logic and evidence, and it ignores the emotions, biases, and prejudices of both writer and reader. Since writers and readers are human beings, however, pure argument seldom exists. Rhetoric employs both argument, a blend of logic 'and reasoning, and persuasion, which includes an appeal to emotions, interests, and other personal concerns.

METHODS OF INDICATING PURPOSE

There are at least four methods of indicating a paper's purpose: the thesis statement, the direct statement of purpose, the controlling question, and the announcement of topic. Each of them has its place, and they should all be mastered.

The Thesis Statement

You've met the thesis statement in previous assignments, but to show you that it's a common technique, we give you some examples taken from important speeches in American history. These sentences appeared at the end of the introduction and were almost repeated in the conclusion.

> The man who has in full, heaped and rounded measures all these splendid qualifications is the present grand and gallant leader of the Republican party . . . James G. Blaine.—ROBERT G. INGERSOLL, "Nominating speech, 1884"

> It is the English-speaking race that has moulded the destiny of this continent; and the Puritan influence is the strongest influence that has acted upon it.—GEORGE WILLIAM CURTIS, "The Puritan Principle: Liberty Under the Law"

> To those of my race who depend upon bettering their condition in a foreign land, or who underestimate the importance of cultivating friendly relations with the Southern white man, who is their next-door neighbor, I would say: "Cast down your bucket where you are—cast it down in making friends in every manly way of all the people of all races by whom we are surrounded."—BOOKER T. WASHINGTON, "Address at the Opening of the Atlanta Exposition"

> I ask that the Congress declare that since the unprovoked and dastardly attack by Japan on Sunday, December seventh, a state of war has existed between the United States and the Japanese empire.—FRANKLIN D. ROOSEVELT, "War Message to Congress"

The Statement of Purpose

Occasionally, a writer wants to be particularly certain that his audience understands his goal or his purpose. Professional articles often begin, "It is my purpose to prove that . . . ," and the writer finishes the sentence with his thesis. Here are some examples:

> It is my purpose today to report what your committee has learned about sexuality on this campus, and what should be done about it.

> In this paper we report that cholesterol is metabolized by *Digitalis purpurea* to several products, among them pregnenolone.—E. CASPI, D. O. LEWIS, D. M. PISTOL, and A. WINTER, *Experimentia*

The statement of purpose is mechanical, but it is effective. It is apt to be used when a scholar is talking to his interested peers, when clarity is more important than grace, or when, in a highly controversial situation, a writer wishes to avoid any possible confusion about his central purpose.

The Controlling Question

There are times when a writer elects to use neither the thesis statement nor the direct statement of purpose. When he faces an antagonistic audience, he may prefer to delay indicating his own opinion until he has conditioned his audience by reducing their prejudices or by producing evidence that will make them more favorable to his thesis. At the beginning he will ask a controlling question that he proceeds to answer in the rest of his presentation. He may not actually state his thesis until his conclusion.

For example, on June 24, 1788, while the New York Convention debated whether to ratify the Federal Constitution, an amendment was suggested that would have limited federal powers. With sentiment running strongly against him, young Alexander Hamilton rose to speak against the amendment. Instead of incurring opposition at once by stating his thesis, he asked, "Now, sir, what is the tendency of the proposed amendment?" He then showed how the amendment would make the United States Senate an un-

stable "vassal." His evidence was great, and after hearing it, the convention accepted his conclusion, "It is necessary that . . . we eradicate the poisonous principle from our government." Had he advanced his unpopular view first, it is conceivable that an aroused convention would hardly have listened to his argument—and the federal government would have been reduced in power forever.

The Announcement of Topic

Sometimes, instead of asking a controlling question in the introduction, writers delay expressing their own point of view by simply announcing their topic. This gives the writer a chance to present his evidence first so that he can unify his message and at the same time prepare his audience for his controversial or surprising view. The announcement of topic is also used when a writer's view may already be known and his purpose is to explain or justify it.

In 1837, when Ralph Waldo Emerson was asked to give the Phi Beta Kappa address at Harvard, he planned to condemn American reliance on European thought and to request intellectual independence. He did not begin with this controversial thesis; instead he announced his topic: "I accept the topic which not only usage but the nature of our association seems to prescribe to this day—the American scholar."

The announcement of topic is often used in straight exposition; for instance, a sociology teacher might announce, "Today I will discuss fascism." Though this approach has its merit, it has a great drawback. Too often it is used as license to wander; a speaker or writer announces a broad topic and then proceeds to ramble all over the place. In contrast to the thesis statement, the statement of purpose, and the controlling question, all of which have very exact predictive obligations, the announcement of topic provides little discipline. The first three guide the writer and tell the reader what he can expect. The announcement of topic, unfortunately, does too little of either.

THE APPEAL STEP

The introduction of a paper has two principal functions. We have been discussing the first: the writer's *establishment of purpose*. The second function is to stimulate the interest of the reader, to convince him to read on. This part of the introduction is called the *appeal step*.

It is nearly impossible to discuss in general terms what will interest people or convince them to read on. We do know there are topics that have what we call current interest. At the time of an international crisis, almost any newspaper article about the crisis will attract readers. A free-lance writer is sensitive to such topics and aware of seasonal interests. For winter issues he may, in June, write articles about skiing and Christmas presents; in January he may write about camping for summer issues.

There are also topics of general interest. Any mother will usually read an article about babies. College students will read about college problems. War, calamity, sex, and violence all attract an audience. Almost invariably, an article that starts out to prove that an important person is wrong about something will attract an audience. We like to read about Jack in conflict with the giant. In fact, we will read almost any article about a controversy.

The trick in making your appeal, then, is to take advantage of the current or general interest. For example, most readers are interested in health. The following article from *Time* magazine demonstrates how the appeal steps should lead provocatively to the thesis, which controls the rest of the composition.

In the basement of Harvard's School of Dental Medicine, biochemist James H. Shaw and his assistants worked for more than ten years with cages full of white rats and cotton rats, with sugar-rich and sugar-free chow, with test tubes and dissecting boards. The twofold aim: to find out how certain sugars promote tooth decay, then to find a way to forestall it. The Sugar Research Foundation, Inc., set up by the sugar industry, bankrolled the project for a total of $57,000. Now in the *Journal of the American Dental Association*, Dr. Shaw reports his findings.

The opening sentence makes plain that the problem is important enough for some men to work ten years on it. This is the appeal step.

The introduction indicates that the article will answer two questions: (1) What causes decay? (2) How can it be prevented? This ends the introduction.

Tooth decay is caused only by food remaining in the mouth—proved by feeding rats through stomach tubes. Even sugar, fed this way, causes no decay.

The first answer begins here.

Sugar, in solution, causes little decay: granulated sugar (as sprinkled on fruits and cereals) causes much more.

Of the various kinds of sugar, fructose (from most fruit), glucose (from grapes and starch foods), sucrose (table sugar from cane or beets), lactose (from milk), and maltose (from beer) are all precipitors of decay. So is a high-starch diet, even when relatively low in sugar. It does no good to substitute raw for refined sugar, but blackstrap molasses causes a marked reduction in cavities.

Saliva is a good tooth protector. Removal of successive salivary glands gave a progressive increase in decay.

The second answer begins here.

Penicillin and chlorotetracycline (Aureomycin) are effective anti-decay agents, as are urea and dibasic ammonium carbonate; other antibiotics and chemicals tested (among them, many of those now commonly blended into toothpastes) do little or no good.

The two answers constitute the body of the report.

Dr. Shaw's conclusion: "We should cut down on sugar consumption, particularly candy. We should be careful about sugar in forms that remain in the mouth because

This is the conclusion.

of their physical properties." Along with his findings, Dr. Shaw also reported that his work has stopped. Reason: the Sugar Research Foundation withdrew its support.

One dependable way to attract a reader is to indicate via your appeal step that you're involved in a controversy. If you can play the part of Jack the Giant Killer and pick a quarrel with an authority or a general opinion, you will catch the interest and maybe even the sympathy of your reader. Notice how Edgar Z. Friedenberg has done that in the following excerpt:

The idea that what separates us from the young is something so passive that it may justly be called a "generation gap" is, I believe, itself a misleading article of middle-aged liberal ideology, serving to allay anxiety rather than to clarify the bases of intergenerational conflict. It is true, to be sure, that the phrase is strong enough to describe the barrier that separates many young people from their elders, for a majority still accept our society as providing a viable pattern of life and expectations for the future. Liberalism dies hard, and most young people, like some Negroes even today, are still willing to attribute their difficulties with their elders and society to mutual misunderstanding.

The author identifies his opponent—the "middle-aged liberal."

I believe, however, that this is a false position. . . .

Here he picks the fight. He is one man against the whole liberal Establishment. He insists, later in this paragraph, that the gap is a serious class conflict.

As the article develops, Friedenberg relies upon his introduction to provide the structural framework. He first refutes the concept of a generation gap and then develops the idea of deep exploitation.

There are at least two common mistakes that writers make in the appeal step. Including a joke or an anecdote that is not related to your topic or thesis reveals a misunderstanding of the appeal step. You may have heard the story of the man who, before he sold his mule, said that it was easy to control; all it needed, he said, was a "soft word." The buyer, however, could not get the mule to move. The seller, called in for help, took a long, heavy club and proceeded to beat the stubborn beast across the rump. At first the mule paid little attention; then he turned his head around slowly and looked at his former master. At this point the man picked up the reins, spoke softly, and, sure enough, the beast went to work willingly.

"But you said this mule is easy to control. All I thought it needed was a soft word."

"You're right. That's what I said."

"Then why the beating?"

"Well, first you have to attract his attention."

This joke is more or less related to introductions, especially to the appeal step, and it conceivably could have been used in the opening of this section. Another story on another subject might have been quite inappropriate. A joke should do more than attract attention; it should focus attention on your subject, or better still, it should dramatically illustrate your whole thesis.

Another common fault is the stereotyped beginning. Whenever a speaker or writer begins, "According to *Webster's,* such and such is such and such," he displays an insensitivity to his audience. Almost any reader or listener has heard such an introduction too many times. It is the cliché of essay and speech openings.

There are many such trite beginnings. You should watch out for expressions that have been overused by every newspaper, advertisement, and speaker. Any student who starts his theme with such expressions as "In this day and age," "In our world today," or "In our modern times" immediately convinces his audience that he is either too lazy to think or simply cannot produce an original thought or expression of his own.

The Conclusion

Theoretically, if you wrote a clear enough introduction and an effective body for your paper, you would not need a conclusion. You would have stated your thesis, and you would have explained or proved it. Almost invariably, however, a conclusion is helpful. It is your last opportunity to demonstrate that you have fulfilled the obligation generated by your thesis or purpose statement. The obvious, perhaps too obvious, procedure in writing your conclusion is to begin the last paragraph with "In conclusion . . ." and to end with an outline-like summary. You may certainly restate your thesis, and you may summarize the body of your paper; but you probably should do either or both with some degree of subtlety. The following two conclusions, written by students who were asked to assist in designing a college building by giving their reactions to an existing classroom, both summarize the writer's objections, yet neither conclusion employs the words *in conclusion* or *in summary:*

```
Only when these three factors—writing boards, acoustics,
and seating—are remedied, will Room 205 become a decent
classroom.
```

So now you have a headache as a result of attempting to take notes with poor lighting, jangled nerves from straining to hear and not being able to, and a backache from a cramped seating position. These are the rewards you receive from trying to obtain knowledge in Room 205.

Whether your conclusion contains a summary or not, make sure that it is an *integral part of the paper* and that it does not refer to a point you have not previously discussed.

There are as many possible kinds of conclusions as there are writers. The form of conclusion that will end one student's theme effectively will not necessarily be effective or even acceptable in another paper. Bear in mind, though, that a conclusion should:

1. Arise naturally out of what has been said.
2. Relate smoothly to the body of the paper.
3. Bring out the main point or points you have made.
4. Make a strong impression on the reader and, consequently, cause him to remember your whole paper.
5. Agree in tone with the rest of your paper. For instance, a frivolous conclusion will not fit a basically serious essay.

The various methods of making a conclusion effective—an unusual or unexpected ending, a rhetorical question, a strong statement of intent or belief, a variation in the length and rhythm of your sentences—will work only if the conclusion as a whole fulfills these five basic requirements.

There is one "natural" way of ending a paper that deserves special attention; it is known as either *completing the cycle* or *closing by return* and consists of returning to an image, an idea, or a statement that occurs in the introduction. The first of the following examples, which are from student themes, contains a return to the same image that was employed at the beginning of the paper. The other example presents a return to the same idea.

Introduction. Every fall, while trees and flowers are dying, a form of America's artificial beauty comes to life: the automobile is reborn. Out of the factory sprouts the stem of our leisure time with all its branches, displaying various shapes, sizes and colors. Each model has its own gadgets, its own improvements, its fancy name, and most of all, its price tag.

Conclusion. Every summer, when trees and flowers are in their bloom, the young automobile is dying. It leaves behind a year of enjoyable driving, and now it is ready either for a trade-in or for the junk yard. Before it dies, however, it brings the birth of this year's new models. Once again, the cycle is completed.

Introduction. "May I help you, Madam?" "Yes, I'd like to see a 15-33, long-point yellow pin-stripe, please." "Surely, I'll see if I have it." To anyone who has ever worked in a department store, these are familiar words. They come from a salesperson, selling his wares, in this case, a shirt. For the past two and a half years, I have been employed by a large Boston department store, selling everything from children's shoes to men's furnishings.

Conclusion. Here it is, two and one-half years later, and I'm still with the Company. On any Monday, Wednesday, or Saturday, I can be found waiting on and diligently answering the questions of my customers. "Could you help me out, sir?" "Certainly, Madam, which way did you come in?"

Often a conclusion returns not only to the concepts established in the introduction but to the title as well.

THE BLUEING OF AMERICA

A sizable segment of the American intelligentsia has been on a kick of revolution talk for the last few years. Only very recently this talk was carried on in a predominantly Left mood, generating fantasies of political revolution colored red or black. The mood appears to have shifted somewhat. Now the talk has shifted to cultural revolution. Gentle grass is pushing up through the cement. It is "the kids," hair and all, who will be our salvation. But what the two types of revolution talk have in common is a sovereign disregard for the realities of technological society in general, and for the realities of class and power in America.

Here, co-authors Peter and Bridgette Berger capitalized on the current interest in the cultural change predicted in The Greening of America.

They set up an intriguing relationship with revolutions of other colors.

Their thesis frames their subsequent structure.

In the body of the article, the authors show that affluent dropouts leave executive voids that will be filled by the children of the blue-collar workers. The authors conclude, in one short paragraph:

"Revolutionary" America?
Perhaps, in a way. We may be on the eve of its blueing.

Closing by return is one of the most effective ways of concluding a paper, but it is also dangerous, for if you repeat a bad introduction in the conclusion of your paper, your theme has two weak spots instead of one.

The additional responsibility of making the thesis memorable—of providing some remarks in the final paragraphs that will attach special significance to the message—is not easy to fulfill. Once a young Vietnam War veteran gave a speech condemning war; in concluding, he said, "The one lesson I learned more than any other is that General William Tecumseh Sherman was right in what he said about war." And then he sat down. Some members of the audience nodded, knowing that the Civil War general had said, "War is hell." The rest did not know Sherman's remark, and there was a momentary buzz of conversation. Finally, the whole audience knew, and everyone nodded. The speaker had given his speech an extra fillip and added to its success. His audience probably still remembers his thesis.

A single dramatic incident, chosen because it most aptly illustrates the thesis, may be an effective conclusion. A pertinent statement by an accepted authority may also be useful, as may a short, pungent, aphoristic condensation of a complex thesis. Likewise, an appropriate, amusing anecdote, a joke, or an analogy can provide effective last-minute dressing.

Since the nature of the conclusion depends so heavily on the nature of the previous parts of the paper, we can give only general suggestions here; for an instructive sampling of conclusions, study the endings of selections in high-caliber anthologies and the closings of articles in quality magazines. Although Aristotle was convinced that all conclusions—he called them epilogues—should contain a summary, most writers work for a more lively and varied content. Few effective writers look at the conclusion as nothing more than, "I've said everything on the subject so I will close." Almost all of them look at the conclusion as the last opportunity to demonstrate that they have completely fulfilled the obligation they assumed when they first announced their purpose.

The Problem
of Unity

A student of writing may fear that the problem of organization limits spontaneity and imagination. The concept does discipline the writer, but it is not a straitjacket. The sonnet and the villanelle are restricted in length, meter, and rhyme, but some of the world's most original poetry has been written within these forms. The prose writer has as many strings as the violinist, as many colors as the artist's palette. The influence of structure on writing is not so much a Procrustean bed as it is a natural framework which has followed man's way of thought and has been worked out and accepted by writers in the past who tried the framework and found it effective. It is based on the way people think and the way they understand.

Of all the aspects of writing, probably the process of organization is the one in which the writer shows most effectively the power of his intellect. The aspects of organization—synthesis, division, ordering, and interrelating with transitions—are the essence of the complex idea he wishes to communicate. Organization is to writing what the skeleton is to the human being, the framework to a building. In short, organization is worth a great deal of attention and effort.

Project

Assume that each of the following sentences appears in either a letter, a paragraph, an essay, or a book. What class of assertion is it? What issues are likely to be raised? On the basis of the issues generated and the structure implied, deduce a pattern that might be used to analyze and develop the idea. Indicate what transitions would be used to move from point to point.

a. Dear Mom and Pop. I want to get married.
b. I have three reasons for acting the way I do—all of them bad.
c. The fourth of July weekend is the time we commemorate the birth of our country and cause the death of our citizenry.
d. To renew one's idiom or one's language is to renew one's conception of one's vision of the world.—EUGENE IONESCO
e. To a large extent, parents with permissive attitudes have children with like attitudes, but there are notable kinds of exceptions.—VANCE PACKARD, *The Sexual Wilderness*

Chapter 7 Development

Recently, a woman sent a manuscript detailing an original and arresting idea to a magazine. Because the manuscript, interesting as it was, seemed to the editors to be somewhat lacking in detail and documentation, it was returned to the author with the suggestion that she strengthen it where necessary and then resubmit it. In a few days the woman replied in effect: "I don't see why my article needs any supporting facts. It is based on my personal observations. And besides, anybody can see for himself that what I am saying is true."

But, [responded the editors] the writer is the eyes and ears of his reader, and those eyes and ears must be alert today as never before, in order to show the reader the facts on which he will ultimately base his judgments.—JAMES F. FIXX

As we stress throughout this text, successful communication proceeds on two levels. There is invariably the sentence which conveys the main idea of the communication. Such an idea is called a *topic sentence* or, in a longer work, a *thesis*. For example:

> Cutthroat competition among newspapers is on the wane in most American cities.
>
> Language provides a way of seeing.
>
> The scientific method derives from definite rules.
>
> Girls tend to have less sex drive than boys.

Such sentences carry thought, but often in a leaky bucket. What do you mean by "cutthroat competition"? What do you mean by "a way of seeing"? What are the "definite rules"? Boys are sexier than girls? Prove it! The explanation or evidence is the second level of communication.

And that is what *development* is all about. Development provides the details that enable communication to clarify and prove the main idea. Consider this report on a book called *The Longest Blade.*

THE LONGEST BLADE

The main reason why <u>The Longest Blade</u> is such a great book is because it is interesting. Probably the single biggest contribution to this interest is the excellent plot, which covers several generations in its sweep and tells many stories. Another reason the book is so interesting is that it contains so many excellent characterizations. The central figure is shown from the time he begins his worldly life till the time he is near death, and, besides the hero, there are many other characters, mostly feminine, that are well developed. It must not be overlooked that <u>The Longest Blade</u> also covers an important era in our history. Everyone will be interested in the clothing, manners, morals, and intrigues. Considering these facts, it is easy to see why Clifton Holton was able to say about this book: "It can take its place along with <u>Gone with the Wind</u> on any bookshelf."

This brief composition is not without some merit. The writer's generalizations add up to a unified thesis: he liked the book. He liked the plot, characterizations, and setting—for whatever reasons—and those are the aspects of a novel that we usually expect a review to cover.

The deficiencies of the review, however, go beyond tautology ("reason why . . . is because"), excessive use of the weak verb *be,* flowery diction ("began his worldly life," which prompts us to wonder when he began his *unworldly* life), and ambiguity (just what is meant by "well-developed" women characters?). The most damaging deficiency is that the review is really only an outline. Each sentence is an unsupported assertion, or an operative sentence whose obligation is not fulfilled. To convey a message clearly and vividly, the writer should illustrate every general assertion. We would have been more intrigued if the writer had told us something of the plot. To what "stories" does the writer allude? What "era in our history" is covered? In what way are the characterizations "excellent"? We must "see" some of the action and characters before we can understand and accept the writer's conviction that *The Longest Blade* is "such a great book." Until the writer provides us with more, all we have is a collection of topic sentences.

Writing is clear and convincing—and interesting—when it is a mixture of the general and the specific, a blend of the abstract and the concrete, a tapestry with a texture of foreground ideas and background exposition and evidence. A collection of generalizations (such as the report on *The Longest Blade*) fails to be convincing because it lacks specific detail. On the other hand, a collection of facts confuses; it needs a generalization to tie the details together. Writing that stays on one level, whether a high level of abstraction or generalization or a lower level of facts and anecdotes, is usually meaningless and deadly dull. In the following sections we analyze the general and specific elements of a paper to help you learn to recognize them and to combine them to form effective compositions.

The "Ladder of Abstraction"

One method of visualizing levels of generalization uses the semanticist's ladder of abstraction (Figure 7-1). At the lowest level of abstraction is a specific, named individual, a collection of many attributes, quantities, and characteristics. In the diagram Smoky is the name of a real, specific, nine-year-old, gray, male house cat. On the second rung of the ladder, Smokey is deprived of the specific qualities of age, color, sex, and name and becomes merely a cat. On the third rung he is divested even of his cathood: he is seen as a pet—whether he is a cat, dog, or canary is not known. Finally, on the top rung of the ladder, the real cat Smoky is described only as "matter," a label that differentiates him from all nonmaterial qualities in the universe (such as courage or the soul).

The point the semanticist makes with his ladder is that when you write about animals, you can make your assertions more meaningful if you refer to cats, particularly a specific cat such as Smoky. When you write on the higher levels of abstraction, as in the composition on *The Longest Blade*,

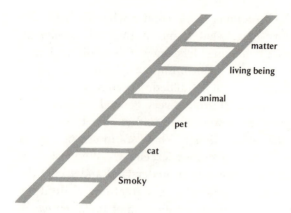

Figure 7–1 The Ladder of Abstraction

your operative sentences will pose more questions than you will answer. You need examples and illustration to make your high-level abstractions clear.

Components of a Paragraph

The paragraph draws the various levels on the ladder of abstraction together. It contains a mix of the general and specific: first, a topic or operative sentence that asserts a conviction and hints at what must further be said; then, the details, or the *development*. In an earlier chapter we referred to this blend as a muted conversation. The topic sentence generates questions; the development answers them.

The following excerpt demonstrates the two parts of a paragraph. Observe how the first sentence, the topic sentence, obligates the writer to proceed with a certain kind of development.

Behind the urge toward "joining" is the sense of the mysterious and exotic. To belong to a secret order and be initiated into its rites, to be part of a "Temple" with a fancy Oriental name, to parade in the streets of Los Angeles, Chicago, or New York dressed in an Arab fez and burnoose, to have high-sounding titles of potentates of various ranks in a hierarchy: all this has appeal in a non-hierarchical society from which much of the secrecy and mystery of life has been squeezed out. The fraternal groups flourish best in the small towns of the Middle West: the drearier the cultural wasteland of a small town, the greater the appeal of the exotic. Americans have an ambivalent

Note that in this topic sentence, an observation, the operative words are mysterious and exotic. Apparently assuming that his reader wonders in what way "joiners" are mysterious and exotic, the writer spends the rest of the paragraph justifying his use of the words.

attitude toward secrecy: they want everything out in the open, yet they delight in the secrecy of fraternal groups, as Tom Sawyer's gang of boys in Mark Twain's book did, and as the cellar clubs and the boys' gangs in the big-city slums still do. Much of the appeal of the Ku Klux Klan lies in this mysterious flimflammery, at once sadistic and grimly prankish. In many ways the American male of adult years is an arrested small boy, playing with dollars and power as he did once with toys or in gangs, and matching the violence of his recreation to the intensity of his loneliness.—MAX LERNER, *America as a Civilization*

A paragraph, taken as a whole, may average a high level of generalization or a very low level. Contrast these two paragraphs by Jacques Barzun:

> I am indeed aware that the movement for abolition [of capital punishment] is widespread and articulate, especially in England. It is headed there by my old friend and publisher, Mr. Victor Gollancz, and it numbers such well-known writers as Arthur Koestler, C. H. Rolph, James Avery Joyce, and Sir John Barry. Abroad as at home the profession of psychiatry tends to support the cure principle, and many liberal newspapers, such as the *Observer,* are committed to abolition. In the United States there are at least twenty-five state leagues working to the same end, plus a national league and several church councils, notably the Quaker and the Episcopal. . . .

> But why kill? I'm ready to believe the statistics tending to show that the prospect of his own death does not stop the murderer. For one thing he is often a blind egotist, who cannot conceive the possibility of his own death. For another, detection would have to be infallible to deter the more imaginative, who, although afraid, think they can escape discovery. Lastly, as Shaw long ago pointed out, hanging the wrong man will deter as effectively as hanging the right one. So, once again, why kill? If I agree that moral progress means an increasing respect for human life, how can I oppose abolition?

The first paragraph mentions specific people and organizations; it abounds with capital letters and proper nouns. Its development is low on the ladder of abstraction. The second paragraph is much more abstract. Several of the sentences in the development are themselves generative; they could be topic sentences for paragraphs lower than themselves on the ladder of abstraction. Both paragraphs, nevertheless, have the texture essential to a paragraph: a general topic sentence and more specific development.

There is also a second distinction between the two paragraphs. In the first the topic sentence needs to be clarified or explained. Its development, therefore, is called *exposition*; the paragraph itself is called *expository*. In the second paragraph, the topic sentence is controversial. The author substantiates it with evidence, or proof, and the paragraph is argumentative.

A paragraph, of course, is usually identifiable on the page by indentation, an arbitrary device that signals a change in thought. A page broken into several paragraphs often appears less oppressive to the average reader, who may be cowed by information so dense that it cannot be separated into a progression of ideas.

Many writers indent only when they have an uncontrollable urge to do so. Others arbitrarily break up a long series of sentences in order to avoid an overly dense page; they rarely let their paragraphs exceed a half page in length. Conversely, since a series of short paragraphs may suggest fragmentary, superficial thinking, some writers avoid having more than three or four paragraphs per page. Conversation is treated differently, of course. The transition from one speaker to another is indicated not only by quotation marks, but also by a new paragraph, as in the following dialogue:

> My teacher thought for a while and said, "The two major characteristics of behavior—"
> "But I am not asking about behavior," I interrupted. "I want to know what you think."
> "Miss Sayles," my professor answered severely, "if you keep interrupting, I never will be able to answer your question."

Though some writers, rightly or wrongly, may paragraph their work arbitrarily, most writers who assemble their thoughts according to the progression of generalization and development will reflect this thought process in their paragraphing, beginning a new paragraph each time they begin a new thought (introduced by a new operative sentence).

In the following paragraph, Howard Mumford Jones weaves several levels of abstraction into his discussion of one basic idea:

> We debunked too much. During the iconoclastic period spirited biographers laid about them with a mighty modern hand. They told us that Lincoln was a small-town politician, Washington a land-grabber, Grant a stubborn and conceited mule, and Bryan an amusing idiot. We learned that there was something to be said for Aaron Burr, but not very much for Sam Adams, Longfellow, or Harriet Beecher Stowe. In place of being American Vikings, the pioneers turned out to be neurotic, dissatisfied fellows unpopular in their home towns, and Columbia, the gem of the ocean, was described as a sort of kept woman in the pay of millionaires. Apparently the only Americans who ever died to make the world safe for democracy died in 1917–18, and made a mistake in doing so. I do not deny either the truth or the necessity of many of these modern biographies. I am no more comfortable than the next man in a room full of plaster saints. But, when the biographers got through, all the heroes had disappeared.

Professor Jones' first sentence is the thesis for a long discussion. It contains two operative thoughts:

    I. We debunked . . . (observation)

    II. We debunked too much (judgment)

In subsequent paragraphs, by demonstrating how German, Italian, and Russian writers deliberately built up their heroes, he defends his judgment. In this paragraph he demonstrates that American writers *did debunk*. While he is expanding upon his observation, he moves up and down four levels of abstraction. If you were to outline this movement, you would come up with something like this:

I. We debunked . . .

    A. During the iconoclastic period spirited biographers laid about them with a mighty modern hand.

        1. They told us that

            a. Lincoln was a small-town politician,

            b. Washington was a land-grabber,

            c. Grant a stubborn and conceited mule, and

            d. Bryan an amusing idiot.

        2. We learned that

            a. there was something to be said for Aaron Burr, but

            b. not very much for Sam Adams,

            c. Longfellow, or

            d. Harriet Beecher Stowe.

        3.

            a. In place of being American Vikings, the pioneers turned out to be neurotic, dissatisfied fellows unpopular in their home towns, and

            b. Columbia, the gem of the ocean, was described as a sort of kept woman in the pay of millionaires.

            c. Apparently the only Americans who ever died to make the world safe for democracy died in 1917–18, and made a mistake in doing so.

    B. I do not deny either the truth or the necessity of many of these modern biographies. I am no more comfortable than the next man in a room full of plaster saints.

    C. But, when the biographers got through, all the heroes had disappeared. (This is his transition to II—". . . too much.")

Note how Professor Jones shows the reader which levels are parallel. In each of the three major points (A, B, and C) under "We debunked," he repeats the word *biographers* or a form of it. At the next level down (1 and 2), he suggests the biographers' relationship to us. "They told us, "We learned" [from them]. By the time he returns to this level the third time, his organization is so clear that he does not even need to say "They told us"; the relationship is implied in his examples by such phrases as "turned out to be" and "was described."

The fourth level down (a, b, c, d) is specific; here Professor Jones gives individual examples. He names names. He returns, however, from the specific to the general. Indeed, his last sentence both restates the idea of the topic sentence and provides the transition that moves the discussion on to how a country suffers when it has no heroes.

Now look back at the book report in *The Longest Blade* (page 80) and see how flat it is. It gets stuck on the second level of abstraction (in this case, plot, characterizations, history) and is devoid of specific details below this level.

Wendell Johnson, a semanticist, used an analogy for his defense of paragraph structure:

> If you will observe carefully the speakers you find to be interesting, you are very likely to find that they play, as it were, up and down the levels of abstraction quite as a harpist plays up and down the strings of her harp. . . . The speaker who remains too long on the same general level of abstraction offends our evaluative progress—no matter what his subject may be.—WENDELL JOHNSON, *People in Quandaries*

The Raw Material: Facts

What we have been saying is that much writing is not specific enough; some writers tend not to get low enough on the ladder of abstraction. This deficiency can be remedied in part if the writer tries, whenever possible, to deal in facts.

Very few terms in our vocabulary are used as loosely as the word *fact*. A fact is an idea, but it has qualities of its own. Thus far we have classified ideas according to the process of abstraction by which they are derived. (See pages 52–59). An observation requires only that you find the right words to describe it. A classification requires that you abstract certain qualities of a class and ascertain whether your specific item has those qualities. A generalization requires that you abstract a commonality, continuation, or recurrence. A judgment requires that you abstract a property that can be measured in terms of quantity (more or less) or quality (goodness or badness). A causal relationship requires that you abstract a cause (antecedent) and its effect (consequence). Any one of these assertions can be a fact.

A fact can be the product of many kinds of thought. A statement is *factual* when it can be verified; it is a *fact* when it has been verified or agreed on. Most people would agree that the following statements are factual:

> Larry Brown gained more than 1000 yards during his best season. (observation)

A Mustang is a product of the Ford Motor Company. (classification)

Most Americans tend to support their republican system of government, even though they may disagree with a particular president's policies. (generalization)

An elephant is bigger than an ant. (judgment)

Commercial cetyltrimethyl-ammonium bromide causes some polysaccharides to precipitate. (causal relationship)

A thought about concrete things and experiences, no matter how it is derived, tends to fall into the category of factual statements. Such thoughts tend to be expressed in a vocabulary that S. I. Hayakawa calls *report language*. In his *Language in Thought and Action*, Professor Hayakawa points out that report language expresses a thought in "such a way that everyone will agree with the formulation." The language used at higher levels of abstraction to express judgments and generalizations that are likely to be controversial or vague is, in Hayakawa's terminology, *inferential language*. The first example above, "Larry Brown gained more than 1000 yards during his best season," is report language, but a sportswriter, using that statement as evidence, might declare, in inferential language, that "Larry Brown was a great football player."

To return to factual statements, let's consider the following example. You might say, "Our halfback, Fred Williams, can run a hundred yards in ten seconds." Chances are very strong that you could verify the statement using a stopwatch. If no one besides yourself has ever seen him run the hundred yards in this time, very likely Fred could run the distance again in order to prove the truth of your statement. The statement is about a concrete object, Fred Williams, and a relatively specific activity. The phenomenon is *verifiable*.

A statement that has been verified by generally accepted standards and can be expressed in report language is a fact. The following would usually be called facts.

That vase weighs one pound.

George Washington was the first president of the United States.

A straight line is the shortest distance between two points.

Actually, these statements demonstrate that although a fact is customarily thought to be a simple idea, there is a great deal of argument about just what is a fact and what is not. We could quibble about whether the sample sentences are facts, despite the "fact" that all have been verified. A pound avoirdupois weighs sixteen ounces; a pound troy weighs twelve ounces; a pound sterling has a varying weight. We could also challenge the second sentence since before the Constitution was ratified the assembly governing the new country elected a presiding officer, Peyton Randolph of Virginia. He is forgotten now, but he actually was our first president. The third sentence, of course, is not true on the earth's surface, as can be demonstrated by geometry.

The following are factual statements. If we agree on the terms and assume that their truth has been verified, they become facts.

> Her name is Amelia.
>
> George Bernard Shaw was a member of the Fabian Society.
>
> Potassium hydroxide is used in the manufacture of some soft soap.
>
> Jim Ryun ran a mile in less than four minutes.
>
> All bodies in the universe have a mutual attraction for each other. (Newton's law of gravitation)
>
> The clock struck twelve.

As you can see, facts can involve vastly different levels of importance and complexity. Notice also that they are usually expressed in words about whose meaning people are in almost complete agreement. For instance, we all know or can learn who or what is meant by the names *Amelia, Fabian Society, potassium hydroxide,* and *Ryun.* We tend to agree on the meaning of the verbs *was, used, ran,* and *struck.* And though it may take some thought about precise definitions, we can agree on the meanings of the common nouns *name, member, soap,* and *clock.* It is this type of vocabulary that is used to express facts; it is, to return to Hayakawa's term, report language.

We can usually have a high degree of certainty about facts. For instance, we can justifiably say that we *know* the following:

> Theodore Roosevelt was president of the United States.
>
> My shoe has a hole in it.
>
> Chicago, Illinois, is on the shore of Lake Michigan.

In your writing, facts and factual statements will often be the raw material from which you will build the development of your general ideas.

Which Thoughts Need Development?

Knowing which assertions need development is one of the truly fine arts of writing and speaking. Before making a decision to give further development to the ideas in a particular sentence, the writer must analyze his audience.

On March 23, 1775, when Patrick Henry stood up to address the Virginia House of Delegates, he knew the temper of his time and his audience. They were aware, as he said, that this was "no time for ceremony," as aware as he of Britain's "warlike preparations which cover our waters and darken our land," as aware as he that "petitions . . . had been slighted." All such assertions would normally have required a vast amount of evidence, but, as Patrick Henry realized, they were not new to his audience. All that was needed was someone with the courage to express what the audience wanted to hear. A British constitutionalist might have charged that there was "not a shred of evidence" in the speech. Nevertheless, when Henry concluded, "I know not what course others may take; but as for me, give me Liberty or give me death!" his audience was greatly moved. Their reaction demonstrated that he had known exactly what support his message needed as well as the susceptibility of his audience at this particular moment.

A situation such as Patrick Henry's is rare. Seldom is a point so clear or so readily accepted that it requires no development. If your audience knows what you are about to say or is already convinced that your point is true, there is little reason for you to speak. Take the assertion that America must turn away from imperialism. If your audience is extremely radical, this statement would require almost no development. It is very abstract; but radicals agree on what it means, and they believe it. You might say to yourself, "This is a platitude for my audience. I will cut it out of my speech." On the other hand, you might think, "This is a very vague generalization. I won't be able to move my speech forward with it, but the assertion is one of our slogans. Therefore, I'll use it, not to convince my listeners, but to rally them." In this case either decision might be right; just remember that if you make an assertion without backing it up with evidence, you are not dealing in exposition or argument—you are merely playing on the emotions of your audience. And if you should make this assertion before a different audience, you would very likely need to cite a great amount of evidence in support of it.

You may think that the need for development is so obvious that we are belaboring the point. If so, picture yourself as the freshman English teacher who annually receives dozens of:

1. Film reviews that fail to mention the title of the movie or the names of its stars.
2. Book reports that omit the title of the book, the names of its characters, or a summary of the plot.
3. Descriptions of high schools that leave out the name, location, and size of the school and make no mention of any specific teachers or students.
4. Attacks on government policies (in regard to foreign aid, deficit spending, Southeast Asia, cooperation with the UN) that fail to refer to specific countries, statesmen, political leaders, sums of money, or actual incidents.

5. Autobiographies that refer to a birthplace without telling where it is; to a parent's occupation, a sport, or a hobby without telling what it is; or to a hometown without naming it.

Without specific details an essay becomes a one-dimensional string of generalizations. Its message has no drama, and its reader is neither enlightened nor convinced. He *is* bored.

Methods of Development

A student writer often learns that he tends to lean on too few methods of development. Writers, even professional ones, find themselves falling into patterns; they write pages and pages using only two or three methods of development and never using some of the other equally effective forms. It would be instructive if you would check back over your most recent themes and see which of the following forms you have used. They are all valuable, not only because they contribute to clarity and conviction, but also because in their wide range they provide variety.

DEFINITION

One of the most common forms of development is the *definition*, which explains what a word or expression means.

Often a writer inserts a definition briefly as an appositive:

> Muslim groups say, for instance, that the role of the black woman is to produce warriors for the revolution. In this light, abortion is genocidal, the deliberate and systematic extinction of a racial group. It is a method of limiting the black population.—*Time* magazine

> Overly frank movies stimulate gymnomania, an exaggerated pleasure from nudity.

Definitions are often longer. In an article from *It's Happening* entitled "The Hang-Loose Ethic," J. L. Simmons and Barry Winograd depend heavily on a term which they feel the need to define. They write:

> The Protestant Ethic was a way of life and a view of life which stressed the more somber virtues, like the quiet good feeling of a hard day's work well done, the idea that a good man always more than earned his pay, and a kind of fierce pragmatism in which the hard and fast, here and now, seeable, touchable aspects of reality were the only things given the name of reality.

The extended definition usually puts the expression in a class (The Protestant Ethic was a way of life) and then shows how the expression is different from other members of the class (which stressed the more somber virtues . . . and a kind of fierce pragmatism).

When you define, remember to avoid being circular, that is, using the word being defined in your definition:

No: A Puritan is a person who believes in Puritanism.

You should also avoid using too broad a class in your definition:

No: A screwdriver is a thing.
Yes: A screwdriver is a tool.

EXAMPLE AND ILLUSTRATION

A writer often needs to give *examples* and *illustrations* to make an assertion clear or to prove it is true. When J. L. Simmons and Barry Winograd tried to explain the "hang-loose ethic," they clarified terms like *spontaneity* and *tolerance* with vivid examples.

> As part and parcel of the importance placed on directly experiencing oneself and the world, we find that *spontaneity,* the ability to groove with whatever is currently happening, is a highly valued personal trait. Spontaneity enables the person to give himself up to the existential here and now without dragging along poses and hang-ups and without playing investment games in hopes of possible future returns. The purest example of spontaneity is the jazz musician as he stands up and blows a cascade of swinging sounds.
>
> Another facet of the hang-loose ethic is an untutored and unpretentious *tolerance.* Do whatever you want to as long as you don't step on other people while doing it. A girl is free to wet her pants or play with herself openly while she's up on an acid trip and no one will think less of her for it. A man can stand and stare at roadside grass blowing in the wind and no one will accuse him of being the village idiot. If you like something that I don't like, that's fine, that's your bag; just don't bring me down.

In exposition usually only one example is necessary for clarification; in argumentation the sentence itself dictates how many examples are necessary. Examine the following sentences and determine the number of examples needed to clarify the statement.

> Most of the girls in my class were bored.
> Some of the girls in my class were bored.

If the assertion is a generalization, it is often sufficient to cite one or two examples and then present evidence that the sample was typical of the whole class under dicussion, as Roul Tunley has done in this passage from an article called "America's Unhealthy Children."

> Despite the protestations of the AMA, lack of money is a formidable barrier to good medical care and it can have tragic consequences. For example, I think of a young mother I know who lives in a large western city and supports her two children on a secretary's salary. Her eight-year-old daughter came down with a cold and was kept out of school for a week.

But, to save money, the mother did not consult a doctor. The child seemed to improve, went back to school on Friday, and the next day was well enough to go to her dancing class. But she came home listless, and seemed tired through the weekend. Around midnight Sunday she became desperately ill, started vomiting and gasping for breath. The panic-stricken mother tried mouth-to-mouth resuscitation. When the child's body went limp, the mother raced across the street to a pay telephone.

Not knowing what doctor to call, she rang the city's medical society, and an answering service responded. After she had explained her desperate need for a doctor, the voice at the other end asked, "Do you have ten dollars?"

"You see," the voice went on, "it's very difficult to get a doctor to make a house call at this hour without a cash payment."

Short of cash and too confused to think of rousing neighbors, the mother slammed down the receiver. Then she looked up and called an ambulance, which arrived in ten minutes. But by this time the little girl was dead. A postmortem was done at the morgue and the cause of death was found to be a virus which attacks the heart. No one knows whether or not a doctor could have saved the child; but no one can doubt that the denial of medical care was a brutal blow to both mother and child.

Uncounted other American children are similarly deprived and billion-dollar research programs will not help them.

In the course of the article, the writer provided evidence to demonstrate that the incident was distressingly typical.

ANALYTICAL EXPANSION

Very often, in both exposition and argumentation, the operative sentence calls for an expansion of the idea itself. In the following paragraphs, try to determine the operative words in the topic sentences that necessitate the *analytical expansion:*

Romeo was not bad-looking. He had curly black hair which he wore long and thick on the sides and he had had his nose bobbed once he retired from the ring. His eyes were dark and flat in expression, flat as Chinese eyes. He had put on weight. He would have looked like a young prosperous exective in Miami real estate if it had not been for the thick pads of cartilage on the sides of his temples which gave him a look of still wearing his headgear.—NORMAN MAILER, *An American Dream*

This is what I wanted to answer to your remark, "You don't love your country," which is still haunting me. But I want to be clear with you. I believe that France lost her power and her sway for a long time to come and that for a long time she will need a desperate patience, a vigilant revolt to recover the element of prestige necessary for any culture. But I believe she has lost all that for reasons that are pure. And this is why I have not lost hope. This is the whole meaning of my letter. The man whom you pitied five years ago for being so reticent about his country is the same man who wants to say to you today, and to all those of our age in Europe and throughout the world: "I belong to an admirable and persevering nation which, admitting her errors and weaknesses, has not lost the idea that constitutes her whole greatness. Her people are always trying and her leaders are sometimes trying to express that idea even more clearly. I belong to a nation which for the past four years has begun to relive the course of her entire history and which is calmly and surely preparing out of the ruins to make another history and to take her chance in a game where she holds no trumps. This country is worthy of the difficult and demanding love that is mine. And I believe she is decidedly worth fighting for since she is worthy of a higher love. And I say that your nation, on the other hand, has received from its sons only the love it deserved, which was blind. A nation is not justified by such love. That will be your undoing. And you who were already conquered in your greatest victories, what will you be in the approaching defeat?"—ALBERT CAMUS, *Letters to a German Friend*

Would you agree that this discussion by Albert Camus results from his perception that to answer the accusation, "You don't love your country," he must go beyond showing that he *does* love his country and show why he might be accused of *not* doing so? That seems to be why he shows that France has deteriorated, but for "reasons that are pure." You can love a country, he says, no matter how fallen, if it has fallen for good reason.

COMPARISON
Often a writer makes a point clear and vivid by drawing a *comparison* to something else. In an essay in which E. M. Forster wished to show how modern India is different from pre-1947 India, he emphasized that the change is political and educational by pointing out that:

> Externally the place has not changed. . . . Outside the carriage windows (the rather dirty windows) it unrolls as before—monotonous, enigmatic, and at moments sinister. And in some long motor drives which I took through the Deccan there was the same combination of hill, rock, bushes, ruins, dusty people and occasional yellow flowers which I encountered when I walked on the soil in my youth. There is still poverty, and, since I am older today and more thoughtful, it is the poverty, the malnutrition, which persists like a ground-swell beneath the pleasant froth of my immediate experience. I do not know what political solution is correct. But I do know that people ought not to be so poor and to look so ill, and that rats ought not to run about them as I saw them doing in a labour camp at Bombay. Industrialism has increased, though it does not dominate the landscape yet as it does in the west. You can see the chimneys of the cotton mills at Ahmedabad, but you can see its mosques too. You can see little factories near Calcutta, but they are tucked away amongst bananas and palms, and the one I have in mind has an enormous tree overhanging it, in whose branches a witch is said to sit, and from whose branches huge fruit occasionally fall and hit the corrugated iron roofs with a bang, so that the factory hands jump. No—externally India has not changed.
> —E. M. FORSTER, from "India Again," in *Two Cheers for Democracy*

CONTRAST
In the following passage, Stokely Carmichael uses the development technique called *contrast* to differentiate between individual and institutionalized racism.

Let me give an example of the difference between individual racism and institutionalized racism, and the society's response to both. When unidentified white terrorists bomb a Negro church and kill five children, that is an act of individual racism, widely deplored by most segments of the society. But when in that same city, Birmingham, Alabama, not five but five hundred Negro babies die each year because of a lack of proper food, shelter and medical facilities, and thousands more are destroyed and maimed physically, emotionally and intellectually because of conditions of poverty and deprivation in the ghetto, that is a function of institutionalized racism. But the society either pretends it doesn't know of this situation, or is incapable of doing anything meaningful about it. And this resistance to doing anything meaningful about conditions in that ghetto comes from the fact that the ghetto is itself a product of a combination of forces and special interests in the white community, and the groups that have access to the resources and power to change that situation benefit, politically and economically, from the existence of that ghetto.—STOKELY CARMICHAEL, "Toward A Black Liberation"

As you can see, comparison clarifies by showing what your subject *is*; contrast clarifies by showing what it is not. Contrast is, in a sense, a type of comparison, but it is a comparison of differences and opposites, not one of similarities.

ANALOGY

One day, as the story goes, Ambassador Joseph Kennedy found his sons fighting among themselves. Rather than lecture the boys on their misbehavior, he gave Joe, Jack, Bob, and Ted each a small stick and asked them to break the sticks, which they did easily. He then took four sticks and asked if any one of the boys could break all four of them at once. To his disappointment, the first boy who tried it succeeded. The Ambassador had read of the idea in a book somewhere, and it had worked there. To console his father, Ted said, "It's okay, Dad. We get your point."

Ambassador Kennedy could have said something platitudinous like, "If you boys stick together instead of fighting one another, you'll be more likely to succeed." Instead, to dramatize his point, he used an *analogy*.

As the next example shows, analogy is a variation of comparison. During a debate in Congress about a highway bill, a United States congressman from an Eastern state objected to the arguments of his colleagues from the Middle West, saying to those congressmen, "You are always against everything."

"You have us wrong," a tall congressman from Michigan replied. "You do not understand us. If you would come out to Michigan, I would show you acres of corn. You would see our farmers spraying the fields. But we are not against corn borers, grasshoppers, and chinch bugs. We are *for* corn! Here in Congress we Middle Westerners are not merely *against* federal intervention; we are *for* good highways—so we want them built by the people in the states which will use them."

An analogy is a form of comparison, but it develops an idea by comparing objects and concepts that are basically dissimilar except for a certain pertinent abstract quality. Words and clothing have little relationship to each other, but Walter Lippmann noted a similarity between them which helped him explain how we should choose our words.

> Words like *liberty, equality, fraternity, justice* have various meanings which reflect the variability of the flux of things. The different meanings are rather like different clothes, each good for a season, for certain weather and for a time of day, none good for all times. In the infinite change and diversity of the actual world, our conceptual definitions are never exactly and finally the whole truth. For, as James said, while "the essence of life is its continually changing character . . . our concepts are all discontinuous and fixed." Like a winter overcoat, none can be worn with equal comfort in January and in July. Yet the summer will end, it too being subject to change. There will come a season and a time for wearing the warmer coat. So it is a mistake to think that we could wear the same coat all the time, and a mistake to throw it away, supposing in the summer that it will never be winter again.—WALTER LIPPMAN, *The Public Philosophy*

STATISTICS

Frequently, a writer cites *statistics* to develop an idea, as in this excerpt from *Look* magazine:

> New York has been considered typical of older United States cities whose overburdened transportation systems have deteriorated until crisis conditions prevail. But New York is not typical of anything. Almost 20 million people, nearly one-tenth of the nation, live in the metropolitan area. Two million people, the equivalent of the combined populations of Boston, Baltimore, and Cincinnati, travel each weekday to the nine square miles of Manhattan's business district. Of these, 140,000 drive in cars, 200,000 take buses, 100,000 ride commuter trains; but the majority—1.4 million— catch the subway. Whichever way you go, it's some ride!—*Look* magazine

Statistics can be as dry as dust, but they can certainly be convincing. An abundance of figures often is necessary to fulfill the obligation of such operative terms as *some, most,* and *all.* Obviously, you need actual or implied statistics of up to 50 percent to indicate *some,* although two examples justify the term. To justify *most* you need statistics to show over 50 percent. *All* is very hard to justify.

Occasionally you may find charts or graphs useful to summarize information in an authoritative way. For instance, in *The Quality of Life,* James Michener, when trying to show that Catholicism is sometimes unjustly blamed for the population explosion, includes Table 1 in his discussion.

Table 1.   Rates of Growth of Catholic and Non-Catholic Nations

Low Rates	Years Required to Double Population	Low Rates	Years Required to Double Population
Belgium	175	East Germany	233
Ireland	100	Hungary	175
Portugal	100	Finland	175
France	88	Great Britain	140
Italy	88	Sweden	88
Spain	70	Russia	70
High Rates		*High Rates*	
Costa Rica	19	Morocco	21
Ecuador	21	Rhodesia	21
Panama	21	Syria	21
Venezuela	21	Pakistan	21
Paraguay	21	Ghana	24
Brazil	25	North Korea	25

Source: *1970 World Population Data Sheet*, Population Reference Bureau.

He then comments:

It would be difficult to find a nation more Catholic than Ireland or one in which the counsel of the priest is more significant, yet Ireland has one of the slowest rates of population growth, requiring a full century to double itself. Portugal, Spain and Italy certainly qualify as Catholic countries, yet their rate stands well below that of the rest of the world.

It is non-Catholic countries like Ghana, Syria and Pakistan that have the runaway population growth, and in these nations the attitude of the Pope has little significance. Obviously, the population explosion here cannot be blamed on Catholic doctrine, and the generalizations yielded by this first set of comparisons is clear: it is the technologically retarded nations of Africa and Asia which produce the highest rate of growth; it is the technologically advanced nations of Europe which have the lowest, and Catholicism has nothing to do with either.

The following paragraph further demonstrates the use of statistics:

The classic study of die-off was John J. Christian's study of Sika deer on James Island in the Chesapeake Bay, West of Cambridge, Maryland. Four or five of the deer had been released on the island, which was 280 acres, and uninhabited, in 1916. By 1955 they had bred freely into a herd of 280 to 300. The population density was only about one deer per acre at this point, but Christian knew that this was already too high for the Sikas' inborn space requirements, and something would give before long. In two years the number of deer remained 280 to 300. But suddenly in 1958, over half the deer died; 161 carcasses were recovered. In 1959 more deer died and the population steadied at about 80.—TOM WOLFE, "Oh Rotten Gotham" from *The Pump House Gang*

TESTIMONY

One of the frequently used forms of development is *testimony*, that is, quoting someone, preferably a deservedly respected authority, to clarify or support an assertion. When a writer feels he has little personal weight as an authority, or if he believes he may be doubted, he may rely heavily on testimony. Since the Democratic Convention of 1968 many people may have thought of the mayor of Chicago, Richard Daley, as a politicking fascist. In writing about him, Daley's biographer, therefore, rarely praised "The Boss" without resorting to testimony, usually from an identified authority, but often from a general reference. For example:

> Only one of his classmates, who later spent many years holding down a desk in City Hall, saw him in a completely different light: "He was a brilliant person, even then. I could see greatness in him. Everybody could. He got along with everybody. People sought him out. He was a brilliant student. He did everything well."—MIKE ROYKO, *Boss*

Sometimes testimony relies as heavily on the "authority's" personal appeal as on his expertise. Are professional athletes and show business celebrities really authorities on breakfast cereals, shaving creams, and cigarettes?

HYPOTHETICAL EVIDENCE
Rarely, a writer will hypothesize a situation which does not exist in order to make a point forcefully:

> Supposing, just for argument, that the biographers of Lincoln could prove, as some of them have tried to do, that he was of illegitimate descent, would you then want that taught in the schools? The conclusive arguments against are: (1) Such teaching would attack the Home, the most precious of all our institutions; for Lincoln is our greatest national hero, and having him illegitimate, even if only back in his parents' or grandparents' generation, would be a destructive influence. (2) That teaching would also attack the institution of National Heroes. Lincoln is our greatest hero; nothing is more beneficial than to have heroes to look up to; we would not look up to Lincoln quite so much if he were in any degree illegitimate; therefore, we ought to hide the fact, if it were a fact. (3) Nothing could be gained by encouraging children to attach scandal to the names of great men. (4) It would be in bad taste to teach in school about the illegitimacy of anyone. On the basis of these and many similar reasons, all decent people will agree that the question of whether Lincoln was illegitimate should never be mentioned in the schools.—VILHJALMUR STEFANSSON, *Adventures in Error*

Stefansson does not hypothesize completely ridiculous arguments simply in order to overturn them later. It is in his interest, however, that the hypothetical arguments should not be *too* strong, since he does intend to refute them. When you utilize hypothetical development, then, be certain that you can support the hypothesis with sufficient strength to carry your reader's opinion in the direction you desire. Be sure that your reader will not be won over by the wrong hypothetical argument.

How Much Development Is Necessary?

With all these devices—definition, example, analytical expansion, comparison, contrast, analogy, statistics, testimony, and hypothetical evidence—at his command, the writer can effectively provide the exposition or evidence required by his generative sentences. But how much development is required?

Some beginning writers think that writing has *just* two levels of abstraction, the topic sentence and concrete development. A good writer, however, as noted earlier, provides a texture of many levels. Within a sentence he may perceive that an abstract word needs a concrete appositive. A sentence in the middle of a paragraph may need two or three subsequent sentences to clarify its contention. Another sentence may need three paragraphs of development, one to clarify the idea being advanced and two to prove it. The broadest generalization will need a book.

The writer must decide every time he sets down a sentence how much exposition or evidence he needs. How generative is his thought? He has three principles to follow:

1. let the nature of the operative sentence determine the type and amount of development;
2. don't be afraid of having too much development; and
3. avoid irrelevancy.

1. Let the nature of the operative sentence determine the type and amount of development. For both the sensitive writer and the interested reader, the type of information that comes after any given generative sentence is predictable. The writer guesses what the reader wants to know; the reader is pleased when the writer anticipates and answers his questions.

Suppose your generative sentence is a classification: "Mistletoe is a parasite." The development of this assertion will require a routine series of steps. Let's listen in on your mental analysis. "The assertion is a classification," you might say to yourself. "Since it is one generally accepted by scientists, my development will not be argumentation, but exposition. The operative words are *mistletoe* and *parasite*. Since my audience probably knows what mistletoe is, I will define only the word *parasite*, because I want to use a special scientific class. To clarify the definition of the class, I will use some examples of other plants that are parasites. Having established the meaning of parasite, I will show by analytical expansion that mistletoe has the characteristics of the plant group called parasites. To wrap up the development, I can turn to testimony and cite an authority who has called mistletoe a parasite. When, in my research, I come across the enchanting fact that Indians chewed on mistletoe to stop a toothache, a sign in my head will flash

'Irrelevant!' and I will resist the impulse to smuggle the information into my paragraph."

Here you determined the amount of development your idea needed on the basis of your judgment that it was "generally accepted," that your audience probably knew the meaning of one of your terms (mistletoe), and that the term requiring most clarification was parasite.

We have already said that you should consider certain aspects of your audience and your assertion in determining which sentences need development. (See pages 88–90). In order to determine how much development they need, you should also consider:

1. The kind of assertion the sentence is. Is it observation, classification, generalization, judgment, or causal relationship?
2. Whether the sentence is expository or argumentative.
3. What the operative words are.

And, in relation to all three of these points, you should consider how many issues must be developed, and what the focal points of your development should be, in order to make your idea clear and convincing to this particular audience.

2. Don't be afraid of having too much development. Since brevity is usually labeled a virtue in writing, you may be surprised that we are telling you not to worry about the length. The sin of wordiness and the virtue of supplying sufficient detail are completely different. The ratio of words in a first draft to those in the final draft is often something like seven to five. A student writing a five-hundred-word theme probably should have a first draft of seven hundred words. However, the two hundred words that he cuts out during revision are hardly ever details; almost always they are overblown generalizations and useless words. Very likely, he will remove three hundred unnecessary words and will add one hundred words, mostly details.

Another consideration is that details often have charm in and of themselves. A series of vague generalizations will bore the reader; but a series of anecdotes, incidents, or even statistics, providing they are made meaningful by the proper generalizations, may be entertaining and will add life and color to the composition. An experienced writer comes to know what information he can jam into his paragraph, justifying it on the ground not only of its relevance, but also of its inherent interest. Note how Jon Landau, in the following record review, has used specific details in the development of his ideas:

> Bessie Smith was by all accounts a loud, hard, often obnoxious, often drunk woman. As the new Columbia two-record re-issue "Bessie Smith —World's Greatest Blues Singer" makes clear, she also was undoubtedly

the finest woman blues singer ever recorded. Starting in vaudeville at an early age she traveled the country with Ma Rainey, an almost equally legendary figure, who taught her the rudiments of blues and jazz style. In the early Twenties she went to New York seeking recording work and auditioned for the black-owned Black Swan label, in which W. C. Handy had a half interest. According to John Wilson, "Just as Miss Smith was about to begin the audition she shouted to musicians, 'Hold it while I spit.' And she spat right on the studio floor." Handy's partner Harry Pace was so disgusted he terminated the audition immediately and Miss Smith went to Columbia where she began recording regularly in 1923.

The last person to record Miss Smith was John Hammond, Sr., in 1933. Hammond is one of the great A & R men in record history; his accomplishments range from pairing Charlie Christian with Benny Goodman to "rediscovering" Bob Dylan. Currently head of Columbia's talent acquisition department, he has remained a lifelong devotee of Miss Smith and has always regarded her as the greatest vocalist he ever recorded. He has now returned to his first love and with collaborator Chris Albertson has prepared for release what must surely be a collector's dream: the entire 160-song catalogue of Bessie Smith's recordings.—JON LANDAU, "Review of Bessie Smith Re-release," *The Phoenix*, August 1, 1970

Lack of detail is a disease of many writers; in college writing it is epidemic. In fact, on college campuses the malady has facetiously been labeled "specific anemia." The cure, fortunately, is simple:

> Learn to be specific; concentrate on details; give names, dates, places, facts, and figures; focus on the visible, audible, measurable; pass on your direct experience—rather than your thoughts, opinions, general ideas.
> —RUDOLF FLESCH, *How to Make Sense*

3. Avoid irrelevancy. The assurance that a writer has little to fear from using too much detail does not, however, give him license to use detail that is not appropriate or purposeful. Do you find any details in the following student theme that should have been omitted?

<u>Tom Sawyer</u> is my favorite book. Partly this is because it is a boy's book with plenty of action in it. The boys play and fight, they run away, they get involved in a murder, and they search for hidden treasure. In short, they do what all boys would like to do and all grown-ups wish they had done. More importantly, however, <u>Tom Sawyer</u> is my favorite book because it is laid in my home town. I was born and brought up in Hannibal, Missouri, and almost as soon as I learned anything I learned the names of Tom Sawyer, Huck Finn, and Becky Thatcher. (I was at least 10 before I knew the real people were Tom Blankenship, Sam Clemens, and Laura Hawkins.) As I grew a little older, I visited Tom's house and imagined myself crawling out his bedroom window and sliding

down the waterspout. A little later I took the guided tour through Tom Sawyer's cave and saw firsthand the spot where he and Becky were supposed to have eaten their cake and the place where Tom was supposed to have seen Injun Joe. For days afterward Becky was my dream girl and Injun Joe the chief character in nightmares that used to bring me out of bed howling. By the time I was 10 or 12 I was allowed to row over to Jackson's Island to swim and fish just as Tom and Huck did. Once I even waited out a thunderstorm there— under the tree that I was sure Tom and Huck and Joe Harper had used for cover years before. I doubt that any book will ever replace Tom Sawyer in my affections, for it's not only a book to me; it's a story that I have relived in Hannibal many times.

All the information is justified. Of the hundreds of ideas and details the author had available about *Tom Sawyer*, he selected only certain ones. Why? Because they were relevant and would best serve to clarify or prove his topic sentence. He cited only those bits of information that showed why *Tom Sawyer* was his favorite book. Contrast this theme with the book report on *The Longest Blade* (page 80). What meaningful details do you find there?

By rephrasing your main thesis into a controlling question, you can make sure that every word in your writing contributes to the answer. Include all the necessary information, but omit anything that seems off target.

Summary

Remember that you may need to develop any assertion that:

1. Is controversial, original, or new
2. Judges or evaluates
3. Suggests a comparison or contrast
4. Applies an unfavorable label
5. Contains a vague, general, abstract, technical, jargonistic, or new term
6. Permits an interpretation other than the one you intended
7. Contradicts generally held stereotyped views

In developing your assertion, think first of your audience:

How intelligent are your readers, and how much do they know about your subject?

Are they favorable, neutral, or hostile to your thesis?

Are they familiar with your vocabulary, or will you need to explain your concepts and define your terms?

Then, with your audience still in mind, ask these questions about the assertion itself:

1. What kind of assertion is it (observation, classification, generalization, judgment, or causal relationship)?
2. Is it expository or argumentative?
3. What are the operative words?
4. What kind of development is required—definition, example, analytical expansion, comparison, contrast, analogy, statistics, testimony, or hypothesis?

As you develop your ideas, avoid irrelevancy, but don't be afraid of supplying too much detail.

A Last Thought:
Development As Pictures

If we think of communication as the transference of an idea from one mind to another, we can see that development plays a very important part in this process. Abstract words have no reality of their own, so they need to be developed into word pictures. And if we can move pictures from one mind to another, we have gone a long way toward transferring perceptions of reality. In this sense, the best writing is pictorial writing, writing that could be used as a script for a documentary film. If the writing is a series of pictures, the camera has something to shoot. If all the writing contains is a sterile group of assertions, all at a dead level of high abstraction, the camera (reader) will have to assemble his own scenes, and they may not be the scenes that the writer intended.

Projects

1. Analyze the following sentences to determine how you might develop them. Estimate the number of words you would need. Where appropriate, analyze the audience you would be addressing; consider the members' awareness of the subject and issues, their usual attitude, and their present feeling. Your analysis will be only an educated guess, but it will be meaningful when compared with that of your classmates.

   a. Dear Father and Mother: I want to leave college.
   b. His girl friend is a real kook.
   c. The United States exhibits the same symptoms of decadence that led to the fall of the Roman Empire.

d. Marijuana has no harmful effect on its users.

e. Sleakerness is a quarkingly micked flixx.

f. In women philogyny is called homosexuality and society condemns it; in men it's called virility and society hails it as an attribute of their heroes.

g. Hank Aaron was never as great a baseball player as Babe Ruth.

h. Religious institutions have historically been the enemy of science.

i. Toads do not cause warts.

j. Messalina is conventionally regarded as the worst of Roman women.

2. The game "Who Am I?" sharpens the process of abstraction and the use of analogy. The person who is "it" decides what famous person he will be. He can be any historic figure, modern celebrity, or a member of any class agreed upon. If he decides to be, say, Julius Caesar, he announces his category as "historic figure." The other players then ask questions phrased in this pattern: "If you were a ——, what would you be?" and "Julius Caesar" responds with one word. The dialogue might go like this:

"If you were an animal, which would you be?" "A lion." (Because lions are warlike, as was Caesar.)

"If you were a corporation, which would you be?" "General Motors." (The response represents an analogy between the importance in its class of the huge corporation; Caesar was as important in his class.)

"If you were a book, which one would you be?" (Here "Julius Caesar" is stumped, because he cannot think of any book about leaders or warrior-writers. He thinks to himself that he must not say *The Decline and Fall of the Roman Empire*, because that would fit just the opposite, so he rather weakly says *Advise and Consent*, because it is about a plot to undo a leader.)

Eventually someone puts together all the abstract qualities they have discovered and shouts out, "You must be Julius Caesar!" Try the game sometime, perhaps in class.

3. Is there a doctor in the house? Look back over all your themes and analyze them for "specific anemia." What sentences should be followed by development and are not? Make a list showing how many times you used each form of development (definition, example, illustration, analytical expansion, comparison, contrast, analogy, statistics, hypothesis). Submit a report of your findings to your instructor.

4. Is there a documentary film producer in the house? Go back over your themes and decide whether a film director could produce a documentary film based on any of them. Could he tell how the people mentioned looked? Exactly how they acted toward each other? Would he know their conversational habits? Could he create sets and find landscapes to fit what you had

in mind? What sounds should he duplicate? In short, do you write for the senses of your reader?

5. Paying special attention to development, trying to use methods that are rare for you, write a theme based on one of the following or similar subjects. Insert enough evidence to prove all your assertions.

a. College slang (perhaps contrast it to that of your hometown).
b. The importance of the automobile to young Americans (perhaps contrast its importance today to the importance it had for your parents).
c. Literature's contribution to your life.
d. The current state of a minority group. (Here many examples and statistics would be appropriate.)
e. Religion in modern suburbia (or rural America).
f. A moral problem troubling a segment of society familiar to you.

Chapter 8 — Style

Style is the selection of words which have the desired effect on the reader and give the expression a distinctive air.—*Aristotle*

The Attributes of Style

Throughout this text we emphasize how four factors—the message, situation, reader, and writer—interrelate during the writing process. When you are writing your early drafts, you tend to organize and develop the paper to fit your message and the situation. You tend to jot down whatever words come to you. In later stages you think more of the right words and the way you put them together. At this stage your writing becomes more of a social affair. You may feel you are communicating to a vast unseen audience, but you have one reader at a time. Your communication is person to person. Your style must affect that single reader, and it must be right for you, the one person writing to him.

To satisfy your reader, your style should be vivid and efficient. To make you feel comfortable and satisfied, your style must reflect your own personality. The "distinctive" air required by Aristotle must be *your* distinction.

Vividness

To say that clarity is a prime attribute of style should be to state the obvious. There are writers, to be sure, who are content merely with self-expression. Some prose writers deliberately leave their work obscure, in the belief that if a reader does not find an idea, he will supply his own. And some poets have exploited suggestive obscurity, believing that, since life is chaotic and meaningless, poetry should be equally so. This "cult of significant darkness" has been very fashionable, but even during its height, many critics demanded clarity. "Obscurity," wrote David Lambuth of Dartmouth, "is not profundity. Neither is it art." "Behind the work of any creative artist," wrote W. H. Auden, "is the desire to communicate his perceptions to others. Those who have no interest in communication do not become artists. They become mystics or madmen." Clarity is the difference between self-expression and communication.

Once you are committed to clarity, you can see the wisdom of working for a vivid style.

Understanding can come from the intellect. But, as Aristotle wrote, you really need more than understanding from your reader. You know that he has the usual human inertia. He is satisfied to be where he is, think what he thinks, and do what he does. You must make him, for some reason, *want* to change, to be a different human being. And that is quite a task.

To get to his intellect, you must involve your reader's emotions. To get him to think right, you must help him to feel right about your message.

WRITE IN PICTURES

Almost 2500 years ago someone is supposed to have said, "A picture is worth ten thousand words." To illustrate this point, we ask you to consider the sentence "Nero was cruel." Although the sentence has meaning, it creates no pictures. The following paragraph puts images on your mental television screen:

> Nero poisoned his rival Britannicus, deserted his wife Octavia, and sentenced her to death. At first he kept the slave woman Acte as the head of his domestic revels, but he soon strangled her in favor of Poppaea. After the burning of Rome—which he, surprisingly, did not cause himself —he almost bankrupted the citizens by heavy taxes. Those who would or could not pay he put to death by crushing them with chariots. After kicking Poppaea to death in a fit of rage, Nero secured the affection of

Statilia Messalina by stabbing her husband. During his courtship of
Statilia Messalina, Nero killed his own stepdaughter Astonia because she
resisted his clumsy attempt at seduction.

Try to re-create particular incidents by describing them in dramatic words.
In the description of Nero, for instance, to say he "killed" Acte is not as ex-
pressive as to say he "strangled" her.

Herbert Spencer, in his *Philosophy of Style,* demonstrated this lesson by
citing two versions of the same message.

> In proportion as the manners, customs, and amusements of a nation are
> cruel and barbarous, the regulations of their penal code will be severe.

> In proportion as men delight in battles, bullfights, and combats of
> gladiators, will they punish by hanging, burning, or the rack.

The first version uses general words to convey abstract concepts; the second uses specific words to convey images.

Since readers tend to be influenced more by images than by abstraction,
you can infer the first rules for achieving vividness.

Cite exact events, names, and places. If you are describing a date at a
football game, tell what game, what quarter, and what girl. Bring your pictures to life. Don't say, "a local restaurant"; say, "Charlie Brown's." If you
are writing your autobiography, tell what town you live in, what high school
you attended, what church or temple you belonged to, what sports and/or
instrument you played. You are right: your writing *will* abound in capital
letters. Don't worry that your reader won't know who Mitchell Marcus is;
if he's the boy you went to consciousness raising with, say so.

Use words that, by their nature, *draw* pictures. Take the word *walk.* Its
deficiency is simply that it does not stimulate an exact image. It describes,
rather vaguely, a means of locomotion that many animals use. On the other
hand, some synonyms of *walk* conjure up exact images:

saunter	The walker is in no hurry; he may be in the park; the weather is balmy. He has time to smell the spring air and listen to the play of children.
stroll	This word creates somewhat the same picture as *saunter,* but our walker may have scenery or leisure in mind; the word is often used with setting as "he strolled through the park."
stride	Now he is in a hurry; his pace is purposeful; he is probably a big man and masterful.
lunge	The walker is a big man, and he is angry, frightened, or forceful; his walk doesn't last long.
skip	The walker is a child, playing, lighthearted.

At the end of many entries in your dictionary, you will find a synonymy, a collection of words that are similar in meaning but have shades of differences. Under *speed* in *The American Heritage Dictionary of the English Language*, you find:

> Synonyms: *speed, hurry, hasten, accelerate, precipitate, expedite.* These verbs mean to move or cause to move rapidly or to increase the pace of a person or thing. *Speed* refers directly to very rapid movement. *Hurry* implies movement or action at a rate markedly faster than usual, sometimes accompanied by commotion or confusion. *Hasten* refers to stepped-up activity that increases progress or brings a desired result much closer to fulfillment. Even more than *hurry*, it stresses urgency. *Quicken* and especially *accelerate* refer to increase in rate of activity, growth, or progress. *Precipitate* implies sudden or impetuous action that causes or impels rapid movement or that causes something to happen suddenly or prematurely. *Expedite* refers to action that furthers the quick and efficient accomplishment of something or accelerates its fulfillment.

Even when you are already familiar with a word's synonyms, you can sharpen your writing and confirm your perception of their meanings by making a checklist of them. A few synonyms for some general, familiar words will show how helpful such a review can be.

Note the different pictures generated by the following synonyms:

kill   slay, murder, assassinate, dispatch, execute, choke him to death

grand   magnificent, imposing, stately, majestic, august, noble, grandiose

frown   scowl, glower, lower

tight   taut, tense

When you have conditioned yourself not to use vague words, you will rarely write a sentence like "He looked at the girl." *Peeked, gaped, stared, peered, glowered,* or *leered* all do much more for your picture.

APPEAL TO ALL THE SENSES

If a picture is worth ten thousand words, why not shoot for a million? Instead of black and white, use living color. Do more. Show how the picture feels, how it smells.

As you read the following selection observe how author David Wilson appeals to all your senses.

"IN SUCH A MAY NOON, IT IS GOOD . . ."

> The path, not much taken any more, leads along the headland on the south side of the island. Every year the ocean chews a little more away and, some day, there will be no path, only field and spruce forest.
> There are strawberries along the way, and cranberries, and, at the edge of the dark wood, blueberries, too. Wild roses, still flatly bearing last year's hips, wait for the warmth of June.

In May, it is still a little chilly on the south side, even when the wind is out of the south. It is off the sea then, and the sea in Maine is always cold, around 40 degrees at this time of year.

But the earth and the rocks are warm, holding and returning the heat of the spring sun, and the air is fraught with a soporific perfume of spruce and juniper. Robins and flickers flirt among the dark trees.

In such a May noontime it is good to throw yourself to the ground, feel the reassurance of the earth under your shoulder blades and the caress of sun on your face, and listen for the silences.—DAVID B. WILSON, *The Boston Globe*, May 21, 1973

Go back over the passage and count the senses to which the author appeals.

PROFIT FROM CONNOTATION

Besides writing in pictures—complete with talkies, technicolor, and smell-orama—you can achieve vividness by exploiting all the levels of meaning attached to words. Some words have only an exact meaning, or *denotation*. Such a word points specifically to its referent, whether it be a thing, concept, or action. Other words have an additional significance, perhaps based on the experiences or emotions of the writer or reader. The word *house*, for instance, has a rather fixed, impersonal meaning; but the word *home* may suggest memories of mother, wife, and child, of fireplaces, toy closets, and the dining table. To some readers, the pictures are warm, pleasant, favorable. If the person hates his father, left home eagerly at the first opportunity, and dreads the thought of returning, he finds the echoes unpleasant.

Although some connotations vary from reader to reader, many words have emotional or dramatic overtones that are relatively similar for all users of the language. These connotations can be pleasant or unpleasant. *Womanly* is a pleasant term, but *womanish* is unpleasant; use *manly* to compliment a man; use *mannish* to describe a woman who is not feminine. With only a few exceptions, any recently coined adjective with the suffix *-istic* is unfavorable: *faddistic, simplistic. Premeditated,* a synonym of *deliberate,* has so long been associated with crime that it is unfavorable, having overtones of evil design.

There are other kinds of connotation besides the favorable or unfavorable. Take, for example, *impending doom* and *imminent doom*: the former has less suggestion of immediacy; we can expect an imminent flood at once, but we may speak of a rebellion that has been *impending* for years. *Policy, strategy, principle,* and *rule* also have different connotations. *Policy* is a definite course of action adopted for its practical wisdom or expediency; it can be long-term and applied in many situations. *Strategy* is a shorter-term plan, method, or series of maneuvers calculated to achieve certain specific objectives. *Policy* and *strategy* are likely to be for nations and institutions; *principle* tends to be a specific basis for action by one person, a guiding sense of right conduct. These three words suggest that interpretation is necessary; *rule* is definite, being made for specific circumstances and occasions.

In another synonymy, the word *practical* implies a rather ordinary ability to accomplish everyday tasks; *judicious* refers to the use of discretion in accomplishing a task; and *sensible* emphasizes the use of good or common sense.

Connotations may change. *Fat* formerly suggested a jolly, Santa Claus

"When a guy like me is broke and owes a buck here and there, he's a goddam deadbeat, but when some big shot goes broke and owes everyone in town, is he a deadbeat? Oh, no! He's overextended."

Drawing by Stan Hunt; © 1972, *The New Yorker* Magazine, Inc.

type; now it conjures images of overeating, bulges above the belt, and potential heart malfunction. The skillful writer keeps abreast of such changes in the language and uses the term with the connotation he seeks.

The year after she graduated from college, Faye Levine went on a trip around the world and wrote a description of her trip, which was published in *The Atlantic Monthly*. From Calcutta she wrote:

> At the YMCA and Salvation Army the silent missionaries gather, with their pale, pale skin and pastel clothes, eating their mild English breakfasts of porridge, toast and tea, and revealing in their eyes and shoulders the hopeless, spiritual invincibility that is their reward for decades spent in leper colonies and rural schools.

Ruddy complexions, loud talk, bright sweaters, and *steak breakfasts* suggest vigor and confidence; *silence, pale skin* and *clothes, porridge, toast* and *tea* do not. Miss Levine uses the connotations of these expressions to demonstrate the mood of hopelessness which comes after little visible reward from a dedicated life.

Projects—Vividness

1. The following words are arranged in groups of approximately similar meanings. After referring to your dictionary, indicate the shades of differences in the meanings and use the words in senses that reveal your understanding of the connotations.

> abandon, relinquish, renounce
> answer, reply, response, retort
> assign, allocate, allot
> contempt, disdain, scorn
> continual, constant, continuous, incessant, perpetual, perennial
> dark, obscure, dim, vague
> defender, guardian, custodian, keeper
> direct, order, command, demand
> lead, guide, conduct, escort, pilot, influence
> progressive, forward, enterprising, liberal
> release, free, dismiss, discharge
> see, perceive, witness, inspect, interview, discern, regard, deem, look,
> behold, gaze, scan, skim

2. Analyze the following essay by George Orwell for the quality of its vividness. Indicate appeals to various senses; note connotations. A way to appreciate exact, effective diction is to show the changes created by using different words. Find synonyms for the italicized words and experiment with them.

In Moulmein, in Lower Burma, I was hated by large numbers of people—the only time in my life that I have been important enough for this to happen to me. I was sub-divisional police officer of the town, and in an *aimless, petty* kind of way anti-European feeling was very bitter. No one *had the guts* to raise a riot, but if a European woman went through the bazaars alone somebody would probably spit betel juice over her dress. As a police officer I was an obvious target and was *baited* whenever it seemed safe to do so. When a nimble Burman tripped me up on the football field and the referee (another Burman) looked the other way, the crowd yelled with hideous laughter. This happened more than once. In the end the sneering yellow faces of young men that met me everywhere, the insults *hooted* after me when I was at a safe distance, got badly on my nerves. The young Buddhist priests were the worst of all. There were several thousand of them in the town and none of them seemed to have anything to do except stand on street corners and *jeer* at the Europeans.

All this was perplexing and upsetting. For at that time I had already made up my mind that imperialism was an evil thing and the sooner I *chucked up* my job and got out of it the better. Theoretically—and secretly, of course—I was all for the Burmese and all against their oppressors, the British. As for the job I was doing, I hated it more bitterly than I can perhaps make clear.—*Shooting An Elephant and Other Essays*

Efficiency

As you rewrite, you can be certain that your reader values his or her time. Whatever you have to say, every one of your readers has something he would rather do than listen. Any argument?

The obvious final line to this observation is that your goal should be to have the word *brief* describe your style. However, brevity by itself is a dubious virtue. If you condense 3000 words to 500 but do not accomplish your purpose, you have wasted your time and your reader's.

What you seek is to get the job done in the least possible words. That is *efficiency,* a word that connotes a healthy concern for your reader's sensibilities.

We suggest that to achieve efficiency, you use standard idiomatic English, sentences structured for emphasis, and economical modes of expression.

USE FAMILIAR WORDS

Your goal, as you write, is to cause your reader to nod and say either, "I understand," or "I agree." If, instead, he blinks his eyes over a strange word, your style has been counterproductive. For an instant you have lost his concentration and you may not regain it. You may be tempted to parade a vocabulary of long words. You may write, "The caitiff osculated the pulchritudinous damsel," but you will sound like a snob or a show-off. If you write that "the rascal kissed the pretty girl," your reader's train of thought will not be interrupted by a trip to the dictionary. You should certainly use exact words and technical words when necessary and properly defined, but you gain nothing if, for pretension and display, you trot out an *esoteric* word. You gain nothing by seeming to be a snob or a show-off. When you have a choice of two equally exact words, select the shorter, more familiar one every time. (At this moment we pause and ask what your reaction was to our word *esoteric*, meaning "known only to a select few." Were you one of the select? Was it any better than *unfamiliar* word?)

USE APPROPRIATE IDIOMS

The literal meaning of many English expressions is puzzling. Think about these sentences. What, exactly, do they say? What, actually, do they mean?

> Did you carry out my command?
> Now, then, what shall we do?
> He made good.
> Take it from me; I know I'm right.
> Go to the foot of the class.
> The man's hard up.
> She wore out her clothes.
> He was named after his uncle.

Expressions whose meaning comes from agreement and custom rather than from the exact meaning of the words are called *idioms*. In addition, the word *idiom* refers to conventional use of prepositions. There are a number of idioms that differentiate American from British English. Americans say, "go to the hospital"; the British say, "go to hospital." Americans say, "What time is it?" The English say, "What time do you make it?" Americans are "on time," but the British are "up to time." Americans and British agree when they "are hungry," but the idiom is different for the Spaniard, who would say, *"Tengo hambre,"* or "I have hunger."

Native users of a language learn idioms almost by osmosis. They get accustomed to *come in handy, mull over, do away with, strike a bargain,* and many others. What seems to be more confusing is the joining of the proper word to some verbs. Idioms that are often misused are:

> We request adherence *to* our policy.
> He is careful *with* idioms.
> Worry is conducive *to* sleeplessness. (Not *of*)
> I agree *to* an idea, but I agree *with* a person.
> He was embarrassed *by* his sister. (Not *at* her)
> The movie was inferior *to* the book.
> Her pie was different *from* the one in the picture. (Not *than*)

We were receptive *to* the idea.

He divided the loot *among* his three accomplices. (Divide *between* two, but *among* more.)

The best way to learn what words are standard currency is to read and listen attentively. Another way is to check such reference works as William Freeman's *A Concise Dictionary of English Idioms,* Harold Whitford and Robert Dixon's *Handbook of American Idioms and Idiomatic Usage,* and Funk and Wagnall's *Standard Handbook of Prepositions, Conjunctions, Relative Pronouns and Adverbs.* More recent but general works include Roy H. Copperud's *American Usage: The Consensus* and Jerome Shostak's *Concise Dictionary of Current Usage.*

STRUCTURE SENTENCES FOR EMPHASIS

Skilled writers use sentence patterns to suggest meanings that go beyond the content of the words. In diction and grammar, these two sentences are equivalent:

The boy is unhappy.
Unhappy is the boy.

Though the same four words are used in both sentences, the word order is different, and, subtly, so is the meaning. The word *unhappy* gets more emphasis in the second sentence. Since the construction is strange, it would be appropriate for an unusual subject or locale as, for example, "Uneasy lies the head that wears the crown."

In general, the words at either end of a sentence influence the reader most. A word that might lose its effect in the middle of a sentence can be more meaningful at the beginning:

The mob suddenly surged toward the Italian embassy, when it was shouted around that the film was not made in the United States.

Suddenly the mob surged toward the Italian embassy, when it was shouted around that the film was not made in the United States.

Suddenly, when it was shouted around that the film was not made in the United States, the mob surged toward the Italian embassy.

The first sentence lacks focus. We cannot anticipate whether the following sentences will be about what happens at the Italian embassy or why the mob changed its direction. Moving *suddenly* to the beginning of the sentence causes the action to seem more immediate. In the final sentence, burying the subordinate clause in the middle suggests strongly that we will learn what happened at the Italian embassy.

When a writer wishes to point up balance of ideas, he will express them in parallel constructions. Arthur Miller wrote, "I left Ann Arbor in the spring of 1938 and in two months I was on relief." The two thoughts are made almost tonelessly equivalent.

Balanced ideas can be extended to a series. The following paragraph shows how parallel ideas may be accentuated by a series of structurally similar sentences:

> The human race, at this juncture in its history, is increasingly exhibiting all of the symptoms shown by the most profoundly disturbed psychopathic personality. Like him, we are as a species becoming conscienceless and violent. Like him, we are becoming predatory and selfish. Like him, we are slaves of impulse and baser instincts.—ROBERT LINDNER, *Must You Conform?*

The parallelism may sometimes be emphasized by letting the reader's anticipation supply part of the sentence structure, as in "Youth is a delight, old age a joy" and "I loved her, and she me." Omitting part of the sentence in this way is called *ellipsis*. Famous examples of the use of ellipsis include Francis Bacon's "Reading maketh a full man; conference a ready man; and writing an exact man" and Benjamin Disraeli's pronouncement "Youth is a blunder; manhood a struggle; old age a regret."

In a series the conjunction is sometimes omitted when each unit of the series is to be considered singly, as in "I came, I saw, I conquered." Occasionally, if the writer desires a strong rhythm and the sense is simple or jolly, he piles up the units quickly, as in the barroom ballad, "They ripped, they tore, they fell upon the floor." On another occasion the writer may play a trick on the reader by getting the series going and then throwing in a last word that doesn't follow the trend of the preceding items in the series. Since there is no conjunction, the reader rushes on to the final unit and gets a mild shock: "The duke played the violin gaily, loudly, badly."

Since equal structures usually signal a similarity of ideas, contrast is emphasized when the ideas are opposed. The sentence "Man proposes; God disposes" is semantically antithetical but structurally parallel. The next examples were used by two American presidents:

> The world will little note nor long remember what we say here, but it can never forget what they did here.—ABRAHAM LINCOLN
>
> Ask not what your country can do for you: Ask what you can do for your country.—JOHN F. KENNEDY

To be efficient, first make sure you have the right word and the right sentence structure. Then, to make sure you have not wasted a word, start to chop.

PRACTICE ECONOMY

You can express most ideas in ten or twenty different ways; often the shortest way is the best. These are some of the most common principles to follow.

Avoid Redundancy

In some writers wordiness is a disease. Some people write not for communication, but because they like to read their own words; they write, "Such are the vicissitudes of this our sublunary existence," instead of "Such is life." The name of the disease is *redundancy*, which is defined as "the use of more words than necessary." *Verbosity* is an extreme form of the disease; words are thrown in so profusely that the writing cannot be remedied merely by cutting out offending expressions. *Verbiage* (or "verbal garbage") is nearly fatal to meaning, so many words being used that the meaning disappears almost completely. When a composition is written loosely, it is said to be *diffuse*, which is the opposite of concise. *Circumlocution* refers to an expression that is stated in a roundabout, indirect, or euphemistic way; it is often an attempt to avoid using an unpleasant term. *Tautology* is a wordiness caused by an almost exact duplication of meanings. The sentence "The English language is one-half redundant" seems concise enough, but the sentence "English is half redundant" uses only two-thirds the words and conveys the same information. The sentence "He walked the entire distance *on foot*" is tautological. Delete the last two words. Other examples of tautology are:

"The reason I am doing this is because . . ."	Condense to "I am doing this because . . ."
mental telepathy	Telepathy is always mental; the first word is unnecessary.
general consensus of opinion	The word *consensus* means "general opinion." Omit three words.
elfinlike	*Elfin* means "like an elf." Omit *like*.
many new innovations	If it weren't new, it wouldn't be an innovation. Omit *new*.

One way to sensitize yourself to economical prose is to note the reverse of it. Many writers amuse themselves by keeping a collection of pretentious, wordy expressions. Can you top these?

England anticipates that with regard to the current emergency, personnel will duly implement their obligations in accordance with the functions allocated to their respective age groups.

A newspaperman, coming across this speech, waded through the marsh-mallows and observed that the hidden message was "England expects every man to do his duty."

> Rumors have been passed stating that particular brands of cigarettes have been banned in various states. However, as of yet, this banning has not been activated.

> There has been legitimate objection that the Council of Economic Advisers' development of the productivity guideposts has included too little participation by those whose experience includes fuller participation in the functions of price and wage determinations. The point is made both in terms of the pragmatics of general acceptance and of the conclusions which are reached.

These two jewels appeared in government publications. Do you know what they mean?

Write with Nouns and Verbs

The power and terseness of the English language lie in its nouns and verbs. The cub reporter writes, "The drunken man walked awkwardly," but the copy editor changes it to "The drunk staggered." "He made the room dark" becomes "He darkened the room." "I move that we lay it on the table" becomes "I move that we table it." Other examples include:

Overly adverbial or adjectival	Nouns and verbs
I am angry about	I resent
He will watch over me.	He will protect me.
He ruled over	He ruled
give in small quantities	dole
feeling of uncertainty	doubt
He made an unpleasant face.	He frowned

Prefer Active Verbs

It has long been fashionable to condemn the passive voice—and to use it. In 1837 a critic called the passive voice "philological coxcombry" and "an outrage upon the English idiom, to be detested, abhorred, execrated and given over to six thousand penny-paper editors." Since then countless rhetoricians have insisted that writers avoid the passive voice.

The stigma attached to the passive voice becomes ironic when we realize that the passive is often a mark of sophistication. Scholars use it more often than do sensationalists. At times writers can scarcely avoid it. When a writer wishes to conceal the agent of an action, he must use the passive, as in "unkind things were said." Likewise, he relies on the passive when the agent is irrelevant or unknown, as in "the message was sent." Active and passive transformations often have different meanings, as demonstrated by "A boy broke the window" and "The window was broken by a boy." You should select what seems appropriate.

There are, nevertheless, three legitimate objections to the passive voice. First, it may foster momentary ambiguity. When a sentence begins, "The dog was given . . . ," we do not know whether the dog is the recipient of the action ("The dog was given a brushing") or whether he is the object of the action ("The dog was given to the girl"). Even though this ambiguity passes, it does demonstrate the potential fuzziness of the passive voice.

Second, the passive is not dramatic. It stresses the object, not the subject or the action of the sentence. In "The child was given a spanking," our attention is focused on the child who received the spanking rather than on the spanking or the person who administered it. In this particular sentence, it may be preferable to focus on the child, but the passive voice can result in too many changes of focus:

> His clarinet was taken from its case, and his music was placed on the rack. His lungs were expanded, and many notes were blown. Before the piece was completed, much beautiful music was played.

This is an exaggerated example, but it illustrates the change in point of view and the flatness characteristic of the passive voice.

Finally, the passive voice requires more space—the reason that is usually persuasive—than does the active. Contrast these two pairs of sentences:

> The dog was given a brushing by the man.   (nine words)
> The man brushed the dog.   (five words)
>
> A dog was given to the girl by her father.   (ten words)
> The girl's father gave her a dog.   (seven words)

Projects—Efficiency

1. With efficiency as your goal, rewrite the following paragraph.

> When we think concerning people who are being bothered by changes in today's modern world, we most often think of the elderly persons who do not like to see any kinds of changes and are kind of upset by them. But changes in things upset the young of today too also. They are not upset by moral rules of do's and don't's or new kinds of ways to do things, or because of faltering traditions and customs. The trouble they have comes from the loss of clarity and direction which changes make a product of. Not knowing their alternative they take a lot of things for granted.

2. Analyze the following selection from *To Be Young, Gifted, and Black* for efficiency. What uneconomical expressions did Lorraine Hansberry avoid in this selection? Restructure the paragraphs and describe the change

in emphasis and meaning. Contrast the short sentences in the first paragraph to the long sentences in the final paragraph. What happens if you break the longer sentences into shorter ones? Do facts belong in short sentences and opinions in long sentences?

> I was born on the Southside of Chicago. I was born black and a female. I was born in a depression after one world war, and came into my adolescence during another. While I was still in my teens the first atom bombs were dropped on human beings at Nagasaki and Hiroshima, and by the time I was twenty-three years old my government and that of the Soviet Union had entered actively into the worst conflict of nerves in human history—the Cold War.
>
> I have lost friends and relatives through cancer, lynching and war. I have been personally the victim of physical attack which was the offspring of racial and political hysteria. I have worked with the handicapped and seen the ravages of congenital diseases that we have not yet conquered because we spend our time and ingenuity in far less purposeful wars. I see daily on the streets of New York, street gangs and prostitutes and beggars; I know people afflicted with drug addiction and alcoholism and mental illness; I have, like all of you, on a thousand occasions seen indescribable displays of man's very real inhumanity to man; and I have come to maturity, as we all must, knowing that greed and malice, indifference to human misery and, perhaps above all else, ignorance—the prime ancient and persistent enemy of man—abound in this world.
>
> I say all of this that one cannot live with sighted eyes and feeling heart and not know and react to the miseries which afflict this world.
>
> I have given you this account so that you know that what I write is not based on the assumption of idyllic possibilities or innocent assessments of the true nature of life—but, rather, my own personal view that, posing one against the other, I think that the human race does command its own destiny and that that destiny can eventually embrace the stars.

Personality

Writing should have life to it. It should be the reflection of an interesting, lively person, writing to someone he respects. We are not merely talking about being clever and original. You can be so clever as to be rude or flippant. You must be considerate. You can be so original as to be obscure. You must use conventional expressions that will be understood. You must, however, try to develop a writing style with a personality so engaging that your reader will actually want to read what you say, want to understand you, want to agree with you.

In your attempt to develop an effective style, you soon realize you must *be* someone. Communication, if it is anything, is a social event. One person talks to another person or several persons. We are speaking of "personality." The more life, the more engaging the personality, the better.

One way you can be yourself is to avoid trying to be someone else. Understandably, you may wish to wear the cloak of respectability. You may feel inclined to write in some stereotyped way because others have done so. Fight off the urge. Avoid wearing someone else's tired old personality.

BARRIERS TO PERSONALITY

Institutionalized Styles

If you wish, you can get a ready-made style easily, as though from a mail-order house. Having it handy, you will be able to express wonderfully banal ideas without doing any thinking at all. If you order the "ad" style, you may receive packages of sports-page clichés:

> That salesman can hit singles and doubles, but he's no good on the home runs. He's bush league.

You can reap a beautiful bouquet of mixed metaphors:

> Let's throw this idea into the mixer and see whether it grows or not. If they shoot it down, we'll know it has too many gremlins in it.

In no time at all you'll be able to master this branch of English, called Madison Avenue.

If you want to enter the military or political world, you can easily order "gobbledygook." Defense department officials are rarely pessimistic; they have a "low confidence factor." They do not start or end anything; they "initiate" or "finalize" it. They sometimes even "accomplish a milestone." Politicians will supply you with grand models of gobbledygook. You'll learn to say, "In my opinion it is not an unjustifiable assumption," instead of "I agree." Some other choice expressions are:

Gobbledygook	Translation
give consideration to	consider
make inquiry	inquire
is of the opinion	believes
comes into conflict with	conflicts with
information which is of a confidential nature	confidential information
protective reaction	bombing the countryside

If you want to become a teacher, you can learn "pedagese." An "under-achiever" is a pupil who is "producing minimally or below his peer group." It may be that his "grade achievement under the multiple-track plan reflects his predisposition toward those factors frequently associated with late bloomers lacking the developmental key of meaningful motivation and without the felt need to effectuate the tasks involved in the learning process." In other words, he "is doing poorly compared with his peers, not because he's

the small society   by Brickman

the small society   by Brickman

stupid, but because he is not interested." Later, he does not merely graduate; he "achieves baccalaureate status."

The writers who use these institutionalized styles deserve some sympathy. Men in positions of responsibility occasionally cannot commit themselves; they need a way to say nothing. There is a certain lure to ingroup expressions; using them gives one a sense of superiority and a feeling of community with the other users. Also, many of the expressions we now ridicule once had specific, needed meanings; *initiate* and *finalize* meant to begin and to end operations with which the person probably had no other connection. The expression *cease and desist* in legal documents indicates not only that an act must stop but also that it must not resume.

Clichés

In addition to ordering a ready-made style, you may acquire a pack of *clichés*. The cliché may once have been a vivid or witty expression, but now the world is tired of it. Fatigued expressions become part of the language and are trotted out with no thought at all. It rains *cats and dogs,* because this is a *tried-and-true* description. The weather report may promise that you will be *warm as toast* or *cold as ice,* or it may strike you as *dull as dish-water*; in any case, you can count on it being *not the heat but the humidity* that bothers you. A girl is *as pretty as a picture, as innocent as a newborn babe,* or *as slow as molasses in January.* An old man who marries a young girl is *old enough to be her father.* Twins are as similar as *two peas in a pod.* A boy who takes too much food has eyes bigger than his stomach; a girl may *look like something the cat dragged in.* If *it all comes out in the wash,* it is a *blessing in disguise.*

Many comparisons are now clichés: *sober as a judge, skinny as a rail, old as Methuselah, nutty as a fruitcake, cold as a statue, honest as the day is long, fine as silk, busy as a beaver, strong as an ox.* Others are dead meta-phors or forgotten allusions. For example, do you know the origin or mean-ing of *cut-and-dried issue, dead as a doornail, toe the line, beyond the pale, dyed in the wool, beat about the bush, pay the piper, swan song?* News-papers drum expressions into our consciousness and wear them out. One of the most overworked words in journalism is *hailed.* Other tired terms are *violence flowed, flatly denied, kickoff, oil-rich nation,* and *gutted by fire.* These expressions have the virtues of brevity for headlines, and they may once have aroused the excitement that sells newspapers. When they occur in serious writing, however, they do not dramatize; they tire.

Clichés may slip up on you because you may not have read enough in certain subjects to know which expressions have been overused. Your in-structor may write "trite" or "cliché" about a phrase you thought quite orig-inal. One way to guard against clichés is to demand that every expression be appropriate not only for the occasion but also for yourself. "Poor as a church mouse" is out of date because churches do not play as big a part in everyday life as they did in the past. "As loud as an atomic bomb" is ques-tionable because such an explosion is not likely to be an experience you share with your reader.

You may often be tempted to use institutionalized language or clichés. A witty or apt expression used by someone before you may have been just right once upon a time, and it is so easy to follow him, and follow him. If you really aspire for your writing to have personality, you should use some-one else's moldy old expressions just about as frequently as you use his toothbrush.

Repetition

Other writers age clichés before you get to them, but you can do your part in wearing out your language. You can fatigue your reader by unwise repetition. A desire for variety can be carried too far, as when the author of the Tom Swift series of boys' books tried so hard to avoid repeating *he*

said that his series of "he ejaculated . . . lamented . . . exclaimed . . . ges-
ticulated . . . queried" and the like has made him the laughingstock of readers for six decades. But within limits a writer should try to avoid using the
same word too frequently. He should select a synonym that will give a more
exact cast to the idea being developed. He should avoid having sentences
that are all the same length or the same structure. He might work within
an average range of, say, twelve to twenty words per sentence. Then he may
suddenly use a short sentence for dramatic effect. He should use a blend of
simple, compound, and complex sentences. This range of language, coupled
with the inevitable variation in levels of abstraction as the writer moves
from general statements to supporting detail, will tend to provide the variety
that characterizes good style.

If the barriers to a style with personality are institutionalized language,
the cliché, and excessive repetition, it follows that the other side of the coin
is to seek out your own personality and find out what traits seem most
attractive.

YOUR OWN LANGUAGE

In the following story, which appeared in the *Boston Sunday Globe,* an
experienced reporter demonstrates his awareness that a writer can tell the
story best in his own language. We have excerpted the sections in which
the reporter quotes his subject.

> "All of my friends are either dead or in jail, and, like man, I've
> known some of the most brilliant kids in Harlem, kids that knew
> everything, kids that could remember the names of all the Supreme
> Court justices in history and click them off from memory. I knew
> kids who knew fantastic things, about the stars and the moon and
> the planets, but they'll never have a chance, no way. Dead, most
> of them, or in some dark jail, or just lost forever, some of them. I
> was a lucky one. I got out, escaped. I mean like I was on everythin'
> from the time I was a little kid. You name it, marijuana, speed,
> meth, heroin, all the drugs. Then I stopped. I had this thing about
> wantin' to be a writer and I guess it saved me."

Lloyd McMillan Corbin . . . explained that his high school gives out three
kinds of diplomas, the least of the three being a trade diploma which
sends graduates "into the business world to practice what they learned at
school on obsolete machines." He earned a general diploma, "a sheet of
paper that states, like, I attended classes for four years, that's all."

> "I don't know why I started to write. I didn't have no kind of
> family life. My parents both work and like most black families we
> don't have what the whites call a nucleus family, you know what I
> mean? But, like, well, somethin' was burnin' inside me to get down
> on paper what I saw all around me. I lived on a block, one corner
> had prostitution, one corner had drugs, and in the middle was the
> numbers, and if one or the other of them didn't get you, well

luck! That's all. When I was a little kid, we started on cheap wine, gut stuff. We'd all chip in what we had and get a bottle. Then when the kick went outa that, we moved to drugs, the easy stuff, then the hard. The price would start small, two bucks a bag, say, and that'd be the tab for awhile, then it'd go up, as soon as you were hooked.

"I came to see it all as a waste of time. I mean life was too mother hard for drugs to be so cheap and easy, then you find out they aren't cheap and easy, and, man, it's too late, too late. It happened all the time. I once had stuff taken from me in school by a teacher's aide and I found out afterwards he used the stuff himself, he was hooked, an addict. But what grieves me is the kids I've seen that are lost, wrecked, smashed, beaten, dead. But like who cares, huh, cause they were niggers?" . . .

"That's cynical, I know, but it's accurate. It's just not good enough for me, as a human being, that I made it, that I can find some cushions somewhere and be able to buy them. I mean, I wrote about drugs and the streets because, well right around the corner from me is a park filled with flowers, but I don't know from flowers, I know about terror and pushers and dead-ends. I was able to get away from it once in awhile, to visit my grandparents who live outside the ghetto, who live in a mostly Jewish neighborhood and I learned about a totally different culture where it wasn't all pocked arms and fright. Oh, man! Those little kids I've known, so bright, with promise . . . and they're gone now, gone, or in jail."

A student of writing must learn that, although there is usually a point to following the niceties of grammar, spelling, and punctuation, he writes most effectively in his own vernacular. When he is asked to write about the nuclear family for a social science course, he may go to the library and do research, but he should cite his own family and those he has observed. Likewise, he should use the language he is familiar with. There is a kind of college dialect which observes conventional and standard usage and avoids slang known only to a few, and the student submitting papers to college teachers learn to handle it; but as a writing student, he practices being himself.

THE TOOLS OF WRITING PERSONALITY

Figurative Language

Very often the first time a student seeks to express his own personality while he writes, he just does not know what arrows he has in his quiver. He has been pressed into a mold for so long that he just has never experimented with the various ways of letting his readers get to know what kind of a person he is.

In the pages that follow we do not particularly recommend any special techniques for your style. We suggest that you try them to see which ones seem right for you. If you like some of them and find they make you happier with your writing, good. If you turn out to be like Somerset Maugham, who noted that metaphors never seemed to come to him naturally, so be it.

Good style is good thinking, expressed well. *Ornamentation*—fancy phrases, long words, foreign expressions, and even some of the devices we will be discussing—can be obtrusive, phony. They may call unwelcome attention to the words and obscure the idea. Some writers do use rhetorical devices and get by with them. We have already discussed comparisons as aids to clarity. We now turn to some other aids ·which give personality to writing.

> His hands held the saucer and cigarette as if they were surgical instruments. The wrinkles of his brow were the worries of yesteryear and today and tomorrow, and the sleepless nights of coronaries and obstetrics, the pains and sufferings that he felt as acutely as did his patients.

These sentences transmit an idea vividly through the use of *figures of speech*. By using such figures skillfully, a writer can create prose that is full of life and fresh in spirit. He can write with pictures and write clearly.

The *metaphor*, one kind of figure of speech, is a device that suggests an idea by an implied comparison. Technically, a *simile* is also a metaphor; but in a simile the comparison is expressed, indicated by the word *as* or *like*, whereas in a metaphor the comparison can be suggested in any way. "He was a tiger in the fight" is a metaphor; "He fought like a tiger" is a simile. In the sentence "He wolfed his food" the verb is a metaphor that could be expressly stated in a simile: "He ate like a wolf." In *Prometheus Unbound*, Shelley writes of "multitudes of white fleecy clouds . . . wandering along the mountains, shepherded by the slow, unwilling wind." The comparison of clouds to sheep is an obvious metaphor. In an interview a Dartmouth quarterback, when asked if he was in shape for the season, replied, "No, I am as soft as a sneaker full of marshmallows." This was a simile.

Two other figures of speech, *synecdoche* and *metonymy*, give drama to prose. *Synecdoche* (pronounced sin-EK-doe-key) is an expression in which a part indicates a whole or a whole indicates a part. *Hollywood* is used to represent the entire film industry; *Madison Avenue* symbolizes all advertisers. A student may ask, "Have you got the word yet?" when he means an entire message. Speaking of an employee as a *hired hand* is synecdoche. *Wings over Britain*, referring to German bombers, is synecdoche, as are *campus life*, *Foggy Bottom* (the location of State Department headquarters), and *Nebraska won*. The last example uses the state name to represent not the state, or even the state university, but an athletic team of the University of Nebraska.

Metonymy, on the other hand, is the use of an aspect or attribute of a concept to stand for the concept itself. For example, a sportswriter may say that the Baltimore Orioles have a strong "bench," which is metonymy meaning that the Orioles have many good substitute players, since the substitutes sit on a bench until they are called on to play. Shakespeare's "A plague on both your *houses*" (our italics) is metonymy. In Genesis we read "In the sweat of thy face," which is metonymy indicating "hard work." In our daily newspapers we often read, "The White House announced today that . . . ," which is a metonymical way of referring to the president of the United States.

Another device that contributes vividness to writing is the *allusion*—a reference to history, literature, or legends. For instance, according to Greek mythology, after Prometheus offended the gods by stealing fire from heaven, the deities resolved to punish man by creating woman. The gods all bestowed gifts on this first mortal female, Pandora, and Zeus gave her a box with instructions not to open it. The curious Pandora immediately opened the box, and, like the winds, out rushed all the evils that were to beset man forevermore. The story sets up a picture of a bewildered woman almost blown over by the outpouring evils, a dramatic scene. Now when a writer speaks of "opening Pandora's box" he means letting loose uncontrollable forces, and he is using allusion.

When a black is called "Uncle Tom," the allusion is to the central character of the abolitionist novel *Uncle Tom's Cabin* by Harriet Beecher Stowe; in the eyes of today's militant black leaders, Uncle Tom was too content with his servitude. Calling someone a "Uriah Heep" labels him with the hypocritical humility of that character from Charles Dickens' novel *David Cooperfield*. A "Pyrrhic victory" is one gained at too great a cost, as was that of Pyrrhus over the Romans in 279 B.C. Pyrrhus, when he had won the battle but sustained heavy losses, exclaimed, "One more such victory over the Romans, and we are utterly undone." Using such an allusion takes advantage of the drama of a whole chapter in history.

Not every writer naturally and easily creates figures of speech. Somerset Maugham lamented that metaphors just never occurred to him. Other people seem to think in figurative language, and one hears or reads expressions like these:

> I don't like to talk with him. I feel dirty when I'm through, as if I'd just walked out of oily sludge.

> If I drove like that in Wichita, I would get a bushel basketful of traffic tickets.

> Yes, it's a fairly neat little lash-up.—(Response of an electronics engineer to a compliment about a computer he has just devised)

Nobody is interested in following a man who, with his eyes fixed on the ground, spends his life looking for a pocketbook. . . . When I paint, my object is to show what I have found, not what I am looking for.—PABLO PICASSO

Youth is the time to go flashing from one end of the world to the other . . . to hear the chimes at midnight . . . to see sunrise in town and country; to be converted at a revival; to write halting verse, run a mile to see a fire.—ROBERT LOUIS STEVENSON

She would rather light candles than curse the darkness.—ADLAI STEVENSON, about Eleanor Roosevelt

You may wish to make your phrases more memorable and even epigrammatic by using *alliteration,* arranging words to make series of similar first sounds.

. . . the wan world of theological thought.

. . . the price of precious peace.

Minimum in mind; maximum in muscle.

By using *oxymoron,* that is, by linking almost exact opposites, you may succeed in coining a phrase that is particularly apt.

He jumped and, as the rushing wind struck his ears, he pulled the cord. For a brief eternity, the chute did not open.

John Lindsay, New York's waspishly hip former mayor.—*Rolling Stone*

. . . the rack on which black and white Americans received their delicious torture.—ELDRIDGE CLEAVER, *Soul On Ice*

The use of figurative language can, of course, go too far. If a writer reaches for figures of speech or uses too many, they can become obtrusive and halt the reader momentarily, blocking the flow of thought. If they are obscure, they can block communication completely. Occasionally, a writer may inadvertently mix his metaphors, that is, present two contradictory pictures, and the result is ludicrous:

The hand that rocked the cradle has paved the way for America's youth.

It is a time of uneasy peace; forged on the anvil of many dreams, the ship of state has sprung a leak.

You must salt away a nest egg for a rainy day.

One way to learn to use effective metaphors is to recognize bad ones. We hope that you are keeping a journal; if so, a valuable entry, often good for a chuckle, is a copy of some strained metaphors. What do you think of our collection?

These bottlenecks must be ironed out.

As State School Superintendent Max Rafferty put it, "When you take off this straitjacket, you introduce a lot of wild cards into the game on which we will have to ride herd."—From the San Francisco Sunday *Chronicle*

The University which rests on a firm foundation has a better ability to unleash a student's mind.

These metaphors create a confused picture. The writers would have been better off sticking to straightforward, simple prose.

Humor

Along with the many other decisions you must make when you write, you must decide how seriously you take your reader, your subject, and yourself. Even if you take them all very seriously, you may decide to treat your subject humorously. Laugh and the world laughs with you; cry and you cry alone. The writer who can turn a deft phrase and amuse his audience will be steps ahead of the writer who cannot. If humor is not your forte, however, you should not strain or warp your authentic self. If you use exact, vivid, and efficient prose, you will be showing the world as you see it, and the result will be the humanness that is the final attribute of good writing style.

Some humor takes the form of gentle irony, as when a writer announcing a serious political meeting writes, "The revels will begin this evening at eight," or when he refers to an important international document as a "conversation piece." By using irony—cool words in times of passion, words of praise to imply blame, or diminutives to label important concepts—the writer creates an air of restraint and detachment.

The following tongue-in-cheek paragraph from an article, "The Enlisted Man," in *The New Yorker* demonstrates the use of subtle irony to make a point that is actually different from what the words say. Try to find the exact words that cause you to realize the writer doesn't think much of the "method."

> Mr. Bedingfield, having established his method, and showing us the diagram, went on to itemize the characteristics of the enlisted man. The enlisted man could be considered as Physical Man, as Professional Military Man, as Psychological Man, as Social Man, and as Spiritual Man, he said. Each of these categories was illustrated by a slide with an appropriate drawing and some writing on it. For instance, Social Man was seen at a bar, or perhaps a soda fountain, with a smile on his face, and under the subhead "Relationships/Activity" it was noted that "the EM needs facilities and spaces which allow him to establish beneficial social relationships/activities." Spiritual Man was shown pouring candy into the Christmas stocking of an Oriental child, and under the subhead "Identity/ Individual" it was noted that "the living spaces and facilities should allow each EM to maintain his identity/individualism." Other large categories were then mentioned. One was Activities, under which it was noted that

"each EM has a basic set of activities which occur within the living spaces," to which the caveat was later added that "activities with similar positions and privacy/community can be grouped into sets of comparable activities termed ACTIVITY GROUPS," and that "activities in compatible sets can occur on the same surfaces and simultaneously with other activities of that set." Another category was Positions, under which it was noted, "Each activity has a corresponding set of positions. Positions generate environmental surfaces and spaces necessary to maintain activities." Among the surfaces were "surfaces for sitting and reclining positions." And the best way of providing these, it turned out, was a chair and a bed.

Humor comes in many ways—especially if it is about yourself or a friend —a play on words, an anecdote, or a current joke, perhaps rephrased slightly to fit the occasion, all serve to remind the reader that the writer is present, a human being viewing and thinking about his subject and his audience.

Learning from Others

There are ways to improve your style beyond those surveyed in this chapter. Robert Louis Stevenson, for instance, recommended that a young writer imitate writers he admires—"play the sedulous ape," Stevenson advised. Benjamin Franklin and Abraham Lincoln, rather than imitating, paraphrased the writing of others and then compared the results.

About learning from others, Donald Hall has written,

> I suspect that a writer's ear is his most subtle, and possibly his most valuable, piece of equipment. We acquire a good ear by reading the great masters until their cadences become part of our minds. The stored memory of a hundred thousand sentences becomes the standard of the writer's own ear.—DONALD HALL, *Writing Well*

There is a value to studying the style of good writers, and fortunately, there are plenty of good models. The editors of many magazines demand that their articles, in addition to having worthwhile information, be written with a distinctive and even distinguished style. Such periodicals include *The Atlantic Monthly, Harper's Magazine, The New Republic, The New Yorker, Playboy,* and *Esquire.* Articles excellent in style are also found in *Daedalus, The Yale Review, The American Scholar, Foreign Affairs,* and *Scientific American.* The prose of contemporary or recent writers of many different political persuasions and literary schools is worth studying; for example, read James Baldwin, Marya Mannes, Eldridge Cleaver, TRB (Richard Strand), Rachel Carson, Paul Gallico, Wallace Stegner, E. M. Forster, Santha Rama Rau, Richard Rovere, Mary McCarthy, Joan Didion, Tom Wolfe, Martin Luther King, Jr., Martin Meyer, Malcolm X, Alan Watts, Sara Davidson, James Agee, Dan Wakefield, George Orwell, John Fischer, Daniel P. Moynihan, Midge Decter, Irving Kristol, Tom Wicker, William F. Buckley, Jr., Jack Kroll, Arlene Croce, and Doris Lessing.

Although there is no standard by which one can judge that any given author is the best English-language stylist, one can certainly say that the prose of E. B. White is among the most respected. About White's style, James Thurber wrote, "Those silver and crystal sentences have a ring like nobody else's in the world." Leonard Bacon wrote, "His most successful moments are due . . . to a high sense of the nobility of the ridiculous tempered with an ingenuous kindness." *Time* magazine called his writing a "kind of precocious offhand humming." Obviously, his writing has *style*.

In addition to writing the children's books *Stuart Little, Charlotte's Web,* and *The Trumpet of the Swan,* White has written for *The New Yorker* and published many collections of essays. For years he commuted between New York City and his farm in Maine, which made it possible for him to write with equal insight about city and rural life.

One of his best essays appeared first in *Holiday* magazine, has been anthologized innumerable times, and is also in print as a book. Titled "Here Is New York," the essay begins:

> On any person who desires such queer prizes, New York will bestow the gift of loneliness and the gift of privacy. It is this largess that accounts for the presence within the city's walls of a considerable section of the population; for the residents of Manhattan are to a large extent strangers who have pulled up stakes somewhere and come to town, seeking sanctuary or fulfillment or some greater or lesser grail. The capacity to make such dubious gifts is a mysterious quality of New York. It can destroy an individual, or it can fulfill him, depending a good deal on luck. No one should come to New York to live unless he is willing to be lucky.

After this introduction, White continues his eulogy with this sentence:

> New York is the concentrate of art and commerce and sport and religion and entertainment and finance, bringing to a single compact arena the gladiator, the evangelist, the promoter, the actor, the trader and the merchant.

After exemplifying these various types, he goes on with his description of the city:

> New York blends the gift of privacy with the excitement of participation; and better than most dense communities it succeeds in insulating the individual (if he wants it, and almost everybody wants or needs it) against all enormous and violent and wonderful events that are taking place every minute. . . .
> There are roughly three New Yorks. . . .
> The commuter is the queerest bird of all. . . .
> A poem compresses much in a small space and adds music, thus heightening its meaning. The city is like poetry: it compresses all life, all races and the accompaniment of internal engines. The island of Manhattan

is without any doubt the greatest human concentrate on earth, the poem whose magic is comprehensible to millions of permanent residents but whose full meaning will always remain elusive. At the feet of the tallest and plushiest offices lie the crummiest slums. . . .

It is a miracle that New York works at all. . . .

Storekeepers are particularly conscious of neighborhood boundary lines. A woman friend of mine moved recently from one apartment to another, a distance of three blocks. When she turned up, the day after the move, at the same grocer's that she had patronized for years, the proprietor was in ecstacy—almost in tears—at seeing her. "I was afraid," he said, "now that you've moved away I wouldn't be seeing you any more." To him, *away* was three blocks, or about seven hundred and fifty feet.

Two outstanding qualities of White's prose are texture and virtuosity. In another part of the essay, only a single sentence separates "The music stops, and a beautiful Italian girl takes a brush from her handbag and stands under the street lamp brushing her long blue-black hair till it shines" from "The Consolidated Edison Company says there are eight million people in the five boroughs of New York, and the company is in a position to know" —a jump from one person to eight million. White's generalizations provide a pattern; underneath the generalizations, the riot of illustration, the coloration, and the metaphor give depth to his highly textured tapestry.

By White's virtuosity we mean that he uses every tool in the writer's kit. In "Here Is New York" there are allusions to Roman antiquity ("gladiators"), to medieval literature ("grail"), to British history ("muddling through"), and to children's literature (the *Wizard of Oz*). There is explicit symbolism ("Harlem symbolizes segregation") and a wealth of metaphor: "The whole city is honey combed with abandoned cells. . . . Broadway is a custard street. . . . batteries and batteries of offices. . . . Standing sentinel at each sleeper's head is the empty bottle from which he drained his release." (Note the alliteration here.) There is joking reference to tired metaphors: "It should have been touched in the head by the August heat and gone off its rocker." There is analogy: "It [Manhattan] is to the nation what the white church spire is to the village—the visible symbol of aspiration and faith." ("Visible symbol" is from the *Book of Common Prayer*.) There is exaggeration or hyperbole. "I heard the *Queen Mary* blow one midnight, though, and the sound carried the whole history of departure and longing and loss." There is antithesis: "lofty housing projects—high in stature, high in purpose, low in rent." And there are varying degrees of synecdoche and metonymy: "No one feeds the hungry IN-baskets"; "New York, the capital of memoranda, in touch with Calcutta, in touch with Reykjavik, and always fooling with something." In fact, there is almost no device that is not represented.

He appeals to the senses: "Street noises fill the bedroom"; "slapped down by a bus driver"; "massive doses of supplementary vitamins"; "voodoo charms of Harlem"; "white plume"; "the love message . . . blown . . . through a pneumatic tube—pfft—just like that"; "burned with a low steady fever"; "casually dressed—slacks, seersucker jacket, a book showing in his pocket"; "Coins rattle to the street"; "the mounted cop, clumping along on his nag"; "cool salvation"; "green salad with the little taste of garlic"; "skirts of girls approaching on the Mall are ballooned by the breeze." There is contrast— harsh sounds and soothing sounds, long sentences and short sentences, simple expressions and long piled-up constructions. There is an amusing description of a "young intellectual . . . trying to persuade a girl to come live with him and be his love," a literary allusion to Christopher Marlowe's poem "A Passionate Shepherd to His Love." "She has her guard up, but he is extremely reasonable, careful not to overplay his hand." In somber contrast there is subdued understatement, a reference to a young couple who have failed to catch the miracle. "The place has been too much for them; they sit languishing in a cheap restaurant over a speechless meal."

Just how much style can a college student expect to develop? Some of you may already have a fineness of writing and an exactness of expression, perhaps even a conscious style that reflects your personality. But all college students can take great strides toward a better writing style and all that can be accomplished with it.

What you must do, of course, is gradually work out your own procedure for writing. George Orwell has suggested that writers answer the following questions as they write:

1. What am I trying to say?
2. What words will express it?
3. What image or idiom will make it clearer?
4. Is this image fresh enough to have an effect?
5. Could I express the idea in fewer words?
6. Have I said anything that is avoidably ugly?

In *The Summing Up*, Somerset Maugham listed clarity, simplicity, and euphony as his goals. One of our students said he was happiest with his writing when it was "light and tight." You will want to select your own goal to fit the nature of your audience, as you perceive it, and your own strengths and weaknesses, as you see them. Ernest Hemingway, if it consoles you, gave up trying to make his sentences sound smooth.

No writer at any one time uses all the devices available to give his writing clarity, effectiveness, vividness, vigor, and variety—in other words, that extra something called *style*. The devices that he chooses to use tend to fall into a pattern individual to him.

With constant effort, you will get results, and your writing will come to have a happy blend of rhythm, precision, originality, vibrancy, color, and harmony; it will have that state of muscular tension, the fat gone and the sinews working together, that makes up your own style. When exposed to such writing, the reader will not consider himself the target of lifeless words; instead he will feel he is taking part in a dialogue with an intelligent, informed person.

Projects—Style

1. React to the following metaphors. Are they fresh, unstilted, generally appropriate for any audience? Are they ambiguous, mixed? Could you devise better ones to demonstrate the same concept?

    a. Effective as a blind lifeguard.
    b. Hysterical as a coop full of chickens.
    c. Awkward as a bull in a china shop.
    d. Thin as the homeopathic soup made by boiling the shadow of a pigeon that had starved to death.
    e. Unplanned as a hiccup.
    f. Restless as a windshield wiper.
    g. Helpful as throwing a drowning man both ends of a rope.
    h. Welcome as a monthly bill.
    i. Graceful as a fawn.
    j. Silly as a loon.
    k. Her eyes were bluer than the feet of a Sicilian wine crusher.
    l. Her face was as expressionless as a smoked herring.

2. Listed below are some expressions that are often quoted, quite out of their original context. We can assume, therefore, that they have been judged to be particularly effective ways of expressing thought. What do you think their appeal is? Is it the message itself, or the way it is expressed? What are some other expressions that have caught your fancy for one reason or another?

    Burning with a gemlike flame—WALTER PATER (*paraphrased*)
    Hail to thee, blithe Spirit!—PERCY BYSSHE SHELLEY
    Pronounce it trippingly on the tongue.—WILLIAM SHAKESPEARE
    The balance of power—SIR ROBERT WALPOLE
    Sea of upturned faces—DANIEL WEBSTER
    Hitch your wagon to a star.—RALPH WALDO EMERSON
    Heaven will protect the Working Girl.—EDGAR SMITH
    When you call me that, smile!—OWEN WISTER
    There is no cure for birth and death save to enjoy the interval.—GEORGE SANTAYANA
    The moral climate of America—FRANKLIN DELANO ROOSEVELT
    Let there be spaces in your togetherness.—KAHLIL GIBRAN

The moral obligation to be intelligent—JOHN ERSKINE

A separate peace—ERNEST HEMINGWAY

Sour grapes—AESOP

Deeds live longer than words.—PINDAR

The ship of state—SOPHOCLES

Love conquers all.—VIRGIL

Man is a reasoning animal.—SENECA

Words are but the shadow of action.—DEMOCRITUS

3. Many skilled professional writers have translated famous passages of prose into gobbledygook. Here are some examples:

> I returned, and saw under the sun, that the race is not the swift, nor the battle to the strong, neither yet bread to the wise, nor yet riches to men of understanding, nor yet favor to men of skill; but time and chance happeneth to them all.—Ecclesiastes 9:11.

> Objective consideration of contemporary phenomena compels the conclusion that success or failure in competitive activities exhibits no tendency to be commensurate with innate capacity, but that a considerable element of the unpredictable must invariably be taken into account. —GEORGE ORWELL, *Shooting an Elephant and Other Essays*

A sentence of Franklin D. Roosevelt's, "I see one-third of a nation ill-housed, ill-clad, ill-nourished," has been translated by Stuart Chase into "standard bureaucratic prose":

> It is evident that a substantial number of persons within the Continental limits of the United States have inadequate financial resources with which to purchase the products of agricultural communities and industrial establishments. It would appear that for a considerable segment of the population, possibly as much as 33.3333 per cent of the total, there are inadequate housing facilities, and an equally significant proportion is deprived of the proper types of clothing and nutriment.—STUART CHASE, *Power of Words*

To sharpen your perception of what to avoid in your own writing, translate the following quotations into gobbledygook:

> I think the true discovery of America is before us. I think the true fulfillment of our spirit, of our people, of our mighty and immortal land, is yet to come.—THOMAS WOLFE, *You Can't Go Home Again*

> We must act, and act quickly.—FRANKLIN D. ROOSEVELT, *"First Inaugural Address"*

> The frontier is the outer edge of the wave—the *meeting point*, between savagery and civilization.—FREDERICK JACKSON TURNER, "The Significance of the Frontier in American History"

> Four score and seven years ago our fathers brought forth on this continent, a new nation, conceived in liberty, and dedicated to the proposition that all men are created equal.—ABRAHAM LINCOLN, "Gettysburg Address"

The writer's duty is to . . . help man endure by lifting his heart, by reminding him of the courage and honor and hope and pride and compassion and pity and sacrifice which have been the glory of his past.
—WILLIAM FAULKNER, on accepting the Nobel award, Stockholm, Sweden, 1950

4. Rewrite one of the following selections. The results should be the best possible example of your style. Use Orwell's six suggestions listed at the end of the chapter. Your instructor may suggest or permit paragraphs by other authors.

The Americans, and especially the Americans who live in the open, have always been story tellers—one need recall only the rivermen, the lumberjacks, the cowmen, or in fact the loafers round any stove at a rural crossroads—but there have been no stories beyond those told by the map-minded breakers of trails, hunters of beavers, and exterminators of Indians. Most of their yarning has been lost to history, but it was a chronicle of every watercourse, peak, park, danger, violent mirth, of Indians whose thought was not commensurate with white thinking and therefore inexhaustibly fascinating, fantasy of mythological beavers or grizzlies, of Welsch Indians or Munchies of the Fair God, of supernatural beings and spectral visitants and startling medicine and heroes who were cousin to Paul Bunyan. It was a shop-talk, trapping, hunting, trailing, fighting and always the lay of the land and oil fields revisited and new fields to be found, water and starvation and trickery and feasts.—BERNARD DE VOTO, *Across the Wide Missouri*

The prosperity of America is legendary. Our standards of living are beyond the dreams of avarice of most of the world. We are a kind of paradise and domestic security and wealth. But we face the ironic situation that the same technical efficiency which provides our comforts has also placed us at the center of the tragic developments in world limits. There are evidently limits to the achievement of science; and there are irresolvable contradictions both between prosperity and virtue, and betwen happiness and the "good life" which had not been anticipated in our philosophy.—REINHOLD NIEBUHR, *The Irony of American History*

5. Assume you are an adviser for one of the new countries in Africa, and you have been asked to write a Declaration of Independence suggested by the American one. Write the first paragraph. It may be influenced by the following paragraph from the United States Declaration, but it must be in your own best style.

When, in the course of human events, it becomes necessary for one people to dissolve the political bands which have connected them with another, and to assume among the powers of the earth the separate and equal station to which the Laws of Nature and of Nature's God entitle them, a decent respect to the opinions of mankind requires that they should declare the causes which impel them to separation.

6. The following passage appeared on an English Advanced Placement Program examination prepared by the College Entrance Examination Board.

Students were asked to locate the rhetorical devices and write a careful analysis (not a paraphrase) of the passage with special attention to the choice of words, phrasing, sentence structure, figurative expressions, tone, and whatever else they considered pertinent. In a 500-word theme, demonstrate how you would have handled this assignment.

"COURSE AND EXAMINATION DESCRIPTION,"
COLLEGE ENTRANCE EXAMINATION BOARD

Meantime our society has lost its own soul. The landscape of Christendom is being covered with lava; a great eruption and inundation of brute humanity has been created. Brute humanity has the power to destroy polite humanity, because it retains the material equipment of modern industry which has recently grown upon man like fresh hide, horns, and claws. Armed with this prodigious mechanism, any hand at headquarters can spread death and ruin over the earth. But whose hand shall this be? Anybody's: the first man's who jumps at the lever, touches the button, and takes possession of the radio.

Yes, but this is so easy, so alluring, that more than one man may attempt it at once. Then the really great war, in the modern sense of greatness, would begin. The whole mechanism in one hand would clash with the whole mechanism in another hand. Will they simply blow each other up, and perish together? Or, at the last moment will they agree to pool their machinery and draw lots as to who shall be boss? Or will one of the explosions miss fire, so that only one party survives, and makes an appeal to chance unnecessary? In any case, it will be a war of extermination establishing an absolute power. There will be no consideration of rights or liberties, no talk of honour, and no nonsensical chivalry.—GEORGE SANTAYANA

7. The Inaugural Address of President John F. Kennedy was a conscious orchestration of stylistic devices. In the speech, which appears below, locate all examples of connotation, alliteration, epigram, paradox, allusion, analogy, repetition, balance, parallelism, anthithesis, metaphor, inverted sentences, and other devices. Then replace them with other expressions the president might have used and, by contrast, try to analyze the particular effect he sought. If, after you have completed your work, you wish to know how a professional rhetorician accomplished such an analysis, see "President Kennedy's Inaugural Address," by Burnham Carter, Jr., *College Composition and Communication*, February, 1963.

Mr. Chief Justice, President Eisenhower, Vice President Nixon, President Truman, reverend clergy, fellow citizens, we observe today not a victory of party, but a celebration of freedom—symbolizing an end, as well as a beginning—signifying renewal, as well as change. For I have sworn before you and Almighty God the same solemn oath our forebears prescribed nearly a century and three-quarters ago.

The world is very different now. For man holds in his mortal hands the power to abolish all forms of human poverty and all forms of human life. And yet the same revolutionary beliefs for which our forebears fought are still at issue around the globe—the belief that the rights of man come not from the generosity of the state, but from the hand of God.

We dare not forget today that we are the heirs of that first revolution. Let the word go forth from this time and place, to friend and foe alike, that the torch has been passed to a new generation of Americans—born in this century, tempered by war, disciplined by a hard and bitter peace, proud of our ancient heritage—and unwilling to witness or permit the slow undoing of those human rights to which this nation has always been committed, and to which we are committed today at home and around the world.

Let every nation know, whether it wishes us well or ill, that we shall pay any price, bear any burden, meet any hardships, support any friend, oppose any foe, in order to assure the survival and the success of liberty.

This much we pledge—and more.

To those old allies whose cultural and spiritual origins we share, we pledge the loyalty of faithful friends. United, there is little we cannot do in a host of cooperative ventures. Divided, there is little we can do—for we dare not meet a powerful challenge at odds and split asunder.

To those new states whom we welcome to the ranks of the free, we pledge our word that one form of colonial control shall not have passed away merely to be replaced by a far greater iron tyranny. We shall not always expect to find them supporting our view. But we shall always hope to find them strongly supporting their own freedom—and to remember that, in the past, those who foolishly sought power by riding the back of the tiger ended up inside.

To those peoples in the huts and villages across the globe struggling to break the bonds of mass misery, we pledge our best efforts to help them help themselves, for whatever period is required—not because the Communists may be doing it, not because we seek their votes, but because it is right. If a free society cannot help the many who are poor it cannot save the few who are rich.

To our sister republics south of our border, we offer a special pledge—to convert our good words into good deeds, in a new alliance for progress, to assist free men and free governments in casting off their chains of poverty. But this peaceful revolution of hope cannot become the prey of hostile powers. Let all our neighbors know that we shall join with them to oppose aggression or subversion anywhere in the Americas. And let every other power know that this hemisphere intends to remain the master of its own house.

To that world assembly of sovereign states, the United Nations, our last best hope in an age where the instruments of war have far outpaced the instruments of peace, we renew our pledge of support—to prevent it from becoming merely a forum for invective—to strengthen its shield of the new and the weak—and to enlarge the area in which its writ may run.

Finally, to those nations who would make themselves our adversary, we offer not a pledge but a request: that both sides begin anew the quest for peace, before the dark powers of destruction unleashed by science engulf all humanity in planned or accidental self-destruction.

We dare not tempt them with weakness. For only when our arms are sufficient beyond doubt can we be certain beyond doubt that they will never be employed. But neither can two great and powerful groups of nations take comfort from our present course—both sides overburdened by the cost of modern weapons, both rightly alarmed by the steady spread of the deadly atom, yet both racing to alter that uncertain balance of terror that stays the hand of mankind's final war.

So let us begin anew—remembering on both sides that civility is not a sign of weakness, and sincerity is always subject to proof. Let us never negotiate out of fear. But let us never fear to negotiate.

Let both sides explore what problems unite us instead of laboring those problems which divide us.

Let both sides, for the first time, formulate serious and precise proposals for the inspection and control of arms—and bring the absolute power to destroy other nations under the absolute control of all nations.

Let both sides seek to invoke the wonders of science instead of its terrors. Together let us explore the stars, conquer the deserts, eradicate disease, tap the ocean depths, and encourage the arts and commerce.

Let both sides unite to heed in all corners of the earth the command of Isaiah—to "undo the heavy burdens and let the oppressed go free."

And if a beachhead of cooperation may push back the jungle of suspicion, let both sides join in creating a new endeavor, not a new balance of power, but a new world of law, where the strong are just and the weak secure, and the peace preserved.

All this will not be finished in the first hundred days. Nor will it be finished in the first thousand days, nor in the life of this Administration, nor even perhaps in our lifetime on this planet. But let us begin.

In your hands, my fellow citizens, more than in mine, will rest the final success or failure of our course. Since this country was founded, each generation of Americans has been summoned to give testimony to its national loyalty. The graves of young Americans who answered the call to service are found around the globe.

Now the trumpet summons us again—not as a call to bear arms, though arms we need; not as a call to battle, though embattled we are; but a call to bear the burden of a long twilight struggle, year in, and year out, "rejoicing in hope, patient in tribulation"—a struggle against the common enemies of man: tyranny, poverty, disease, and war itself.

Can we forge against these enemies a grand and global alliance, north and south, east and west, that can assure a more fruitful life for all mankind? Will you join in that historic effort?

In the long history of the world, only a few generations have been granted the role of defending freedom in its hour of maximum danger. I do not shrink from this responsibility—I welcome it. I do not believe that any of us would exchange places with any other people or any other generation. The energy, the faith, the devotion which we bring to this endeavor will light our country and all who serve it—and the glow from that fire can truly light the world.

And so, my fellow Americans, ask not what your country can do for you: Ask what you can do for your country.

My fellow citizens of the world: Ask not what America will do for you, but what together we can do for the freedom of man.

Finally, whether you are citizens of America or citizens of the world, ask of us the same high standards of strength and sacrifice which we ask of you. With a good conscience our only sure reward, with history the final judge of our deeds, let us go forth to lead the land we love, asking His blessing and His help, but knowing that here on earth, God's work must truly be our own.—JOHN F. KENNEDY, in *Inaugural Addresses of the Presidents of the United States*

8. Divide the class into committees of four or five students and have each committee make a study of the writing that appears in a number of periodicals, reporting its findings orally to the class. Assign different tasks to each student, for instance, seeking devices for vividness, vigor, and variety. Possible categories for study are headline rhetoric, sports page lingo, the language of the advertising man, preacher prose, and academese.

9. It is agreed that the King James Version of the Bible has had an influence on English writing style, but there is disagreement about whether the influence has been beneficial. Select a magazine article or an essay by an author whose styles you admire and, by comparing it to a section in the King James Version, decide whether your author seems to be influenced by Biblical style, and whether you think he should be influenced. Suggested technique: Contrast sentence length, ratio of compound-complex-simple sentences, uses of tenses and voice; list figures of speech and other rhetorical devices for both writers; and contrast their euphony, cacophony, alliteration, and assonance. You may wish to refer to a translation of the Bible into modern English, the Revised Standard Version. Write a 500–750-word theme in which you analyze both styles, state your conviction, and support it.

10. Write a theme on a very abstract subject and, using your very best style—with perhaps an emphasis on rhetorical devices—attempt to clarify your ideas and persuade your reader. (Do not let the abstractness of the topic keep you from being specific.)

Suggested topics: Americanism, democracy, pacifism, God (or "godliness"), existentialism, nonviolence, freedom, urban life, conservatism, enlightened self-interest.

11. In your out-of-school leisure reading, you encounter newspapers and magazines, each of which attempts to develop and reflect its own style. Examine several of the periodicals with which you are already familiar and identify both the kinds of style represented and the specific methods of achieving them. You may discover that everything you read is written in the same style, perhaps "subway journalese," or "sophomore collegiate." If you do make such a discovery, examine critically some of the following publications: *The New York Times, The Christian Science Monitor, Time, Newsweek, The Progressive, Ramparts, Partisan Review, McCalls, Ladies' Home Journal, Playboy, Mad.*

12. Using either your course anthology or some articles in a serious magazine, analyze a prose style you like or dislike. Count the number of words in each sentence; contrast the frequency of simple, compound, and complex

sentences. Read aloud and describe the sound patterns, including alliteration, assonance, and rhythm. Locate and label all figures of speech. If present, single out such sins as redundancy, mixed metaphors, cacophony, gobbledygook, and stilted diction. You may wish to compare the writing of two authors. Write a 500–750-word theme about the results of your research. Besides the writers mentioned in the chapter, the following authors should provide provocative models: Kenneth Burke, George Santayana, Thorstein Veblen, Ernest Hemingway, William Faulkner, James Gould Cozzens, Dwight Eisenhower, Warren G. Harding, Marshall McLuhan.

Part  *Rewriting*

Chapter 9 Rethinking

I twist and turn; I scratch myself. My novel is having trouble getting under way. I suffer from abscesses of style, and phrases itch at me without coming out. What a heavy oar a pen is, and what a heavy current an idea becomes when it must be dug into! I fret so much about it that I am greatly amused. Today I passed the whole day with the windows open and the sun on the river in the greatest serenity. I have written one page and sketched out three others. In a couple of weeks I hope to have hit my stride; the colors in which I dip my brush are so new to me that I open my eyes in astonishment.—Gustave Flaubert, *Letters (To Louise Colet, end of October, 1851)*

The first part of this book was aimed at developing skills, attitudes, and habits that contribute to good writing. The second part divided the process of writing into basic steps and made suggestions about how to take these steps in a way likely to help you write well.

Now we turn to a later stage in the writing process, the one that really separates the passable from the very good—the difficult, irritating yet rewarding process of rewriting.

While you write your first draft, you should write at top speed. Although we like to think that you unconsciously think of organizing and developing and using the appropriate word, if you pause to worry about them, you may dim your flashes of creativity. You will probably jot down some unrelated sentences for an introduction, establish a thesis or purpose, and then begin to gather momentum. If you have really caught the muse, you race along through the body of the paper and jot down some conclusions. Good. This speed may reflect a highly inspired creative section of the total writing process.

It is not the part that identifies you as a genius, or as the heir to Chaucer, Shakespeare, Ernest Hemingway, or Tom Wolfe. The moment that marks the master is what Russian Nobel Prize novelist Alexander Solzhenitsyn calls the "final inch." It is at the same time the most burdensome, most difficult, and most exciting.

When you finish your first draft, you will feel protective about it. One of the French terms for "first draft" also means "my baby." If anyone were to criticize your baby at this point, you might hit him. When you read your first draft, you may smile fondly and see your path running clearly to a Pulitzer Prize. You just cannot be objective.

A student, usually an excellent writer, wrote these paragraphs in class.

The city's theater world of music and drama has to offer its patrons and audience a wide field of entertainment. The music world has the taste for Rock to Classical as the drama has the pre, post and Broadway hits to amateur college productions. The theater of music and drama world vary from largely builded structures to small renovated movie theaters, from expensive elegant taste of comfort to the downstairs of churches and centers. The Theater season extended from September to late May which Summer Happenings schedule takes the off Season and offers Rock in the Arena and drama productions by college drama groups and the like. Inevitably, the city is bursting with entertainment throughout the year.

In our society, and our city is no exception, we have generation gaps, Democrats versus Republican, Christian versus atheist, marriage versus celibacy, conceit versus humility all of them contrast our need to cultivate us to be US! As we have these distinctions in our ideas, beliefs, lifestyles and personality, so we also have distinctions in entertainment. In music, there are four basic groups ; Rock, Folk, Jazz and Classical. Again, our city satisfies and suits every taste.

After class, when the teacher read the paper and told the student he could not understand it, the student was hurt. About two weeks later the teacher and the student were rummaging through the student's folder, and the student reread the paragraph and smiled ruefully. "You have made your point," he said. The point is that distance and time are necessary for objectivity, and you need objectivity to revise your paper.

When you produce a draft and set it aside even for the minutes required to walk down the hall for a Coke, it becomes a thing apart. It is no longer so much a part of you, and you can look at it from a new perspective. It is now that you may have some objectivity, some distance.

During rewriting you will eliminate the weak parts. You will accentuate the strong ones. You will look again at your thinking. You will look again at your expressions. You will try to accomplish what you originally set out to do. It is rewriting that Lord Bacon had in mind when he wrote, "Writing makes an exact man."

Most of us write and talk with some degree of rationality. Either because of some natural talent or because of past training, we carve out a subject, establish a point of view, and make more or less logical assertions. We tend not to contradict ourselves; instead we provide the reasonable evidence necessary to justify our thinking.

But we do make mistakes, and it is the writer's task to be sure he is not tripped up because he got mixed up in his thinking; it is also his task to make sure that all the necessary material is provided for the reader to come to the same conclusion that he did. I. A. Richards wrote that "rhetoric is the study of misunderstandings and how to avoid them."

When you have a draft in front of you, especially if it has slept a night, you may be able to adopt a skeptical attitude toward your own work and give it the critical scrutiny that is necessary for really excellent writing.

When you revise you must, first of all, check your thinking. You must lay out your reasoning, check on possible fallacies, and correct them.

Step One: Get Yourself into a Rational Frame of Mind

During revision you do not need to become your own worst enemy, but you must tell yourself that during the heat of inspiration you might have become somewhat uncritical. You will need to condition yourself by expecting to find some loose thinking. If you can occasionally laugh at what you have done, you are on the right track. This excerpt from a satiric essay, written by Max Black for *Scientific Monthly*, may get you into the right frame of mind to recognize sloppy thinking.

PRINCIPLES OF REALLY SOUND THINKING

Think Only As a Last Resource

The really sound thinker knows thinking to be an uncomfortable, disturbing, and antisocial occupation. Consider the attitude of Rodin's statute "The Thinker." This is not the favorite posture of a successful executive or a regular guy.

Modern life fortunately provides a number of defenses against the early onslaught of thinking. The radio is always close at hand—use it. The company of others, preferably of the opposite sex, is to be strongly recommended. If the irritation is too severe, one may retreat to bed until restored to a healthier frame of mind. . .

Conscientious adherence to the next principle will go far to palliate the discomforts of unavoidable and involuntary thinking.

Trust Your Feelings

The logic texts have created the fiction of Logical Man, coldly calculating the probabilities of alternative hypotheses, willfully blind to human sentiment and passion. Do you want to be this kind of philosophical monster, interminably vacillating between conflicting conclusions? Of course not. In any matter of serious concern, you will *feel* strongly that a certain conclusion *must* be right. This is the clue to success in really sound thinking. Let yourself go—think in technicolor.

Suppose you are worried about the possibility of war with Russia. You will notice in yourself a tendency to think of Stalin as a blood-thirsty ruffian, dripping with the gore of murdered innocents. Dwell upon the notion—let your blood pressure rise. In a short time you will *feel* strongly enough to be able to stop *thinking* altogether. In really sound thinking, it is the conclusion that counts, not the premises. Trusting your feelings will quickly provide you with satisfying, heart-warming conclusions.

The two principles of really sound thinking can be illustrated by the following maxims, widely accepted by successful practitioners.

1. *If you must stick to the point, be sure it's blunt.* The natural human reaction to contact with a sharp point is violent motion in reverse. Such animal wisdom is deeply significant. It's the dead butterfly that stays on the point. Cultivate judicious irrelevance.

Example: Does John Smith deserve a raise in salary?

Blunted point: Doesn't everybody deserve a raise?

Really sound reasoning: Of course they do! Who is John Smith to be favored at the expense of everybody else?

2. *What's in it for me?* Remember that a really sound thinker is practical. And what can be more practical than concern for one's own interests? The chief advantage of this maxim is the strong light it throws upon the truth of many a debatable proposition.

Example: Should educational facilities be improved in the South?

Really sound reasoning: What's in it for me? Nothing—I don't live in the South.

Conclusion: NO. (Notice the directness and incisiveness of the method.)

3. *It all depends on who says it.* Men are easier to classify than arguments—attend to the man, not the argument. . . .

Example: Should Congress be reorganized?

Really sound reasoning: Who says so? X? Oh—he ran for the Congress three times unsuccessfully.

Conclusion: You can't trust *him.*

4. *A million people can't be wrong.* It would clearly be undemocratic, not to say snobbish, to think otherwise. We can't all be Gallups, but we have a ready fund of popular wisdom to hand in the form of proverbs. Make frequent use of such axioms as "Human nature never changes," and "An ounce of experience is worth a peck of talk," and, especially, "It will all be the same in a thousand years." The last is particularly consoling.

Example: Can we prevent another war?

R. s. r.: I've seen men fighting. You'll never change human nature. After all, it will all be the same in a thousand years.

This method can be successfully supplemented by the use of identical propositions, such as "East is East, West is West," "Business is Business," "A man's a man for a' that." These are best introduced by the words "after all." Even a logician can hardly dispute the truth of such tautologies.

5. *The exception proves the rule.* Corollary: The more exceptions, the better the rule. This popular maxim hardly needs recommendation. It has the great advantage of allowing us to make simple generalizations in an intolerably complex world.

Example: You say women are no good at physics. What about Madame Curie?

R. s. r.: The exception proves the rule! (Absolutely conclusive, as R. s. r. should be.)

6. *It's all right in theory but it won't work in practice.* We might almost say: *Because* it's right in theory, it won't work in practice. This maxim is very useful in puncturing the pretensions of experts.

Example: Should we support the United Nations?

R. s. r.: (You know what!)

7. *Consistency is the hobgoblin of little minds.* None of the great thinkers from Socrates to Korzybski have been consistent. Who are you to improve upon their practice? The sciences are notoriously full of unresolved contradictions. If scientists don't care, why should you?

Example: You say that we ought to work for universal free trade, but insist on raising American tariffs.

R. s. r.: I contradict myself? Very well, I contradict myself.

Project—Revision

Analyze the following student essay and make suggestions for revision. What idea is most important and should be emphasized as the thesis? What ideas should be left out, if any? What expressions are operative in that they make assertions that need explanation or proof? What subtopics need expansion?

ANA

Ana is a very mysterious young lady. Ana is from California and knows a little about everything. She is one of my roommates in the dorm. Ana is very smart and picks up her studies very well. Lately I have been very worried about her, because she's been cutting classes. She told her reasons why, "My teachers made me see how I was wasting my time in college." "All they do is knock college and tell us we're wasting money." I can't understand the attitude taken by Ana's teachers. As a result Ana won't be returning like so many others second semester. I don't know what we can do to keep students happy at school.

Step Two: Find Out Whether
You Have Really Said Anything

Case History 1: "Sadder but Wiser"

In order to see how the step-by-step process of revision can work, assume that you have been asked to look at a theme written by a former high school dropout who has just returned to school. It is your job to criticize the paper, encourage the writer, and direct him through the thinking that will help him prepare a worthwhile end product. Here is his first draft:

After searching intensely during a break I took during my high school education, I found that in order for survival in this complex world, an education must be attained. I base this theory on my many experiences after quitting school and leaving home at the age of sixteen. Many people think getting a job without an education is very difficult, but this is false. Getting a job, any job, is easy, but finding one that you enjoy doing is hard. Without the necessary education you cannot compete for anything worthwhile. You have but one quest in life, to fill your belly. So, after months of deliberation, I came to the conclusion that in order to live and not just exist, an education must be secured.

Now read the theme again and try for some second thoughts. If you concentrate on the grammar, spelling, and punctuation, you may miss the opportunity to make this a really important paper. Forget the mechanics. Is any idea in the paper worth expressing? We would say Yes. The theme shows considerable wisdom. Although every sixteen-year-old *knows* that an education is necessary, every year discontented students leave school. They also know they can get a job. Jim over on the other side of town got a good job working at a McDonald's. A meal "on the stand," nine to five, nothing to do nights but run around, no work on Saturdays, just go to the flicks. Mom makes the bed and cooks the meals; Pop pays the rent and furnishes the family car. What a deal!

But the writer of this paper has gone beyond this limited perception. He makes a fine distinction and an important one. He balances two ideas against each other: what the dropout expects and what he gets. The paper has sufficient merit to make revision worthwhile—if his revision goes far deeper than proofreading. You must help the student to *revise*.

First, help the writer to dig out his central thesis. His purpose seems to be to resolve an unsettling problem for the potential dropout. His parents and the guidance counselor say he won't be able to get a job, but he *knows* he can. Who is right? The writer must dramatize what happens to a young man who has not finished his junior year in high school.

With this purpose in mind, then, you can move on to the development, the lack of which is the worst deficiency in the paper. There are many operative expressions in the paper that have done no operating.

searching intensely	He should describe his efforts. He should let us see two kinds of action: head-scratching thought and day-after-day pavement pounding.
a break	How long? From what high school? In a city, suburb, or small community? The writer should let us *see* this young man in dreary, disconsolate action—first confident, and then increasingly despondent.
survival in this complex world	What is meant by "*survival*"? Since he says, "Getting a job . . . is easy," we would think that the "filling his belly" type of "survival" would be easy. Apparently, the writer is speaking of another type. He will need to delay using this phrase or make it clear by showing in detail what it is that the dropout cannot achieve.
many experiences	The writer should dramatize these. We need to *see* this action. He should use the old trick of mentally preparing a television documentary. What scenes would the camera shoot? He needs to supply details.
getting a job . . . is easy	He should show this. The writer should list the "opportunities" and how he learned about them. Want ads? Word of mouth from the "fellows"?
one that you enjoy . . . anything worthwhile	These expressions set up two perhaps contrary descriptions of a potential job. We need some examples to show the kind of job that the dropout might find both enjoyable and worthwhile.

The writer must now rewrite the paper, putting in the required details. His paper already has some elements of organization: The first sentence is the introduction; the last is the conclusion. The writer can refine these ideas later; for now, ask him to separate them from the rest of his composition to emphasize the fact that he is working on the body of the paper.

At this point, although the theme has a three-part organization (introduction, body, conclusion), its body has no internal organization. After looking at the key ideas the writer plans to develop, you might decide that a combination of chronological and topical structure makes sense. Perhaps the writer could start out with the "getting a job is easy" concept. First he might describe the odd jobs he had while in school; he was confident—in spite of his parents' warning. Perhaps he even got ahead of the game before leaving school by getting a job—at a drugstore? Garage? Pool hall? Men's club? On a construction crew? The money began to roll in. (How much did he make? $1.75 an hour? An astronomical $5.00 per hour?) Then the first big disillusionment: the building job was completed, and he had to buy a jalopy to get to a new site. Extra expenses! He had to get up two hours earlier. And work on Saturdays. Or perhaps business got slack, and our hero was the first to be laid off. Tell the writer to let us *see* the situation. He should make us weep.

In the next paragraph our hero trudges the pavement. There are still plenty of jobs, but after his previous dismissal, he knows what to expect from most of them. Traveling with a crew of magazine salesmen made up of a hustler and a bunch of other dropouts? Making phone calls for a shady outfit selling chances on a Cadillac? A construction job for which he must pay a hundred-dollar-union-initiation fee?

Exact details pay off. We have the ideal rhetorical situation here. The writer is a firsthand authority; he knows something interesting that his reader doesn't know. Did he cool his heels in an employment office while a college graduate walked right in ahead of him? Such an observation would be priceless to demonstrate the central point.

So far the structure of the body of the paper has been: Part One, Happy Anticipation; Part Two, Gradual Disillusionment. In Part Three should the writer take a step backward to enlarge his perspective on the scene? He can begin to think and to indulge in some speculation valuable for his reader. He can discuss what the dropout can expect; he can look into the future and cite hypothetical details, or better, he can describe what has happened to some of the men he encountered during his own jobs. What have they done? What did they, his fellow workers, advise him to do? What did he learn about himself? What kind of job does he now feel will satisfy him? Again, remind him to be specific. Would he like a job in which he does something for humanity? What, exactly? How much money per year does he now feel he needs? What kind of a neighborhood does he like? What type of car?

What hobbies? What vacations? What should his life be like? End of Part Three.

Soberly our hero describes his return to school. In his conclusion he must be honest: school is no more fun than it was, but it is not as bad as the last job he had. And it is nice to be back with the winners; the losers are still out looking for jobs.

With this kind of planning, you can help the student write a worthwhile draft. After his draft is written, he can refine the organization. At first, he will stress chronology; it all happens in order. The topical structure will emerge soon. Part Two of the body can be pointed up with an introductory comment: "Slowly what I thought would be freedom became a new—and far less promising—prison." He can open Part Three with a comment such as, "Finally, I began to look around, not just at myself, but at people who had done what I was doing. The picture was not encouraging."

To get past the purpose, organization, and development stages may take two or three drafts. When the writer has completed these, however, he can focus on more minute aspects of his paper. He will probably have refined much of his grammar and diction in the process of telling a better story, but there is very likely more polishing to be done. For the sake of illustration, let us assume that, in the case of our former dropout, the sentences from his very first version still exist, even after he has taken several steps in his revision. If we scrutinize these sentences, we will immediately see that loose thinking has resulted in some ambiguity.

. . . in order for survival in this complex world, an education must be attained.

Notice that it sounds as though it is the education that wants to survive. The writer should change this to "in order to make something of this complex world," or—better—"to make something of this complex world, I needed an education." Now look down to the final sentence. Find the same trouble? This time the writer seems to be saying that an education wants to "live and not just exist." He should rephrase his sentence to something like "in order to live and not just exist, I had better finish school."

this is false.

Strictly speaking, the word *this* should have a clear antecedent; without one, the pronoun is vague, and the sentence is imprecise. Compare these revised versions of the sentence with the original and see if they are clearer and more effective: "Many people think . . . but they are wrong" or ". . . but this belief is false."

The next step is to look at the diction. In the case of our writer, he should first cull questionable usages, with an eye to refining awkward phrasing.

in order for survival	Better: "in order to survive" or "to survive."
one that you enjoy doing	Redundancy: "one you enjoy" is sufficient.
I came to the conclusion	"I concluded."

Normally, at this level of revision we would experiment with alternative word choices to find words that are exact or vivid; the version with the most exact and dramatic diction will be the most detailed and will convey the ideas most clearly. At this level of revision the writer in our example should ask himself, "Is my description active and precise enough yet?" If he has written, "After weeks of reading the papers," should he have said, "After weeks of searching through want ads"? He should scrutinize every phrase this way, trying to bring the reader into his narrative with every word he uses.

After you are satisfied with the body of his theme, advise the writer to return to his introduction. Perhaps the key to a good appeal step is suggested by the words "Many people think. . . ." If he could quote some dire threats from newspapers or magazines about the difficulty dropouts have in finding work, he could then catch the reader's attention by having the temerity to say, "Dr. So-and-So is a nationally known authority, and I am only a high school senior, but I know he is wrong."

After the writer has reworked his introduction, he should look at his conclusion. He may feel that experience is the best teacher, but perhaps he will admit that at times he wishes he had been willing to take someone's advice.

A last step in revision is to take another look at the title. "Sadder but Wiser" is trite, and since the writer seems to feel he has profited from the experience, "sadder" hardly seems appropriate. Furthermore, the title would fit hundreds of student themes about "a lesson learned." Nothing in the title tells us what the message of this particular paper will be. Since the subject is so timely, perhaps the word *dropout* should be included in the title. Maybe just the title "Dropout" would do. Could we make something out of "The Return of the Dropout"?

THE OBJECTIVE: SIGNIFICANCE

As you can see from the preceding analysis, your first task when you revise your own paper is to decide whether you have said anything at all. Reading his own work, one kind of writer reads what he thought he wrote; the other reads what he did write, as it will appear to his reader. One sees intended meaning; the other sees his expressed meaning. You should try to be the latter type of writer and face the possibility that what you have written amounts to precisely zero. While you were writing your early draft, you were wise to charge yourself with the dream that a masterpiece was in the making. It was good to think big. Now that you are revising, you must be very rational. You must try to see what you really have said.

Case History 2: "Education Through Reality"

The following paragraphs were written by a student who became almost too fluent a writer; his words and sentences often sounded so eloquent that he never quite developed a critical sense about his own ideas. All through his college career, he was plagued with either A's or F's—nothing in between. At one point a professor wrote on his paper, "This is the most beautiful job of saying nothing I have ever seen." Does the student say anything in the following composition?

A person enters a new world through realization; a spark ignites a fire of thought and the fantasy of the past is devoured by the present reality. This person enters college, not by choice, but due to the needs of present-day society. Previously he had gone to a small boarding school of little acclaim and yet after five weeks of college, he realizes that the college consists of definite individuals, but mostly toys played with by a childlike society. If the individual is broken, replace him, don't mend him. To the other school, each person worked as a part; without one of the parts, the school could not produce. If a new part took its position, the old would have to adjust in time.

What of the people? What is different about them? People? Are they really people? One is afraid of speaking honestly; one is afraid of being seen as he really is. People, you say? What has happened to their individual beliefs, their ideals, their concepts of truth, honesty, and justice? Hushed, hushed by fear, uncertainty, and confusion. And what of the few who do speak? A "conference in confidence," only to be put before the class in the form of a question, and to be chewed, digested, and given back far from its original form. Who would want to speak? Play with your toys, humanity, for as you break, you destroy what is good in an individual. In five weeks he has learned more from people than college could ever teach him.

This paper expresses the germ of the idea that society somehow blights a sensitive individual, which is, of course, sometimes true. But not always. The idea with no qualification at all is probably not true. And with the qualification that society *can* or *sometimes* does thwart an individual, it becomes almost platitudinous and banal. On the basis of what the student has written, a person who believes the thesis will continue to do so, but one who disagrees, especially one who is enthusiastic about the beauty and value of the college experience or who is oriented to think that society helps the individual, will not even understand what the writer is talking about.

At first, this student was hurt by his instructor's criticism. "You are saying it in nice words," said the student, "but what you are really saying is that I should junk the paper."

"Yes," the instructor replied, and then he described to the student an essay he had received earlier. "The first version of this paper was almost a joke. It even had the title 'My Summer Vacation,' and all it was was a string of sentences about going to the beach, working at a resort, going to parties every night, and going to bed late. Hundreds of boys have exactly those same experiences every summer. Buried in the account were references to tennis lessons for black and Puerto Rican students and to a fight with some other boys; there was even a hint that he had been seduced by a forty-year-old woman."

"I talked with the writer," continued the instructor, "and a week later another paper came back. All the stuff about the summer vacation had been condensed or dropped. The title was 'Reluctant Maturity,' and the student now went into detail about how he had been bored while teaching tennis to rich kids and their parents but had gotten a kick out of giving free lessons to bright-eyed, brown-skinned children. In the course of his tennis instruction he had begun to realize that a woman was only pretending to be interested in tennis; and he had come to know a lonely, divorced, and frightened human being. One of his sentences read, 'I never did get into bed with her, and to this day I am not sure that was what she wanted, but I knew her and liked her better than any adult I have ever met.' In the last section of his paper, he wrote about how he had been beaten up by the other tennis teachers to punish him for giving free lessons and spoiling their business. He concluded: 'That was the summer that was. I learned that what I want most in life is to work with underprivileged children. I learned that adults have small, frightened, inner thoughts which even they do not wish to recognize. I learned that it is not all beer and skittles in this world. When you try to do what you think is right, you still might get whacked for it. That, I would say, is a fairly large summer.'"

The student who had written the first paper went back to his dormitory and started all over. He called the result "Culture Shock," and he described how it felt to go from a small, private, Episcopal prep school, where he had had a half-hour conference each week with the headmaster, to a large urban university. He described how he had arrived too late to be admitted officially to his university dormitory and how he had spent the first night in his room —but with no blanket, mattress, or pillow, just cold metal springs. "Welcome to the U," he had thought just before he dropped off to a fitful sleep. As he wrote, he recalled other incidents that demonstrated his thesis about the difficult adjustments he had had to make—and he worked them into his paper, which was ultimately very successful.

As you think of your purpose, and particularly as you examine your introduction and conclusion, you must ask yourself: "What am I trying to say?" "What question am I answering?" "Is the question worth asking—or answering?"

Case History 3: "My Family Trips"—in which a student gets lost

A student wrote a paper discussing the many trips his family had taken during his boyhood. The final sentence of his introduction read, "In a panorama of personalities, situations, and settings, by coming in closer contact with people different from those I had known, I had become aware of the distinctions and distinct*ness* of my own personality." His paper ended with, "Traveling has accomplished what my parents intended it to: it has broadened my horizons, physically, mentally, and emotionally, and also has made me aware of my position in the world."

Although the thesis that "travel is broadening" may seem to be a platitude, it can be developed in especially meaningful ways; many accounts of a young person's experiences as a traveler have become best sellers or important literature. Ralph Ellison's "Did You Ever Dream Lucky?" and Ray Mungo's *Total Loss Farm* are recent examples. In *Gift from the Sea* Anne Morrow Lindbergh has written beautifully on the value of a vacation.

The question about the student's paper was, therefore, not whether his thesis was worthwhile, but whether he stuck to it. According to the paper, the family traveled from Teaneck, New Jersey, to the Civil War South, to the rolling prairies and billowing skies of the Middle West, and to the national parks in the Far West. The paper was a travelogue—the sun even "set slowly in the west"—and when the student looked at his thesis while he was revising, he realized he was off track. Although his paper was supposed to be about how travel had affected him, he had talked only about the travel itself, not about its effect. In his revised version, he related the journey to his resolution to major in both history and law before going into politics, his thought being that a legislator should understand the background and traditions of his country.

Case History 4: "Three Stories"—in which a student discovers she has something to say about all three

In an essay she titled "Rituals in Reality," a student discussed three short stories: Isaac Babel's "The Story of My Dovecot," Shirley Jackson's "The Lottery," and Lionel Trilling's "Of This Time, Of That Place." She was satisfied with the unity she had achieved. She had analyzed the three stories to show that modern man still accepts legend and myth. In the first story a young Jewish boy adjusts to the religious fanaticism of his father and to the prejudice of the Russian peasantry. In the second story a town adjusts to the ritual of drawing by chance the name of a person who must be sacrificed. In the third story a teacher dares not jeopardize his own career to defend a bright but nonconformist student who gets in trouble for rejecting the myths and traditions of the school.

In reconsidering her theme, the student–writer was momentarily nonplussed. Is this enough? she asked herself. All I am really doing is retelling the stories. The student finally decided she was *not* merely retelling the stories; she was, indeed, interpreting them. *Exegesis*, or critical interpretation, is sufficient to make a worthwhile paper. Carlos Baker published many articles about Ernest Hemingway's stories and Cleanth Brooks has written extensively about the message of William Faulkner. In her paper the student was discussing a comment that three artists had made about society. The stories were credible, and it was important that the theme be identified. The student was right; her paper had passed the test of significance.

Case History 5: "From the *Messiah* to *Jesus Christ Superstar*"— in which a student discovers a change in religion

A student reread his comparison of Handel's *Messiah* and Webber and Rice's *Jesus Christ Superstar* and realized that all he had done was to tell the story, first of one and then of the other. He reminded himself that if he was really comparing the two works of music, he should point out their similarities and differences, letting the nature of one contrast with, and thereby illuminate, the nature of the other. The *Messiah* should tell the reader something about the modern rock opera; better yet, it should tell him something about our time or, at least, the counter-culture of which *Superstar* is a part. The student subjected his paper to this double test: (1) Does it set up a thesis? (2) Is the point significant?

As he searched through his draft for a thesis, he noticed that Handel seemed to be celebrating the story of Jesus' last few days, while the rock opera was asking questions. Intrigued, he counted question marks and discovered that *Superstar* had 110 of them, and *The Messiah* had none. He concluded that in Handel's time the story of Christ was accepted as given, whereas today man questions the nature of God and the relationship between man and Jesus. As the student saw it, *Jesus Christ Superstar* suggests that Christ was very much a man and Mary Magdalene very much a woman—and man can be comforted by their humanity. He then went on to hypothesize that the uncertainty shown in *Superstar* is not necessarily bad; it removes a crutch that many people relied on in Handel's time. *Superstar's* message, wrote the student, is that modern man, uncertain about what is "up there," must learn to solve his problems on his own "down here."

Case History 6: "A College Freshman versus Plato"— in which a student develops confidence

A student in a Western Civilization class had read that Plato condemned literature because it excited the reader to false imitation and thus interfered with intellectual and moral development. The student, although he could accept Plato's belief that literature cannot imitate "eternal Forms of Ideas which are entirely spiritual," still believed that literature has value, and he said so in an essay on the topic. He boggled as he reread his paper, though, and realized that he was contradicting Plato. He decided, however, that he *could* be bold, because he had some insight that Plato had lacked, namely Freud's perception that "vicarious emotional outlets are necessary as defense mechanisms for mental soundness." He found further support for his ideas in the writings of John Dewey and in his own experience with literature. He had recently read Chekhov's *The Cherry Orchard* and had found in it a clear comment on his own society. In his paper the student wrote:

The decayed elite, the faded gentry in my own hometown, like Chekhov's Russian landowners on their country estates, failed to see what they must do to keep up with history. . . . Chekhov's semifeudal landowners refused to cut up their "Cherry Orchard"; the old rich in my hometown fought to save their sycamores. . . . Plato may be right that literature cannot be true, but it is not inherently "deceptive and misleading". . . . I <u>know</u> that Christopher Marlowe's <u>Doctor Faustus</u> and Chekhov's <u>The Cherry Orchard</u> are not true, but almost because they are not true I can look at them with a special feeling of disinterest. I am involved, but I am not involved, and I can now judge a series of incidents so close to what happened to my town, but not really true, that I have learned more, I think, than if the story were true. . . . Something which increases a person's knowledge should not be censored. Poets should be encouraged, not banned.

The student decided that an argument over a value is always important. Instead of dodging a fight with Plato, he decided he would give his challenge more focus; his introduction began:

As a dutiful Episcopalian I have frequently sung a hymn written in 1668 by Peter Sohren. When I came to one sentence, I think I knew that the poetry was probably rather bad, but I assumed that I should believe what the words said:
<u>Sing praise</u> . . .
<u>For Socrates who, phrase by phrase</u>
<u>Talked men to truth unshrinking,</u>
<u>And left for Plato's grace</u>
<u>To mold our ways of thinking.</u>
After thinking about these lines, I am sure the poetry is not for me—I do not think <u>grace</u> rhymes with <u>phrase</u>—and I do not agree with the words. I do not feel that I am less an Episcopalian when I believe that Plato should not be permitted to "mold our ways of thinking."

These case histories have, we hope, shown you that as you work through your first revision, you must question whether, and how clearly, you have centered on a purpose. Ask yourself whether the purpose is significant. Relying on your own sensitivity (which has been awakened by your asking these questions, and which will be sharpened as you continue to do so), determine whether, as a result of your thinking, reading, or personal experience, you could possibly have something to say on the subject to an informed and unknown reader.

Step Three: Find Out Whether You Have Said Something That Is Just Plain Dumb

As you read your first draft, assuming you have adopted the proper skeptical stance, you should expect to find some questionable thinking. You will not be alone. A famous United States senator found that he had made a terrible mistake in an article he wrote for the *Harvard Law Review* and demanded that the whole issue be retracted. He found the mistake so late that the issue had already been printed and all that was possible was for the pages to be removed, making the slenderest *Review* that had ever been mailed. We suspect you will find your howler before you submit your paper to your professor.

THE OBJECTIVE: IDENTIFICATION AND REMOVAL OF FALLACIES

During your proofreading you may find word choices that convey false impressions.

> During the intermission thirty *odd* students came into the auditorium.
>
> My mother objected to my *fast* friends.

You may also find and correct errors in fact. At this point we are more concerned with *fallacies,* or errors in logic. Knowing them helps you refute fallacies when you encounter them in the writing of others and helps you avoid fallacies in your own writing. In general, fallacies fall into four classes, and you should be able to recognize them all.

1. ERRORS OF INSUFFICIENT EVIDENCE

Hasty Generalization

Errors occur when we generalize on the basis of too small a sample. You may meet a young Italian, think he is a jolly person, and conclude that all Italians are sunny in temperament. You may order some shrimp for the first

MISS PEACH   By Mell Lazarus

time, dislike them, and conclude that you will not order seafood again. You may read *The Golden Bowl,* find that it is too slow-moving, and decide that you will read no more of Henry James' sixty-three novels. In such cases you are guilty of hasty generalization.

Post Hoc Ergo Propter Hoc

Some of the fallacies have Latin or Greek names that have not been re-placed by English. The Latin expression *post hoc ergo propter hoc* means "after this, therefore because of this." This error occurs when we decide that because B happened after A, A must have been the cause. *Post hoc* reasoning is the cause of much superstition. A football team wins two games, and the coach decides his team won because he wore the same cap on both occasions. A student sits by the window in a classroom, does well on an ex-amination, and decides it is lucky for him to sit near a window. The Demo-cratic party gets tagged with the title "War Party" because a war happens every time it gets into power. A Democrat would argue that this is *post hoc ergo propter hoc.* The cause for the war, he would maintain, lay in what the other party had done before the Democrats came to power. A corporation gets a new president. If its business suddenly gets better, is it cause and effect or *post hoc*? Did business get better in general, or did the new presi-dent actually initiate effective new procedures?

Ad Ignorantiam

Ad ignorantiam is an "appeal to ignorance." It assumes that, since a belief has not been proved false, it is true. A student says, "I told Professor Stim-mer that he was unfair. Since he hasn't answered, that proves it must be true." We accept in legal practice the theory that a man is innocent until proved guilty; in logic to do otherwise is to commit the fallacy of *ad ignorantiam.*

Card Stacking

The name card stacking is a metaphor, referring to the inevitability that if we could select only the cards we want, we would hold a winning hand. When Brother comes to Mother and complains, "Sister bit me," Mother may conclude that Sister deserves punishment—until she learns that Brother has withheld the information that he bit Sister first. Tourists in Pakistan at first become incensed at India, for the Pakistanis complain that India stole the Kashmir from them. When the tourist moves on to India, however, he loses his warm feeling for the Pakistanis, for the Indians tell him how Pakistanis murdered Hindus in Kashmir. Then the tourist realizes, correctly, that there is a long history of abuses on both sides, which the contestants understandably tend to ignore.

Very often this card stacking is unintentional; we are all often guilty of *selective recall*; we tend to remember only what supports our convictions. Card stacking may be caused by viewing a problem or a statement out of context. We may read a single sentence from a long speech and get a misconception. We may not know what went before the sentence or what happened afterward. Since card stacking is, by definition, a *deliberate* withholding of evidence or a selection of evidence that supports the writer's conclusion, selective recall and perceptions out of context are not technically card stacking, but their results are the same.

Correction of Fallacies Based on Insufficient Evidence

When you encounter errors based on insufficient evidence (hasty generalization, *post hoc, ad ignorantiam*, or card stacking), you can correct or refute them simply by providing more evidence or by indicating that there is no contradictory evidence. In a case where cause and effect is claimed, you can apply the tests outlined by John Stuart Mill:

1. Agreement: Was the quality assumed to be the cause always present?
2. Difference: When the antecedent was there, did the consequence always occur? Conversely, when the antecedent was not there, was the consequence absent?
3. Residue: When the antecedent is surrounded by other qualities, can we determine all the consequences of the other qualities and thus end up with just one consequence, the one claimed for the antecedent?
4. Concomitant Variation: Does the consequence vary in amount as the antecedent varies?

In the case of *ad ignorantiam*, look for the missing evidence. If this is impossible—for instance, if a maligned person is dead or otherwise unable to answer a charge—request fair play; you can ask that your reader not make up his mind until he has had an opportunity to examine more information.

2. FALLACIES OF IRRELEVANCE

Often when we are asked to make up our minds, the information we are supplied with is not sufficiently related to the problem to be of value when we make the decision. Occasionally, when we look at our rough drafts, we find that we have presented as evidence some material that has simply nothing to do with the issues. Such information is irrelevant, and it may appear in many forms.

Bandwagon

Most of us feel rather more comfortable when we are voting or running with the crowd, and many appeals are made to this understandable instinct. Being on the winning side can have many advantages. When the election is over, we may share the fruits of victory, and in any event, we will have the pleasure of having our opinion supported by the majority. However, if we voted in anticipation of the joys of winning or *because* we want to be with the pack, we have "climbed aboard the bandwagon" and thus committed a fallacy. A variant of bandwagon is snob appeal, which is a suggestion that all really distinguished and respectable people believe the assertion. Reverse snob appeal, or the plain-folks approach, is an appeal to everyday community life. The writer suggests that the reader should accept his assertion because good, common, unassuming people do.

Appeal to Force

In an appeal to force, the force may be physical—"If you testify against Muggsy McGinnis, you will end up in a concrete coffin in the East River" —or the appeal may use other threats: "Unless you stop investigating auto safety, we will expose your personal life." The threat may be veiled: "Senator Touch, I represent three hundred contributors to your party treasury, and we. . . ." All these threats may be understandably persuasive, but they should be recognized for what they are. They should have no part in helping a man make up his mind.

Ad Hominem

The expression *ad hominem* means "to the man." In the midst of an argument a person may leave the issues and relevant evidence and point out alleged deficiencies in his opponent's character. When, in the investigation of Senator Joseph McCarthy that led to his censure, a lawyer listed the evidence of misconduct on the part of the senator, McCarthy countercharged that his accuser's partner had once been a member of a Communist organization. Whether the charge was true or not, it was not relevant to the study of McCarthy's own record; Senator McCarthy was guilty of *ad hominem.*

Tu quoque ("You Did It Too.")

During an argument one member may respond, "Why are you charging me with this? You do it too." A group of Democratic investigators charged the governor of the state with accepting campaign contributions from architectural firms and then giving them contracts for government buildings. The defenders of the Republican governor responded that the previous governor, a Democrat, had done the same thing. An old proverb, "Two wrongs never made a right," is appropriate here, but the main objection to the assertion is that it is irrelevant. The question was whether this governor's practices were illegal or unfair; whether the previous governor used the same practices had nothing to do with this particular question.

Red Herring

In an oral examination an instructor asked a student what person had most influenced a certain writer. Rather than say, "I don't know," which would have been the direct truth, the student said, thoughtfully, "In the first place, it was not X." The instructor took the bait and said, "What makes you think that?" The student took five minutes answering the second question, and then it was another student's turn. The student had thrown out a red herring, some information to throw the discussion off the track.

Fallacy of Opposition

The fallacy of opposition is an attempt to condemn an idea by pointing out that the "bad guys" are for it. A few years ago, when a senator criticized a policy of the State Department, the secretary answered, "That is certainly something that Red China would like to have us believe." The statement may have been true, but it was irrelevant and an attempt to curry emotional favor. In addition, it contained a veiled hint that the senator held a Communist viewpoint.

Inappropriate Authority (*Ad Verecundiam*)

Advertisers often commit the fallacy of inappropriate authority. The "testimonial" provided by professional athletes, television comics, and Hollywood celebrities, who swear that they could not live without certain brands of aspirin, mouthwash, deodorant, underwear, and gear shifts, should only be ludicrous, but market analysts find them effective. An intelligent advertising man is aware that the celebrity is not used because of his testimony but because he attracts attention to the product. A man's attention is caught and held for a moment by a picture of Betty Bikini asking for a small cigar. After he reads the ad, he is not convinced that Betty really does smoke cigars, but he has a favorable associative memory about the cigar and knows its name. When he sees the cigar at a tobacco stand, he has a pleasant memory, and he may buy the cigar.

Appeal to Pity

The appeal to pity is also called *argumentum ad misericordiam.* When a teacher grades a paper, he may be impelled to soften a grade if he knows the student is having family or financial trouble. This practice may be pedagogically sound, but the teacher should realize that his analysis of the paper has been affected by pity. Pity was an important factor in the senatorial election in Illinois in 1966. Voters recognized that both candidates were respected, both deserving. Voters who liked the Republican disliked voting against the Democrat because he had a long, distinguished record and they hated to turn him out to retirement. Just before the election, however, the daughter of the Republican candidate was murdered, and pity set in in favor of her father. At the same time in Massachusetts, two excellent candidates, both with extremely good records, were also running for the Senate. The strength of one man lay especially in his civil-rights record, but his opponent was black, and out of a hundred years of guilt, many votes went to the latter that might have gone to the former. Fortunately, all four candidates were unusually able and thousands of people voted objectively; but many voters were uncomfortably aware that their votes were cast on a nonrational basis.

Ad Populum

Ad populum is an appeal to the prejudices and biases of the reader or audience. A trial lawyer must be a master of this appeal, and many lawyers have strong convictions about what biases or prejudices they can expect of jurors. Many lawyers prefer male jurors for women defendants. They prefer jurors who hold unimportant jobs if their clients have claims against large corporations. These are not the practices of unscrupulous lawyers; they owe it to their clients to secure sympathetic jurors. However, the fallacy must be recognized for what it is, an example of *ad populum.*

The so-called glittering generality, that is, the phrasing of an idea in vastly favorable terms is often *ad populum,* as when a politician speaks of foreign aid as the "American policy of warmheartedness to its less fortunate neighbors." The use of "good" reasons instead of "real" reasons is also *ad populum,* as when a farm-state senator defends foreign aid because it is "humane for the underprivileged" when his real reason is that he wants to dump his state's farm surplus. There may be elements of truth in the glittering generality, and the "good" reason may be part of the reason for a belief;

but when they are examples of muddy thinking or deliberate deception, they must be recognized as fallacies and treated as such.

Genetic Fallacy

No matter how an idea is derived, it should be criticized on its own merits. An original idea may have come from coincidence, a whim, or a mistake. If the birth of the idea is attacked rather than the idea itself, a genetic fallacy is committed. When the news of Jesus Christ began to reach Jerusalem, scoffers said, "Nothing good can come out of Galilee." The criticism was a genetic fallacy.

Correction of Fallacies of Irrelevance

Many of the errors of irrelevance (bandwagon, appeal to force, *ad hominem, tu quoque,* red herring, opposition, inappropriate authority, appeal to pity, *ad populum,* and genetic fallacies) originate in subconscious drives and emotions—fear, pride, pity, or competitiveness—and these forces are potent. When we detect these fallacies in ourselves, we can only back away and try to talk ourselves out of being swayed by our emotions. When we recognize them in the arguments of others, we cannot always succeed by saying, "But that's irrelevant!" More often we can succeed by suggesting, "Before we continue with our discussion, let's decide just what the issues are and what evidence we agree is acceptable. What authorities are we to trust? Are they experienced, free of bias, and supported by equally reputable authorities?" Still another procedure is to ask, "Would you mind developing that point further? In particular, will you tell me why it is relevant? Will you detail your argument a little more?" Occasionally, you can get the opponent to talk himself out of a fallacious conviction.

An honest, responsible writer must confront himself with the question of the extent to which he should use emotional devices. He knows that in many cases to ignore emotion is to imperil his cause and that to be blunt is often to be tactless or unkind and thus to antagonize his audience. Pragmatically, however, he recognizes that he cannot depend on winning an argument every time if his case is based on purely emotional appeals. As you write, assemble the best possible case that you can. If your analysis is clear and your evidence is overwhelming, you will rarely need to appeal to the emotions of your audience.

3. FALLACIES OF AMBIGUITY

Francis Bacon long ago referred to some fallacies in man's thinking as "Idols of the Marketplace"—the confusion caused by shortcomings in language. The English language is not perfect, and intentionally or otherwise, its users can create inaccurate impressions.

Amphibology

The fallacy of amphibology stems from the fact that some constructions in the language permit more than one interpretation. Some examples of amphibology are amusing, like the slogan during World War II that brought smiles when it appeared on signboards: "Save soap and waste paper." Some amphibology is intentional, as when the Delphic Oracle told Croesus that if he went to war with Cyrus, he would destroy a mighty kingdom. Croesus went to war and destroyed a mighty kingdom—his own. Some advertisers exploit amphibology and phrase slogans that are not dishonest, yet not honest either. For instance, an advertisement for Brand X aspirin may claim that "three out of four doctors recommend this type of pain relief." First, the implication is made that three out of every four doctors were questioned, but if we look again, we realize that this may not be so. Second, the implication is that Brand X is the "type" being recommended; whereas it is aspirin that is being recommended, and there are dozens of brands of aspirin.

Equivocation

Equivocation is the intentional or mistaken use of a word in a sense different from that understood by the reader. William Wordsworth is supposed to have said, "I believe I could write like Shakespeare if I had a mind to try," whereupon his friend responded, with a smile, "Yes, all you need is the mind." Wordsworth obviously meant *inclination* for the word *mind* but his friend equivocated and interpreted *mind* as *intelligence*. Benjamin Franklin used equivocation humorously when he wrote, "If we don't hang together, we will hang separately." When a candidate promises a supporter, "You will get what you deserve after the election," the supporter may find that the politician has equivocated. Another candidate is identified as "liberal" by his supporters, who later wonder whether the campaign oratory meant the opposite of "stingy" or of "conservative."

The Tyranny of the Metaphor

Occasionally, an inexact metaphor obscures meaning. For example, the term *Renaissance* imperfectly describes what happened during the years 1500–1600. The word means "rebirth" and, to be sure, there was a rebirth of interest in classical education and culture, but much that happened was completely new—a *birth* rather than a *rebirth*. As a result many students have a misconception about the period. Similarly, Henry Adams' use of the dynamo to characterize history since 1250 is unfortunate. We think of a dynamo as a creator of energy; Adams thought of it as something running down and losing its power. Other writers have misunderstood his metaphor and confused Adams' interpretation of history. The symbol of the United States as a bearded old man has caused foreigners to think of the United States as patriarchal and conservative. In order to understand national economics, students used to be encouraged to compare the federal government to a man who pays his bills at the end of the month; this comparison left a whole generation incapable of understanding Keynes' concept of deficit spending. Michelangelo's paintings of God have caused many to think of Him as a magnificent old man. When modern theologians said that this was a faulty picture, the old man disappeared, and we were informed that "God is dead." What died was a God that never was.

Correction of Fallacies of Ambiguity

Ambiguity of many kinds may plague even the most experienced writer. To rid ourselves of this disease, we must first proofread skeptically to make sure no unintentional meaning is possible. To avoid equivocation, we do well to heed the wise man who said, "If you wish to converse with me, define your terms." Finally, when using figurative speech, we must be certain that our metaphors convey only the message intended.

4. FALLACIES BASED ON THE MISUSE OF LOGIC

Complex Question

Occasionally, you may get trapped into making a statement or implication you did not intend. The classic example of this is the question, "When did you stop beating your wife?" Any response brings trouble. The question permits no direct answer that will indicate innocence. This sentence is considered comical, but James G. Blaine probably lost the 1884 presidential election because he could not properly field a question by a New York clergyman, "Don't you think the Democrats are the party of Rum, Romanism, and Rebellion?" Blaine's attempt to untangle the question did not satisfy New York's Irish Catholics, and he lost their crucial vote. Liberal candidates are often embarrassed by the question, "Are you going to continue the trend to fiscal irresponsibility?" Either a Yes or a No answer involves damaging admissions; if the candidate tries to explain his position, an opponent may charge him with hedging or avoiding the question.

Begging the Question

Begging the question, also called circular reasoning, consists of restating one of the premises as the conclusion, albeit in different words. A college girl comes back to the dormitory enraptured about a new boyfriend. "Oh," she raves, "He is so neat." Her roommate asks, "Why do you like him?" and she answers, "I like him because he is so wonderful." This is no answer at all; about all it says is "I like him because I like him."

The Garbled Syllogism

A writer with a slight knowledge of logic can often phrase his argument in logical terms when his argument is not logical at all. He can toss around words like *premise, ergo, therefore,* and *recognized authority,* and make his argument sound much more convincing than it is. This technique, since it is an appeal to emotions and biases, is probably *ad populum,* but it often seems so reasonable that it can be untangled only by using the techniques of logic. Very often a syllogism will turn out to be faulty because it implies that one of the terms has been distributed when it has not. A student might not want to go to college because it is not one of the "prestige" schools. His argument might go like this: "Prestige schools are worthwhile. X is not a prestige school. Therefore I will not go to X College." The term *worthwhile* has not been distributed, which means that there are other colleges that are worthwhile. If our student friend has not been accepted by a "prestige" school, we can feel sympathetic to him for the blow to his ego, but we could argue that his misfortune should not keep him from profiting from an education at X College.

Correction of Errors in Logic

Very often you can straighten out your own thinking by taking out a scratch pad and jotting down your arguments. As you look at them, you may recognize circular reasoning. The fact that grammarians have for many years defined an adverb as "a word that modifies a verb, adjective, or another adverb" and that Calvin Coolidge announced that the only cure for unemployment is work indicates that begging the question can be hard to recognize. Sometimes faulty arguments seem so good that you may believe them yourself. However, if we recognize the possibility that circular reasoning, complex questions, and garbled logic exist, we can often eliminate them by learning to identify them. We can ask that arguments be spelled out more carefully. In the case of the complex question, the best answer may be to ask for a restatement of the question. Another device is to slip between the horns of the dilemma: "I have never beaten my wife." In other cases a careful response may work: "Your question is very complex. I cannot answer it with Yes or No."

Conclusion

The old battles of epistemology, logic, and psychology are still fought every day. Susie, in high school, asks, "Mother, may I wear a halter to school today? All the girls are wearing them." The ensuing discussion may open on three fronts. Mother may contest Daughter's statement on epistemological grounds: "I am sorry, Susie, but in this family we do not conduct ourselves on the basis of what others do. There is a right and wrong, and we think it is wrong for you to wear such clothes to school." Mother may challenge Susie on the basis of the evidence provided: "I am sorry, Susie, but I drove by your school yesterday, and I observed that only a few of the girls were wearing halters." Mother, without saying so, has accused Susie of the fallacy of card stacking. Mother must think of her daughter's emotions. If she responds: "I do not care what the other girls are wearing. You will do what I say, and I say No!" Mother has forgotten the emotive aspects of the argument; if she is often in the habit of doing so, we can assume that she and Susie will be involved in all kinds of conflicts.

In your everyday life you will encounter problems of logic; very often you may not have the time to analyze the assertions and arguments. When you are revising your own work, you *will* have time. Scrutinize every conviction you present to be sure that you have arrived at your conclusions soundly. Be sure that you provide your reader with the proper apparatus to check your logic. And finally, be sure that you provide all the relevant evidence that he needs.

Projects—Fallacies

1. What fallacies are illustrated by the following sentences? In your discussion try to use terms explained in this chapter.

   a. Did you see the way those Indians made it rain? Just as soon as they stopped dancing, it really poured!
   b. All Germans are warlike and belligerent.
   c. Democrats stand for freedom, liberty, equality, and prosperity.
   d. Don't waste the evening listening to Schoenberg; everybody who's really "with it" will be down at the Unicorn listening to Oscar Schlopp sing Australian Aborigine protest songs.
   e. God never lies. The Bible is the Word of God. The Bible clearly teaches that God exists. Therefore, God must exist.
   f. I first met Baboon and Haggis cigarettes at the Henley Regatta. Where did *you* meet B & H?
   g. Neighbors, Ah growed up raht heah in Crockett County, an Ah knows that when yew make me yoah new govanuh, yew an me'll fahnd this

heah state a better place to live in, her havin' a country born and bred, Godfearin' little old cowboy up theyah in the cayupitl.

h. There are two philosophies—two ways of life—in the world today: the great capitalist free enterprise system and the godless, enslaving Communist conspiracy. We must choose today between them!

i. Why can't East and West live together in peace by joining in a federated world government, where heavy industry would be state-owned, small commodities privately produced and marketed, and social legislation would ensure a decent standard of living to all without greatly vitiating the advantages of the talented and well-born?

j. Can I be trusted? Well, take a look at my autographed portrait of Cardinal Smith.

k. Consider joining the American Nazi party. It is a small, fraternal group, permitting large individual participation. It is active, vibrant, alive; its objectives are clear and comprehensible.

l. Don't pay too much attention to Ustislav Keldysh's ideas on space flight; after all, he's a Communist party member.

m. About a month after Uncle Ngobjebe refused to sacrifice to the Jujube, he was eaten by a lion. Impiety is always revenged by the gods.

n. Surfers of the world unite! History is a mighty wave, and we alone know how to ride it.

o. Joe Palooka says, "Gletch Slop-on Deodorant has made me the only clean-smelling boxer in the business."

p. America is a nation governed by laws and founded upon a doctrine of human rights. Every American, therefore, tacitly assumes liberty and justice as the basis for his acts, abides by his understanding of the law, and respects his neighbors.

q. Better dead than red! (*or* Better red than dead!)

r. Love is truth. I love all men and therefore have all truth in my heart. Why, then, should I read books, which can add no truth to that absolute truth which is mine?

2. An Episcopalian, a Mormon, and a Muslim were discussing their religions. The discussion was very gentlemanly and conducted in a spirit of honest inquiry, but in the course of the dialogue, the Episcopalian said, "I do not like to be critical, but I must confess that I have difficulty appreciating religions that were founded under the circumstances yours were. Mohammed was a poor camel driver who claimed the Angel Gabriel told him all about the Old Testament, but actually the report is more like the ideas held by the Jews in Medina at the time. The founder of the Mormons is supposed to have written his message down on gold plates, but the plates were lost." Almost in unison, the Mormon and the Muslim responded gently, "How can an Episcopalian talk thus? We all know that your church was founded so Henry VIII could get a divorce!" What fallacy did the Episcopalian commit, and with what fallacy did the other two respond?

3. A story is told about a farmer who bought an old horse from a back-

woodsman. "Him no look well," the owner said, "but him plenty pull." Later the enraged farmer sought out the seller, exclaiming, "This horse is blind!" The response was, "That's what I told you. This horse, him no look well, but him plenty pull." Was the sales talk an example of card stacking or equivocation? Support your decision.

4. As an exercise in recognizing causality in the familiar social problems listed below, try to find areas where your antecedent is present in varying degrees or not at all. Check the antecedent's relationship to the consequence that interests you.

  a. The effect of United States' foreign aid on new countries.
  b. The effect of United States' military aid on new countries.
  c. Comparison of the effects of communism and capitalism since World War II on developed (industrialized) countries.
  d. The effect of a winning season on attendance at home professional sports events.
  e. The effect of night games on attendance.
  f. The effect of advertising on a company's gross sales (The Hershey Candy Company does not advertise.)

In class report on how you will try to validate your results and cancel out all common causes and factors that might contaminate your results.

5. Write a theme analyzing the dependability of a news story. If the article is straight "news," you may wish to discuss the source. Is the author identified? Was the information approximately the same in several newspapers and in a weekly news magazine? (See especially "The Week in Review" section of any Sunday *New York Times*.) If known authorities are quoted, check their backgrounds in biographical reference works. (Are they properly trained and experienced? Do they have any reason for bias or prejudice?) If your article is an indication of recent trends, as suggested by such headlines as "Sharp Increase in Crime Rate," "F.B.I. Announces Increase in Violent Crime," "Public School Official Predicts Decrease in Enrollment," determine how the figures were derived and by whom. For help in the analysis of such pronouncements, see *Social Indicators*, by Raymond Bauer, published by the M.I.T. Press, Cambridge, Massachusetts, 1966.

Chapter  Revising

Easy writing makes damned hard reading.—*George Gordon, Lord Byron*

I write. I write again. I write again. . . . Then I take the third; I literally fill the paper with corrections. I then write it out fair for the printer. I put it by; I take it up; I begin to correct again; it will not do. Alterations multiply; pages are rewritten; little lines sneak in and crawl out. The whole page is disfigured; I write again; I cannot count how many times the process is repeated.—*John Henry Cardinal Newman*

Almost every enterprise has a weakest point. In the newspaper industry, for instance, hundreds of men cooperate, work for hours, and spend thousands of dollars to get a paper into the hands of a newsboy—and then the eleven-year-old throws it into the snowbank outside the door, and the subscriber never sees it. All too often the writing process is analogous to this disrupted chain of events. A student will do extensive research, take copious notes, create a preliminary outline, scratch his head, worry, create, and prepare the first draft of a potentially superb paper, and then—eager to have done with it—he will turn the paper in without looking at it again. Every writer, whether novice or expert, must have the discipline to move past the first draft. Lack of revision, all too often, is the flaw—like the newsboy's bad aim—that prevents the paper from reaching its target and fulfilling its potential.

It is while revising his manuscript that a writer learns what he can do. An applicant for a Rhodes Scholarship, required to submit an essay as part of his application, stopped at the home of his adviser and asked how to go about it. The adviser, a writing teacher, welcomed the student to his home and insisted that he stay there until he had rewritten the essay many times. The applicant, now a lawyer in San Francisco, reports, "I got the scholarship all right, and I learned more about writing that night than before or since. At three o'clock in the morning my adviser's wife got up and made us some coffee. At eight o'clock we had breakfast, and for the first time in my life I saw what I could do with words. I had written something I was proud of."

At first, revision may be sheer drudgery, but as the desired form begins to emerge, the work becomes exciting and exhilarating. When John F. Kennedy was a student at Harvard, he was, at first, "far from diligent," but in his senior year he was so stimulated by his honors thesis that he did, as he said, "more work than I've ever done in my life." According to the President's father, at this point his son learned to appreciate excellence.

Some Basic Principles

The almost conventional nature of the early steps of the writing process has led to certain principles of writing that can be summarized as follows:

1. Every composition written for exposition or argument should have a central purpose or thesis, which is made clear in the introduction and referred to in the conclusion.
2. The body of the paper should fulfill the composition's central purpose by proceeding in orderly steps or subtopics. There should be sufficient detail to clarify or prove all generalizations or other operative sentences.
3. Ideas should be expressed exactly and vividly, with variety and originality—and as briefly as possible.

There are, to be sure, excellent papers which are exceptions to these principles, but at the least these principles are insurance against poor writing and almost always a step toward good writing.

As we have stated elsewhere, most writers prepare a sketchy outline and then hurry through their first draft. Dorothy Canfield Fisher compared the first draft to skiing down a slope that is a bit too steep. She pushes off. There is tingling excitement and alarm as she picks up speed. She scribbles down the words as fast as she can, page after page, some words being only marks and abbreviations she may not remember later.

The result may be hardly more than a collection of disjointed sentences or fragmentary paragraphs. If a particular section does not satisfy the writer, he rushes on, perhaps even leaving some blank lines or pages. Later he goes back over the weak sections and fills in the blanks.

While revising, you must seek the ultimate development of your thought and expression. Only as you experiment with your own ideas and language will you be able to develop your own technique. At best we can but suggest alternatives among which you can choose. Many of them are reminders of what has been discussed before, but cast in the new light of the revision process. Try out the suggestions. Once you have tried them—and only then—will you be able to see what works for you and what does not.

There is an important distinction between *proofreading* and *revision*. When you proofread, you are looking for possible improvements in grammar, diction, spelling, and punctuation. Almost every time you look at your paper you proofread; you pencil in a comma or make sure the *i* is right in *perceive*. Essentially, you are examining your paper word by word. When you are revising your paper, however, you are examining it from a much broader perspective, and you are taking certain conscious steps to improve your paper as a whole.

Different writers may take the steps in revision in different order, but all revise with the unity of their work in mind. In revising, be sure that your introduction looks forward to the central point of the rest of the paper and that the conclusion looks backward to the preceding parts. Make sure that the body of your paper fulfills what your introduction obligates. Stand back and look at your subtopics and review their order, proportion, and relationship. In yet another step, evaluate the completeness of your paragraphs. Have you supplied the detail that your internal sentences require? Have you been sensitive to the obligations generated by observations, classifications, generalizations, judgments, and causal relationships? Look at the language, and, finally, do the proofreading. Look at spelling, grammar, punctuation, and manuscript conventions. *Re-vision* requires that you "look again," as the word itself says.

Developing the Critical Stance

When a writer examines his own work, he tends to be protective. That is natural, and it may be true of you. To help you take the critical stance, we have provided some sentences from the papers of *other* students. What would you have done with them?

"With a gleaming smirk on his face, he stuck his head out the window of his Mack truck and screamed, 'Get a haircut, you hippie.'"

Question: Does a tough truck driver "smirk"? Or "scream"? Can you smirk and scream at the same time? Would he "snarl"? How about this, "With hate on his face, the truck driver yelled. . . "?

"Since the dirty cafeteria is near the bargain basement, I purchased an absolutely darling T-shirt (89¢) for my cousin that reeks of hamburger "

Question: Does the cousin reek? How about "Since the bargain basement is near a dirty cafeteria, the darling T-shirt I bought for my cousin reeks of hamburger"?

"My allowance was supposed to be used for banking purposes."

Thought: Wordy. Better: "My allowance was supposed to be saved." Do you prefer "I was supposed to bank my allowance"? Why?

"Despite the rampant political apathy of the past year, you must not say that Young America has given up."

Question: Can apathy be "rampant"? How about "pervasive apathy" or "wide-spread apathy"?

"She is a member of the female sex."

Thought: Come now. "She" and "female" are tautology. There must be some way to get rid of this whole sentence.

"If you can believe half of what you hear, opening a college nowadays is like opening a can of worms; or like opening a boutique in a nudist colony; or like opening a parcel from the Weathermen."

Question: Do people still know who the Weathermen were? That was a group well known in the sixties, but now? Is "can of worms" a cliché? Does the metaphor about the nudist colony sound a mite forced? Start over.

"The university which has a firm foundation has a better opportunity of unleashing the student's mind."

Question: How is that for a mixed metaphor? What is the author trying to say, really?

"Ted told a man drinking a Coke with a tired expression that we were here to do some custodial work. We would not bother the patients."

Question: Does the Coke have a face? How would you unload this sentence?

"The really good student is in short supply."

Thought: The sentence may be all right, but what do you think of the briefer "The really good student is scarce"? You do not always find a better expression.

"The cost of living is expensive."

Question: Could the sentence be shortened? "Living is expensive."

"Meetings will be held out of doors provided that the weather permits."

Question: Could the sentence be shorter? "Meetings will be outdoors if the weather permits." Too terse? Maybe.

"In the first amendment of the U.S. Constitution it is stated that. . . ."

Question: Could the sentence be shorter? "The first amendment . . . states that. . . ."

"I told my fellow teammates that. . . ."

Question: Isn't this more tautology? Teammates *are* his fellows, aren't they? "I told my teammates. . . ."

"When living in a dormitory, there are almost always some
things you must sacrifice."

Thought: *Thing* is such a general word you usually can improve it; the inverted "there are" form of a sentence can often be shortened. "When living in a dormitory, you must often make sacrifices." This correction places the introductory modifier closer to *you*, whereas the original was awkward.

The changes we are making may seem trivial, but Mark Twain said once that "the difference between the almost right word and the right word is really a large matter—'tis the difference between the lightning bug and the lightning."

Eliminate the Negatives

There is no special order to the process of revision, but basically you are trying to prune out the bad and improve the good. First, then, we remind you of some negatives.

Among the most distracting or confusing faults you should search out and eliminate are truisms, redundancy, confused grammar, ambiguity, and faulty punctuation.

TRUISMS AND PLATITUDES

You can improve your writing by avoiding the unnecessary or the obvious. If you ask yourself, "Is this something my reader already knows?" you may screen out superfluous statements and avoid boring your reader.

A *truism* is an idea so obvious that it need not be uttered. President Calvin Coolidge was guilty when he commented soberly, "When men lose their jobs, unemployment results." Often a writer will present a truism in such a pretentious way that it is called a *platitude,* a trite, self-evident statement expressed as though it were important and original. Do you recognize these platitudes?

> We ought to do our duty.
> All of us, someday, will die.
> Paris is, indeed, a city.
> TWA is still TWA.

WORDINESS

Earlier in this text we discussed the various forms of wordiness (redundancy, circumlocution, tautology, and some cases of euphemism). While you are revising, try hard to remove wordiness. To tune up your sensitivity to wordiness, we provide some examples:

According to the *American Heritage Dictionary*, *boo* is defined as. . . .	Better: *The American Heritage Dictionary* defines *boo* as. . . .
most unique	It's *unique* or it's not.
Donate to us the implements and we shall finalize the assignment.	"Give us the tools and we shall finish the job." (This is the way Winston Churchill expressed it.)
The basic essence of logotherapy is the idea that. . . .	The essence of logotherapy is that. . . .
used for economy purposes	used for economy
due to the fact that	since
The senator is a very ambitious man. He was encouraged by his wife to seek higher office. The office he finally decided to run for was that of vice-president. (twenty-nine words)	Encouraged by his wife to seek higher office, the senator, a very ambitious man, finally decided to run for vice-president. (Twenty-one words; more important, this version is one sentence, instead of three, with minor ideas subordinated.)
In our modern era of today	Today,
I was born in the city of Los Angeles.	I was born in Los Angeles.
Memory and intelligence are connected together by virtue of the fact that they are dependent upon each other.	Memory and intelligence are connected by their dependence upon each other.
Throughout the entire story.	Throughout the story.
The explosion of knowledge, especially in the area of fields of the physical and social sciences, has changed our ways of thinking.	The explosion of knowledge, especially in physical and social sciences, has changed our thinking.
Frankl's book was written during the time of World War II.	Frankl's book was written during World War II.
Silently Gautama nodded his assent.	Gautama nodded. (Something is lost here perhaps. You may wish to keep the original.)

What would you do with these expressions?

Perhaps Bob Dylan foresaw the period of ugliness America was entering into.
Do we not have any feeling of compassion left?
Dr. Victor Frankl spent three years of his life in Dachau and Auschwitz, the most infamously known of the concentration camps.

MISS PEACH by Mell

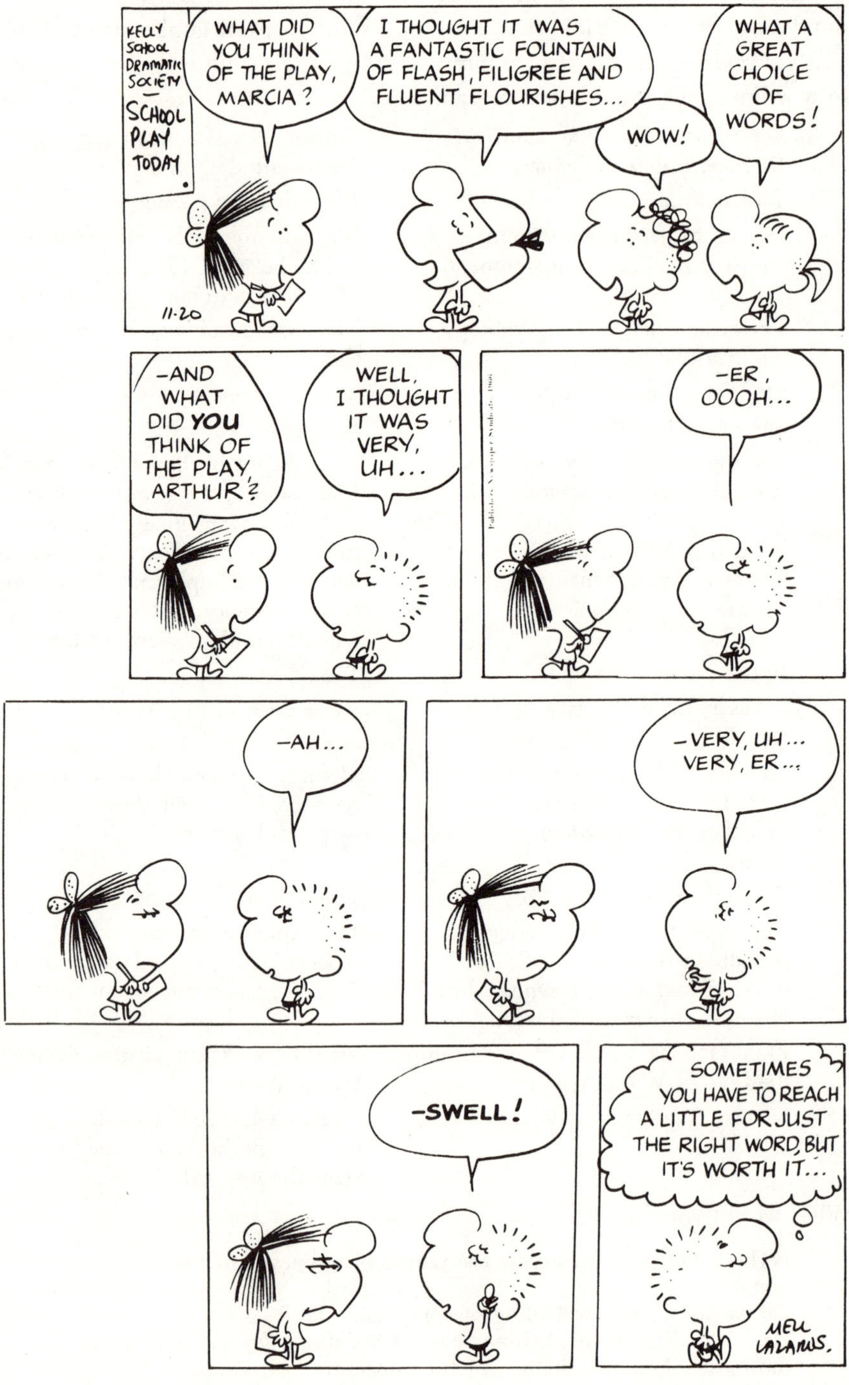

CONFUSING GRAMMATICAL CONSTRUCTIONS

English is a code. If your reader has been trained in this particular language, you would be foolish to write for him in Swahili or Khmer. The conventional American sentence is a grouping of words that approximates most nearly what an American reader has been trained to expect. If you fail to use standard patterns, you may obscure your meaning. For example, the following sign in a cafeteria in London delighted everyone and informed no one for months, until it was finally removed. The sign read, "Let all those who are going out first." Fortunately, such sentences, which do not communicate at all, occur rarely. But we hear many sentences that confuse *momentarily*, because of phrasing, spelling, or punctuation.

> *Momentarily confusing:* I like Bob and Betty likes Bill.
> *Instantly clear:* I like Bob, and Betty likes Bill.

When we read, "The man told John he had to go," we are not sure whether it was John or the man who had to go.

Take a close look at the following:

> Before leaving class, your exam should be completed. (Sounds as though your exam is thinking of leaving class.)
>
> To understand college students, they have to be considered as professionals, professionals at being students. (Sounds as though students are trying to understand students—which might be a good idea.)
>
> Our plan, hopefully, will succeed. (Sounds as though our plan is doing the succeeding in a hopeful manner.)
>
> While trying to master Zen Buddhism, the short moralistic stories, called *koan*, often confuse you. (Sounds as though the *koan* are trying to master Zen.)

These faulty grammatical constructions are called dangling modifiers because the elements are separated from the words they describe. They are worse than ambiguous; they may yield a ridiculous second meaning that will set your reader snickering while he temporarily forgets all about your message.

The New Yorker magazine has for a long time reprinted some of the more humorous of these boners, along with appropriate comments. Here's one *The New Yorker* picked up from the *San Francisco Examiner:*

> *The sentence:* "On the floor of the Cow Palace, smiling and waving triumphantly to the crowd, was Jerry Lucas, the man who holds the NBA record for consecutive games played by a forward without any visible emotion."
> *The comment:* It's when he's *not* playing that his feelings well up.

Worse than the fault that causes confusion or a guffaw is the construction that obscures completely:

Confusing: The design was approved by the committee which was most exciting.

Clear: The design which was most exciting was approved by the committee.

Another common grammatical deficiency is faulty parallelism, as in this sentence: "In their plays, Čapek and Shaw speak out against loss of identity and automation." Here the ambiguity can be shown diagrammatically. Where does the parallelism begin?

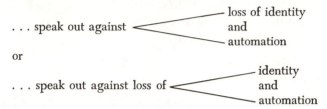

The careful writer would rephrase the sentence: ". . . speak out against automation and loss of identity."

RHETORICAL AMBIGUITY

Rhetorical ambiguity is a confusion set up when one word has two meanings.

> She could not have been more *disinterested.*

Strictly speaking, *disinterest* means "impartial, without bias or prejudice, fairly" as when you select a disinterested judge, one who does not profit by a decision either way. Recently the word has come to be used to mean "without interest, or having no enthusiasm or concern," equivalent to "uninterested." Care and frequent reference to the dictionary are the required antidotes in these cases.

FAULTY PUNCTUATION

Faulty punctuation often causes confusion. An eminent historian once complained bitterly about a passage that appeared in his book, pointing out to the printer the following sentence:

> The American Indians, who took delight in torturing their captives, deserve to be called savages.

The printer had contributed the commas; the author had written:

> The American Indians who took delight in torturing their captives deserve to be called savages.

"What's the difference?" the printer asked.

"All you have done," the author responded, "is to make me guilty of overgeneralizing about American Indians. You've had me condemn *all* Indians, when actually some tribes were very peaceful and helpful to the white encroachers."

Objective: Coherence

As you revise one part of your paper, you will have to revise others. As the body changes so must the introduction and conclusion. A paper that sticks together, whose parts fit together smoothly, is said to have coherence. How do you make sure that the body of your paper fulfills the obligation of the thesis, that the beginning and end seem to be going in the same direction, that the internal parts meld?

All during the writing process, you likely will be making outlines, usually simple topic headings to show what is to be in each section. During revision you may wish to boil your paper down to a few headings. Keep your outline simple. Check your original outlines. Have you changed them? Why?

Now analyze your thesis as a generative sentence. If your thesis is a judgment—for instance, if you are writing that the Beatles have made a significant contribution to music—be sure you have faced the right issues. In this case you would ascertain what the basis of your judgment is: What *is* "a significant contribution to music"? Have you raised the second question? Did the Beatles make such a contribution? If your thesis is an observation, classification, generalization, or causal relationship, check to see whether you have based your paper's structure on the appropriate questions.

At this time you may want to dig out scissors and paper clips, perhaps a pencil with a dark lead, and probably some tape. To focus your attention on your organization, make the structure as obvious as possible. You might circle the thesis statement, underline the topic headings, and indicate the topic sentences with stars in the margin. If these key sentences are evident, you will be able now to check them not only for appropriateness and order but also for proportion. If one of your points obviously takes up little space, you will notice this at once, and you may decide either to eliminate it because it is unimportant or to expand it to balance with other sections.

When you delete a section, delete it lightly; you may put it back in later. You may want to cut the paper into sections and ink in a topic heading at the top of each section. Rearrange the parts according to what your analysis tells you is appropriate. Consider alternative ways of ordering those parts. Try shuffling them randomly. What is the effect? Does any new order have merit for the reader you have in mind?

Probably, the first question you will ask yourself after you have created a brief outline is, "Do my major points build toward my thesis, or toward an answer to the reader's questions?" The following case histories deal with various students' answers to this question.

Case History 1: "The Salem Witch Trials"—in which a student discovers a thesis

When studying an outline of his work, a writer may find that if he organizes his paper in a certain way, an unexpected and interesting thesis emerges. For example, a student writing a theme about the Salem witch trials discussed his major points in chronological order:

1. The first hints.
2. The accusations.
3. The trials.
4. The deaths.

As the writer reviewed his organization, he thought, "Most of my readers will know, at least in general terms, that there was a witchcraft scare, that some women were murdered, and many were prosecuted. What does my outline tell that they do not know? Really not very much, I guess. I had better look again. Let's see. Under each point are the facts of the case—dates, places, names, and incidents. What is there besides these facts that make it possible for me to infer anything of significance? What will my reader want to know? I begin to see a paradox here: the colonists came to America to avoid persecution and yet here they are, persecuting other people. Why? Maybe a discussion of this point will make my report worthwhile. I will refine my purpose; instead of writing a chronological report of what happened, I will try to explain *why* it happened. In my introduction or in the first part of the body I will briefly relate *what* happened; then in the second and largest part of the body, I will try to show the insecurity of the time. It was a time of misfortune. The Massachusetts Bay Company had just lost its charter, and property ownership was in jeopardy. It looked as though the Devil was getting the upper hand. One especially zealous preacher, the Reverend Samuel Parris, encouraged his pupils to tell their wild stories of how they had been 'bewitched' by certain women. The purpose of my paper will be to explain the events. I will subordinate the factual history and reorganize the body of my paper.

1. The special tension of the times.
2. The stimulated imagination of the children.

Now the paper gives me a chance to do something creative: I am hazarding an explanation that is a more detailed analysis than Arthur Miller's *The Crucible* but suggests that the playwright may be sound in his view. I'll refer to the play in my introduction."

Case History 2: "Which Comes First?"—
in which a student discovers missing points

Occasionally, a scrutiny of one's major points will indicate that an important point has been forgotten. A student was asked to answer the question, "Who comes first, the artist or the scientist?" Earlier the instructor had reported that a critic theorized that the artist, using some special sense, sees a truth and writes about it. Then the scientist comes along and "proves" what the artist has suggested. After thinking it over, the student decided that the critic was right, and she dashed off her paper. She discussed Sigmund Freud's theories in relation to Henrik Ibsen's play *Hedda Gabler*. The student showed that twenty years before Freud formulated his theory of the Electra complex the Norwegian playwright had created a character, Hedda Gabler, who acted the way Freud later predicted such a woman would act. Hedda adored her father and wanted to be like him, but could not be. She wore boots and was preoccupied with horses. She refused to recognize that she was pregnant. She dominated her husband and tried to dominate her lover. She tried to play the man's role in all her relationships. When she was frustrated, she took vengeance on her enemies. She burned her lover's "baby"—the manuscripts he had written with Hedda's rival—and she maliciously destroyed the hat of an aunt who represented everything she, Hedda, hated.

When the student reread her paper, she realized that she had not told her audience enough about Freud's theories. She, therefore, inserted a whole new section discussing the Oedipus and Electra complexes, sublimation, phallic symbols, role identity refusal, and misplaced aggression. She indicated that Freud had advanced these theories between about 1900 and 1910. Then, after pointing out that Ibsen had created a character in 1890 who exhibited all the same symptoms, she had a reasonably good argument, with all its major points fully detailed, to support the thesis that the artist's perception precedes that of the scientist.

Case History 3: "College Dropped-Ins"—
in which a student seeks proportion

A student who started to write a paper about dropouts soon realized that she had little to say that had not been said many times before. As she read her draft, she began to be aware that there is also a type of student, the "dropped-in," about whom nothing had been written. She changed her thesis to "The College 'Dropped-in' is a Serious Problem." Her first outline was:

1. Definition of a "dropped-in."
2. "Dropped-ins" unfairly take college seats that students with better motivation should have.

3. The fate of the rejected student whose place is taken by the "dropped-in."
4. Situation not the fault of the college admissions officers.

The writer decided that point four could be omitted by showing in the definition section that a dropped-in cannot be identified by tests and admissions procedures. Point three had been in the writer's earlier draft about dropouts, but it was relevant to the new topic. Under point one the student defined the dropped-in as a person who goes to college for questionable reasons: because his parents force him to, because society dictates that everyone must have a college degree, or because society believes that college is the best place to find a spouse. The dropped-in has no personal motivation that makes college worthwhile or makes him worth the while of the college and its faculty.

As the student's thoughts took shape in her mind, she saw that the body of her paper would have a three-part structure that would show why the dropped-in is a problem:

1. Without motivation, he tends to do poorly and flunk out.
2. Having no direction, he selects courses irresponsibly.
3. He takes the place of a student who might have better motivation.

Although she realized that some students select courses because of good teachers, special interests, or personal and other legitimate needs, she knew of too many students who planned their curricula around their desire to have no courses before 10 A.M., after 3 P.M., or on Friday, no laboratories, no heavy reading, and no writing. She talked to some dropped-in seniors and jotted down the subjects they had taken. Their curricula were fragmentary, with courses, for example, in Russian foreign policy, but none in Russian government or history; courses about foreign policy from 1810 to 1900, but none covering the periods before or after; courses in subjects like astronomy in which the student had had no interest and whose content he had quickly forgotten.

To develop the third point about displaced candidates, the student decided to argue that several friends, who had not been admitted to any accredited college but had done well when they took correspondence courses in the army, could have done as well in college because they were highly motivated.

The student was still not satisfied with her analysis of the problem. She kept thinking, "What if my reader says, 'So what?' after he reads my paper?" She resolved to condense her paper as much as possible and add still another section. The section already written would present the "problem," and the new section would advance a "solution." She would suggest that poorly motivated students be permitted to take a year off from their studies. She began to read on the subject and found that the "year off" idea has a history. The Church of the Latter-Day Saints customarily encourages its young men to travel for a year to do missionary work. The system is valuable because the tour provides a chance for the young men to decide what they want to do. In the 1880s parents in New England let their sons and daughters take a *Wanderjahr* (a "wanderyear"); frequently, the young people would audit lectures in the universities of Europe to decide what they wanted to study. Our student also came across some statistics showing how well Korean War veterans did when they returned to complete their educations.

Now the student had the whole structure of the paper. Her purpose would be to recommend a solution for one of today's educational problems, the poor academic performance of the dropped-in. In the first section she would show that the difficulties were at least partially attributable to poor motivation; in the second part she would show how a year off for travel, volunteer service, or work of any sort could save such students. Almost organically, this paper grew before the writer's eyes.

Case History 4: "Martin Luther"— in which a student reinterprets his research

In the previous two examples a section of a theme was either incomplete or missing. Occasionally, however, the writer faces the opposite problem: a section mushrooms completely out of proportion and leads nowhere or, worse yet, misleads the writer.

A Lutheran student was writing about Martin Luther. He had written his first draft, which he thought was a straightforward factual report. As he revised it, he tied his account of Luther's break with the Church to the modern ecumenical movement, stating that before the Protestant and the Catholic churches could merge again, the causes of the original separation must be understood. All well and good, he thought. In his draft he had dealt with three reasons for Luther's break with the Catholic Church:

1. Luther objected to the corruption of the Church, especially the selling of indulgences.
2. He questioned the infallibility of the Pope.
3. He believed that only two of the seven sacraments were valid.

As the student surveyed his paper, he saw that his discussion of the first point occupied three-fourths of it, and he began to suspect that, as a twentieth-century student who was somewhat anti-Catholic, he had filtered his information through his own bias. In his research he had encountered the sentence "Whereupon he [Luther] rose from his knees and slowly and sadly walked away," and the student now saw that it was at this point that Protestantism had begun. The symbolic walking away had come while Luther was "climbing the Sacred Stairs at the Lateran," when "the thought arose in Luther's mind that justification came by faith alone, and that physical acts availed nothing. This was the first of several doubts Luther had about the Church, and it resulted in his revolution against it."

The student began to question his interpretation of his own notes. He had overexpanded the section on the selling of indulgences and had neglected the basic cause for the split, which was, he now thought, that Luther had come to believe that only God can save man—that neither man nor any other earthly power, including the Church, can help in any way. Thus, to Luther, the Church was a minor part of spiritual life. The error was not that the Church sold indulgences to the rich; it was that the Church granted indulgences at all. This put the Roman Church in a new light for the student. In a subsequent draft the student described the basic conflict Luther had with the Church, his belief that it must play a minor role, that it cannot grant indulgences, that the Pope is not infallible, that sacraments are symbolic rather than literal acts, and so on. The student recast his entire paper to develop the thesis that Luther broke with the Church not because (as the student had originally believed) it was a haven for embezzlers, but because the Church was the proponent of a theological view different from his own.

Retouching the Introduction
and Conclusion

These case histories illustrate the kind of thinking you must do when you take an overview of your paper. You will need to make sure that the body of your composition fits your thesis, and vice versa, and that you have the proper points in the proper balance and order.

Once you are satisfied with the message and the organization of the body, you will want to look again at your conclusion and introduction. Often at this point you will find your introduction dull, general, and inappropriate, like this one:

Every age and every society has its fill of social problems, and this year is no different. Right now, to a degree never seen before, America's young are getting hooked on hard drugs. The problem I would like to discuss is the drug question—what can we do about it?

The writer decided to try for a fresh introduction. He knew that most of the people in his community would have read about the college student who had recently plunged nineteen floors to his death after having been arrested for drug possession. He knew that almost everyone would have some ideas about how the boy's death could have been prevented. He decided that although he was no authority on drugs, he could provide a new dimension. He wrote:

Two nights ago the parents of Craig Burke drove five hundred miles almost without stopping. They were racing desperately to the side of their son, hoping to reach him before he succeeded in one of his repeated attempts to commit suicide. They did not arrive in time, and for the rest of their lives they will torture themselves, worrying about what they could have done.

I do not claim to know how the life of Craig Burke could have been saved, but—as a young person constantly exposed to the arguments of adults who want to keep us out of the drug culture—I know the arguments that do not work.

In this case the student opened with a specific incident and led up to his more general thesis. As you revise your own introductions, you might bear the same pattern in mind. Sometimes your introduction will consist solely of a strongly phrased thesis statement, but more often it should funnel into your thesis or statement of purpose. You may start, as the student we just quoted did, with a specific illustration of part of your point and broaden out to the whole thesis, or you may start with a reference to a general, important, timely problem and narrow to your specific thesis.

When you revise your introduction and conclusion, put yourself in the place of the reader. Ask, "What is my reader's state of mind now? Is he convinced? Hostile? Maybe a little tired of my hammering at him?" One student wrote a very good paper about the apathy of modern college students. He piled up incident after incident, illustration after illustration to prove that his peers do not vote, do not participate in political campaigns, and do not write to their congressmen—at least in any appreciable numbers. He cited the high absence records of his classmates in college, their use of professional theme writers to prepare fraudulent term papers. He had his case so well established that even he was a little tired of it. He resolved to try in his conclusion for some detachment, to let his readers off the hook a bit, to give them some perspective on the subject. This was his revised conclusion:

A story is told about a man who, while walking through the fields in the country, came upon a stallion tied to a post. The man saw the beauty of the animal—its slim lines, its luminous black coat—and was awed by the perfection of the animal. He spied a farmer standing near the horse and expressed the desire to see the horse run. The farmer untied it, slapped it on the rump, and the horse galloped through the field. As it ran, it seemed even more beautiful than before, and the man was even more enchanted. But suddenly the horse ran straight into a tree.

"Why," the man exclaimed, "that horse must be blind!"

"Not blind," the farmer calmly replied, "he just don't give a damn."

Modern students are not blind to the problems of our time; they are not blind to where their conduct is taking them. They have been beaten across the rump with so much pressure, so many crises, and so many false values that now they just don't give a damn.

A humorous story is not always a strong conclusion. It may blur your focus or damage the tone of your essay by seeming frivolous. Your own sensitivity must guide you. Your originality and imagination may suggest various conclusions, and it is up to you to select the best one for your particular paper.

Objective: Completeness

The focus of your revision tightens. When you were revising your paper's organization, you primarily considered larger elements: whether the major points in the body added up to the thesis you had phrased, whether the appropriate points had been established, whether one point got too little attention or another too much, and whether the points were in the most effective order. Finally, you looked again at the thesis, then at the introduction, and then at the conclusion. Now it is time to scrutinize the individual paragraphs and their details.

First, examine your paragraphs to see what operative sentences you have left vague and undeveloped. Look for barren assertions such as "Herbert is dominated by his wife." The phrase "dominated by his wife" is operative; alone it gives no true picture of the couple's relationship, but expanded, it tells the reader a great deal:

Herbert is dominated by his wife. When he was invited to his friend's wedding, his family arrived in the family car. His wife and his teen-age daughter sat in the back seat; he sat alone in the front, like a chauffeur. No wonder he spends his evenings alone in his study classifying stamps.

Hypothetical development does not pass as evidence. Consider the following paragraphs from a student theme about the difficulty a man faces when he reaches retirement:

The average middle-class man of today started work early in his life. This work was often necessary to supplement the income of his parents, who often had families much too large for their income. Starting with a paper route at 10, he worked his way up to being a venerable "soda-jerk" at a neighborhood ice-cream parlor. If he was conscientious, he made it through high school. College was for the rich. The war came, the World War or the Korean conflict, and John Doe found himself behind a rifle. He shot and was shot at. Wars end and he found himself a job with a local manufacturing concern. Marriage and family followed. Unionization gave the man a constant salary growth and an enviable living condition. Promotions came with time, and the man saw his off-spring doing much that he could not do when he was their age.

With the growth and eventual independence of his children, John Doe's mind turned toward himself. "Why should I work when I can live off retirement benefits?" With a tear in his eye and a gold watch in his pocket, John Doe retires. He has doomed himself to death.

After working steadily for forty years, John has forgotten how to live.

Essentially, this paper is argumentative. The author begins it with the sentence "To the average man, retirement is a paradise ahead," and then goes on to show how Mr. Average Man, when he does retire, discovers that his dreams were pure fantasy. Retired, with time hanging heavily on his hands, he becomes restless and bored. "His children detest his meddling in their affairs," the student writes.

When an author's purpose is to change the beliefs of his reader, however, hypothetical examples such as those the student used will not do, for the reader knows that anyone can make up such examples. This paper lacks hard, concrete *evidence*. To show that our senior citizens are not content with retirement, the student must dig up statistics. How many men come out of retirement not because they need money, but because they are bored? Maybe he can quote his grandfather. Surely, he can describe how some of his aged friends frantically struggle to keep busy and to feel useful.

In this paper the student calls his hypothetical man John Doe. If he had, instead, described the retirement dilemma of an actual person, perhaps his grandfather, he would have succeeded with what is called the "psychology of securing confidence." As we have mentioned earlier, whenever pertinent, the writer should cite facts and exact dates, and use correct professional terms to indicate to his readers that he knows what he is talking about. For example, in the paper about Ibsen and Freud discussed on page 185, the student reported that Freud died in 1939, whereas Ibsen had died in 1906; that Ibsen wrote *Hedda Gabler* in 1890, and he could not have heard of Freud's theories until at least a decade later. In discussing Freud, she used Freud's terminology. All this attention to detail created an aura of authenticity.

The writer will be in a constant dilemma as to how much detail to supply. He knows he should write as though his unknown reader were the whole educated community. And though he applies the test "Can a trained mind, not expert in my subject, understand what I am saying?" his answer cannot be exact, and he worries lest he bore his audience with an excess of information. The danger of supplying too much detail can be averted, at least in part, by the writer's making sure that the details and the examples are in themselves interesting. The writer may put in more details than necessary to clarify or even convince, but if his details are vivid and entertaining, his reader will not complain. When Dale Carnegie wrote *How to Win Friends and Influence People,* his thesis was simple; it could have been developed in a paragraph. Instead, he inserted chatty little anecdotes about celebrities —and a million people bought the book.

An excerpt from a student theme illustrates the problem we are discussing:

By means of certain techniques an author can introduce deeper meanings than his simple plot suggests. He may use symbols to emphasize his theme or to generalize the message he wishes to convey.

Some readers might have a rather clear understanding of what these sentences mean, but some—perhaps many—would not. The problem is how to clarify the message for the uninformed reader without boring the knowledgeable one. The student reasoned that even the informed reader would be interested in knowing how certain highly respected writers used symbols. He turned to a short story by Katherine Mansfield, a play by Edward Albee, and a novel by William Faulkner in the belief that both levels of readers would find the explanation profitable and interesting:

In the short story "Bliss," Katherine Mansfield accentuates the immaturity of her protagonist by giving her the name "Bertha Young," which hints that she is as young as at birth. When Bertha's rival is mentioned, the reference is often juxtaposed to the ripening of a pear tree. To make sure that the reader catches the relationship of the second girl and the mature tree, her name is Pearl (Pear + l). In the story, a black cat continually chases a gray cat. Bertha pointedly ignores the two cats, just as she remains ignorant that her husband is chasing her rival.

In Edward Albee's Who's Afraid of Virginia Woolf?, the two leading characters, George and Martha, have created a son in their imagination. The game they play of talking about him shuts out their insufferable actual life. Their fearful reluctance to end the fiction by having the son die points up the author's belief that man must hold certain beliefs, true or not, if he is to endure real life. The similarity of the end of their pretense to the death of Jesus Christ suggests that religion is one of the fictions that man creates for support. When they "kill" their son, they are forced to face up to their problems—perhaps Albee is suggesting that man is better off with the crutch of imaginative (or religious) support. We must not forget that it is hardly coincidental that their names are the same as those of George and Martha Washington. Is Albee telling us that Americans are strong only because of the myths they maintain?

In William Faulkner's Light in August, there is no place on earth where Joe Christmas can go, and he is finally murdered. This is a gruesome story, we think? It can't happen here, we say? Perhaps Faulkner thinks differently. Joe Christmas has the same initials as Jesus Christ. The parentage of both is very unusual. They were both thirty-three years old when put to death; the story has frequent references to the cross and to crucifixion. Is Faulkner telling us that mankind had the same fate for Jesus, the founder of Christianity?

> In this way the authors can suggest subtly a great deal more than the observable action and characters do on the first level of perception.

The student's statements about the symbols required an involved development because the concept was complex. In such a case the writer has a choice: either he avoids making such a provocative assertion (he deletes it from his paper), or he gives it the full treatment it requires. In the preceding paper the student found that he needed so much space to develop the two generative sentences quoted on page 192 that they became the thesis of his entire theme. In his first draft these sentences had been buried in a paragraph with a series of equally undeveloped thoughts.

Objective: Authenticity

Once you are satisfied with the significance, organization, and development of your message, you should step back from it and ask: "Is this something that one human being should say to another? Does it reflect my thought? Is it somehow more than a treatise that could be churned out by a computer? What quality in it makes it authentically mine?"

Case History: "Up Against the Wall, Male Chauvinist Pig!"— in which a girl unleashes her anger

A girl had written a fairly good expository paper. She had described how rock music became the essence of the youth culture. Ever since "American Bandstand," she wrote, it had

> filled the lonely spaces of my life. . . . The music became a sort of other world where I daydreamed a whole vicarious living made up of other people's romances and lives. It was what got me together with other people. After spending hours in front of the mirror learning how to dance, I would go to parties and dance for hours at a time. I was part of every person there and everyone there was part of me.
>
> Rock music was the only thing we had of our own, the only values we had which weren't dictated for us. We wore "hip" clothes, did "groovy" things, and became society's flower children.

As the girl read her paper, she grew madder and madder. It wasn't only that she realized she was describing how she had locked herself into a conformist culture; it was, as she later wrote, when she had "connected with the women's movement" that she had become aware of another, and not very appealing, aspect of rock. She then began to write what she herself had never thought about before—her sudden conviction that rock music is nothing more than an out-and-out exploitation of women.

The paper that emerged was authentic in every sense. It was a message from one angry, liberated human being to all the world.

What I was seeing was not all those different groups, but all these different men. . . . All the names on the albums, all the people doing the sound and lights, twirling the dials, all the voices on the radio, even the DJs between songs— they were all men. . . .

There are, of course, some exceptions. After all, Woodstock Nation is 51 percent female. I remember hearing about some all-girl bands on the West Coast, like the Ace of Cups, and I also remember reading about how they were laughed and hooted at with a general "take them off the stage and give them a good f---."

Her blistering account poured out her anger, about the "chick" singer who can only "make it at the stag parties," the screaming of the groupies for their sex thrills, the put-down of the girl who realizes that it's her body, and not her soul, that is the target for rock lyrics.

She saw herself in Stokely Carmichael's remembrance of going to Westerns as a child and cheering wildly for the cowboys—until one day he realized that, being black, he was really an Indian and all those years he had been rooting for his own destruction. She remembered how many rock songs, like "Under My Thumb," were all about revenge and were filled with hatred for women.

Then she took her paper one step further and ended this new version on an optimistic note: how women can take rock music and make it more than it is.

When the Beatles sing "Let It Be," it's all about decadence; when Aretha Franklin sings it, it's about pain, humiliation, and love. A different one coming from a different place, it is a hymnal of hope. I knew we could use all that charged rock energy. . . . We can quit being, at best, exotic domestic animals that come with their masters or come to find masters. We do not all have to end with Janis Joplin, incredible sex objects with an out-of-sight voice, with no alternative to an uptight and unhappy way of life. We can put it all together better than the men can. We can. And we will.

The moral of this story is that, even in the last stages, the writer must be sure to seek his own authentic self if he wants a really superior paper. He must be a person writing to persons—and his message must be *his* message.

Objective: Polish

By the time you reach this stage, your manuscript is probably a mass of insertions and scratched-out phrases. You may want to retype or rewrite the whole theme, perhaps triple spacing it to leave room for the changes you will begin to make.

The previous steps in revision undoubtedly have expanded your manuscript. You have added details, definitions, statistics, and illustrations to the body of your theme, and your introduction and conclusion are considerably longer than they were when you started. Now you must *condense*. You must cut and cut and cut, stopping only when the prose bleeds. You must also check exactness. Verify every name, every date, every detail. George Bernard Shaw wrote in *Advice to a Young Critic*, "Get your facts right first; that is the foundation of all style." After you have read your paper enough times, you will tend to believe everything you have written, so you must therefore verify, verify, and verify. A student once entered an essay contest, and his paper was given a superior rating by two of the three judges. The third judge gave the essay a very low rating, explaining later that the student reported that three lifeboats were sent to rescue a trawler, whereas the judge remembered reading that there were only two lifeboats. An error in a statement for him counterbalanced all the merits of the paper.

As you read through your paper this time, think of the factors of style. Consider alternative words, especially alternative verbs. If a word does not seem quite right, look for synonyms in either your dictionary or a thesaurus. Avoid pretentious, flowery words, of course, but try each synonym, deciding what each does to the message of the sentence. Random, even haphazard experiment may refine your thoughts and add a great deal to your paper. The author of the paper about Freud and Ibsen that we discussed earlier used the following sentence: "The ideas in the play are the same as in Freud." She then tried out "The ideas . . . illustrate. . . ." and "The ideas

. . . foreshadow. . . ." The sentence that finally emerged from this experiment was, "In *Hedda Gabler,* Henrik Ibsen anticipated Freud's analysis of the dynamics of human behavior."

The same student wrote the following two sentences, which could have profited from condensation:

> "Hedda had to return back to the estate."
> "Brack alone had the power to dominate over her."

Do you see words that can be eliminated? Try leaving out *back* in the first sentence and *over* in the second. Condense the second to "Brack alone could dominate her."

Condensation is a ruthless yet profitable art. Many students reject it at first—until they have cut a fifth of the words in an essay and found that their thoughts are intact and clearer. See for yourself. As an experiment, try covering the right-hand column below while you condense the sentences in the left-hand column. To cut properly, focus on small units of expression.

Most of the students eventually achieve baccalaureate status.	Delete the last three words; substitute *graduate*. Delete *of the*.
I got a job working in a factory.	Delete *working*.
Today's businessman wants to acquire as many sales as possible.	Condense to "Today's businessman wants to increase his sales."

To understand how a writer's mind should function during revision, study the following columns. The expressions in the left-hand column should give rise to the reactions in the right-hand column.

Many *modern* elementary school *systems are providing an advanced program of education* . . .	This section is wordy. Whether the school is modern or not is irrelevant; I can indicate that I am talking about present-day schools by simply using the present tense of my verb. *Systems* is unnecessary; all I need is *Many elementary schools. Are providing* can be shortened to *provide* or *offer. An advanced program of education* is wordy; I know it is education, and I know it should not be *advanced program,* because it seems to be limited to math and languages.
for some of their students, most commonly *centering around the fields of* math and languages.	The qualification *for some of their students* can probably be assumed and thus deleted. *Centering around the fields of* is pure pedagese and is better omitted entirely. If I simply write, *Many elementary*

In order for this program *to be beneficial to these and future students,* careful consideration of the participants must be given. . . . Before a student is selected for this advanced study, *tests of both academic and psychological stability should be administered and corrected.*

schools now offer advanced courses in math and languages, all I need is there, and I have eliminated over half the words.

Redundant. I need only *for this program to benefit students,* and once again I have removed over half the section.

As *it now stands,* pupils are chosen *to participate* solely on the basis of their *previous* academic record. . . . Obviously this might result in serious psychological problems *on the child's part.* . . .

Wordy. Why not just *he should be given academic and psychological tests?*

Wordy, a cliché. *Pupils are now chosen* is all I need. And I can delete *previous.*

The idiom and brevity here suggest problems for the child. Try: *Students are now chosen solely on their academic record.* . . . *Obviously this might result in serious psychological problems.*

A *battery of tests* should be administered to all children *that would predict their aptitude and whether* or not *they have been working to their fullest capacity.*

A *battery of tests is a* cliché, and it is wordy. I'll just say, *Tests.* Misplaced modifier here. Sounds as though the children will be expected to do the predicting. I'll put the modifier closer to the noun: *Tests that diagnose aptitudes and determine whether the student has been working up to capacity should be administered.* I won't say *fullest capacity,* which is tautological; *capacity* is sufficient.

After the results of these tests have *verified the fact* that the child is *totally* capable of advanced study, then, *and only then,* should the student be selected.

This whole section is wordy and repetitious. I'll substitute: *Only when the child has demonstrated his capability for advanced study should the school consider him for the program.*

This point being reached, *the child and his parents should be confronted.* If teachers, parents and child agree *on the helpfulness of the program,* then the child should be admitted.

I should recast the entire passage to reduce the duplication: *At this point, the child, his parents, and his teachers should determine whether he ought to be admitted.*

After condensing the passage, the writer would still have to develop his ideas. Presumably, the school authorities have some reason for their present policy, and the writer, by citing cases where students have been upset and frustrated by more school work than they can handle, must show that the authorities are wrong. Then he must show, in detail, that tests exist or can be developed that will determine mental and emotional capacity. If possible, the exact tests should be named and described.

The writer may realize, as he probes the situation, that the school authorities are right, in which case he will either change to another topic or do more research to substantiate his new view. At any rate, his paper has profited from the revision process called condensing. Even if he has said little as yet, he is no longer wasting the reader's time. The passage at this stage of the revision would read, after some additional rephrasing, something like this:

> Many elementary schools provide advanced courses in math and languages. . . . For these courses to benefit students, school authorities should be extremely careful about selecting participants. . . . They should give academic and psychological tests to determine whether students can handle advanced work. Pupils are now chosen solely on their academic records. . . . Only when the child has demonstrated his capability for advanced study should the school consider him for the program. At this point the child, his parents, and his teachers should determine whether he ought to be admitted.

As you polish your writing, strive for exactness, vividness, and variety. Make sure you have used your key words properly. A student once received a low mark on a term paper about Ernest Hemingway because she misused the word *spiritual*. She thought it meant "basically interested in religion"; using it thus, she conveyed the impression that she believed Hemingway constantly expected a mystical revelation. Another student mentioned in his conclusion to a paper on Thoreau that what he had just written was the "definitive" paper on Thoreau's concept of art. What the student *expressed* was a boast that his effort was the final and complete paper on the subject; what the student *thought* he was saying was that he had "defined" Thoreau's concept of art.

Ambiguities, either structural or verbal, must be detected and removed. When you reread your paper, try to perceive every possible meaning of the words and expressions you have used. Cover the right-hand column below while you try to catch the double meanings in the left-hand column.

She had outlived her ambition without realizing it.	We can't tell whether her ambition had not been realized or whether she did not realize that she had outlived her ambition.

I was originally born in South Dakota, but I've spent most of my mortal life in Nebraska.	How else were you born besides *originally*? Where have you spent your *immortal* life?
Have you spent all your life in Vermont?	Not yet.
Loosely wrapped in a newspaper, she carried three dresses.	She may get cold.
When I called his roommate, he said he'd be out of town for a few days.	I'm doubly confused: I don't know who did the saying or who will be out of town.
The bag is light and empty you can pack it easily in another bag.	Is the bag light and empty or do you mean that when it is empty you can pack it easily in another bag?

One frequent ambiguity occurs in students' attempts to end their papers: "In conclusion, Descartes must be considered the father of. . . ." The writer probably means that he is concluding, but it sounds as though Descartes were concluding.

Earlier we mentioned that at this stage of your revision, you should consider alternative words, especially alternative verbs. This is the time to strengthen your verbs. Using a felt-tipped pen with transparent ink or any heavy pencil, preferably one with colored lead, read through the entire paper again and mark every form of the verb *to be* and every use of the passive voice. If you do not find your paper filled with marks, your style is well on its way to being vivid and dramatic. But if you have marked many forms of *be*, look closely at those weak verbs and try to find stronger, active-voice verbs to replace them. In the following draft of the paper referred to earlier about the Salem witch trials, we have underlined the weak verbs:

After many trials and many hangings came an event which was responsible for causing public sentiment to stir. The event was the death of Giles Corey. He was a man over 80 years old and had been "carried away by the delusion for a time." His testimony was to be used for the conviction of his wife; the old man, however, refused to plead one way or the other. After three such scenes were demonstrated, he was taken into an open field, stripped, and thrown on his back; a heavy weight was placed upon his body until he was pressed to death. It took this unfortunate incident to stimulate the residents of Salem to think seriously about the way they had been acting.

Could events like this continue? The answer was no, for the

public sentiment against the hangings became so powerful that even Stoughton, the chief justice, retired from the bench. What actually broke the spell, what actually caused the downfall, however, <u>was</u> that the accusers began to strike too high. They aimed at the ruling class, at relatives of the magistrates, at the president of Harvard, at the wife of the governor, and at Mr. Willard, the godliest minister in Boston. Accusation of Mrs. Hale, wife of the minister of the First Church, "hit the nail on the head." Although Reverend Hale <u>had</u> <u>been</u> one of the leaders of the witchcraft delusion, things looked quite different when they came directly to him. His eyes <u>were</u> opened; the whole community under his influence became convinced that the "afflicted" children had "perjured themselves" and from that moment their power <u>was</u> gone. The awful delusion began passing away and Salem began returning to its senses.

A shift in viewpoint can convert the weak verbs to active, strong expressions. The writer should have the townspeople performing the action:

. . . the townspeople tried so many suspects and hanged so many "witches" that they gasped at their own brutality. When they tried Giles Corey, an 80-year-old man who acted as though deluded, they knew they had gone too far. Because Mr. Corey refused to testify against his wife, they took him into an open field, stripped him, and threw him on his back. Then they placed a weight on his chest so heavy that it crushed him to death. Their own cruelty caused them to think—to realize with horror what they had done.

Eventually the witchcraft fervor grew so strong that even Stoughton, the chief justice resigned. The accusers began to strike too high. They hurled accusations at relatives of the magistrates, at the president of Harvard, at the wife of the governor, even at Mr. Willard, the godliest minister in Boston. Reverend Hale, the minister of the First Church, had cried "witch" as loudly as any man; but when his parishioners accused his own wife, he changed his perspective rapidly. His eyes opened; he convinced the community of its overzealousness. Soon the delusion vanished, and Salem returned to its senses.

Instead of "Columbus was a man of the Renaissance," Paul Horgan, in *The Conquistadores,* wrote, "Columbus was the son of his time, the dawning Renaissance, when the spirit of discovery of man's arts and sciences was breaking across the western world."

To express his basic thought—"Jessamyn West usually writes light fiction; this time she has gone into more somber work"—Webster Schott, in a review of *A Matter of Time,* (Miss West's book about a woman with terminal cancer) wrote, "Jessamyn West is a nice lady who writes nice fiction. Lately she has been having midnight thoughts."

According to Samuel Taylor Coleridge, there is in the sentences of the greatest writers a "reason assignable not only for every word, but for the position of every word." When you are fairly comfortable with the words you have selected, look again at your sentences and arrange each element in them effectively. Compact your sentences and give them texture. A sentence may be particularly interesting because it has many ideas compressed in it:

> There Jim sits.
> There Jim sits, quietly.
> There Jim sits, quietly, in slow decay.

Make your prose as compact as possible, being careful, however, to avoid a howler such as, "Coming from St. Louis' rain and slush, Palo Alto's climate is heaven sent."

The selection below contains one idea per sentence:

> All societies are governed by laws. The laws are really hidden. These hidden laws are not spoken. They are profound. They are assumptions. The assumptions are by the people. Our society is like all societies. A writer has a job. An American writer has a special job. His job is to find out the laws and assumptions. Our society has a special quality. The quality is that we smash taboos. We still have to pay attention to the taboos. American writers will have a hard time finding our laws. They will also have a hard time finding our assumptions.

The staccato effect is monotonous, amateurish, and wasteful. Note how James Baldwin conveyed the same ideas:

> Every society is really governed by hidden laws, by unspoken but profound assumptions on the part of the people, and ours is no exception. It is up to the American writer to find out what these laws and assumptions are. In a society given to smashing taboos without thereby managing to be liberated from them, it will be no easy matter.—JAMES BALDWIN, *Nobody Knows My Name*

Earlier in this chapter we showed you a paragraph about a man overwhelmed by his wife. Now look at another version of the account:

> Herbert's wife dominates him. When they attended his friend's wedding, his wife and daughter sat in the back seat. They were dressed in frilly, bouffant dresses. Herbert sat in the front seat alone. He collects stamps for a hobby.

In the next version note the effect of a change in sentence structure. Even if your views on sexism cause you to think the husband gets what he deserves, you will see that his point is advanced more effectively.

> Herbert is dominated by his wife. When he was invited to his friend's wedding, he arrived in the family car. Enthroned in the back seat, all frilly and bouffant, sat his wife and teen-age daughter. Alone in the front, like a chauffeur, was Herbert. No wonder he spends his evenings alone in his study classifying stamps.

This second version opens with two passive verbs, to emphasize Herbert's docile nature. The construction of two sentences is reversed, so that in this version they begin with *enthroned* and *alone,* to emphasize the status of the wife and daughter in relation to Herbert. The metaphor of his family's being "enthroned" is in poignant contrast to the simile of Herbert as chauffeur. Only the last sentence, which mentions Herbert's one positive act, awards him an active, transitive verb all his own.

As you revise the structure of your sentences, seek variety. In the margins of your draft, jot down the number of words in each sentence. If your sentences are all long, unload some of them. An abrupt terse sentence can be effective. It can catch the reader's attention. Try it. Indicate also in the margins whether your sentences are simple, compound, or complex—and make any changes necessary to correct an overabundance of any one type. Observe what patterns your modifiers follow, and try for other patterns. Here are some unusual constructions:

> He shook hands, a quick shake, fingers down, like a pianist.—SINCLAIR LEWIS

> The jockeys sat bowed and relaxed, moving a little at the waist with the movement of their horses.—KATHERINE ANNE PORTER

> Calico-coated, small-bodied, with delicate legs and pink faces in which their mismatched eyes rolled wild and subdued, they huddled, gaudy, motionless and alert, wild as deer, deadly as rattlesnakes, quiet as doves. —WILLIAM FAULKNER

> Joad's lips stretched tight over his long teeth for a moment, and he licked his lips, like a dog, two licks, one in each direction from the middle.—JOHN STEINBECK

All this carpentering, experimenting, reordering, fleshing out, condensing, and rephrasing may well form a product that, at this moment, is not *you.* The English language has a huge collection of patterns and word choices, and each writer must select what suits him best. Remember your fourth objective, authenticity. Is this you talking? If it is not, polish your sentences to satisfy yourself. Which sound better to you?

> Luther rose from his knees and walked slowly away.
> Luther rose from his knees and slowly walked away.
> Slowly Luther rose from his knees and walked away.

All three sentences are effective, logical, grammatical, clear, and exact, but especially if you have read them aloud, you may feel more comfortable with one version than with the others. Remember, however, that you are striving for something even beyond authenticity. You are striving for *artistry*. Somerset Maugham complained that

> many writers without distress will put two rhyming words together, join a monstrous long adjective to a monstrous long noun, or between the end of one word and at the beginning of another have a conjunction of consonants that almost break your jaw.—SOMERSET MAUGHAM, *The Summing Up*

If you are to avoid such troubles, you must experiment and select, mumble your sentences to yourself, and polish till you have what satisfies you. Give your paper the same care you would give a cherished work of art.

The Final Step: Proofreading for Grammar, Spelling, and Punctuation

Glory of glories, you have finally worked through all the steps of the rewriting process. Significance, logic, coherence, completeness, authenticity, artistry—all are yours. At this point, you feel your paper is finished, and you probably cannot bear to look at it one more time. But remember the sad fate of the newspaper: all that work is wasted if the newsboy throws it into the snowbank. You must, once again, reread your work to be sure that the grammar, spelling, and punctuation are conventional and effective.

How do you begin? One step at a time. First, check the grammar. Look through your previous compositions to see what barbarisms you have committed before. Comma splice? Misplaced modifier? Singular subject and plural verb? Since there are only so many mistakes you can make, you might prepare a checklist of those you usually make—and then set out to avoid them. Read the paper aloud, thinking about sentence structure, repetition, sound, and rhythm.

Then shift to punctuation. Here it is important once again that you read aloud. Read interpretively, as though you were talking to a small child. Pause here; put stress there. Does your punctuation, insofar as it can, reflect the vocal inflections so important to meaning? Don't use too many commas.

If too many are needed, recast your sentences in shorter form. Just before you read your manuscript for punctuation, you might want to read the punctuation examples in the handbook section of this textbook (pages 305–311). Read the examples aloud, inflecting them more heavily than you ordinarily would.

Would you have been able to use the punctuation necessary to convey the ideas expressed below?

> That student thinks his teacher is the best in the school.
> That student, thinks his teacher, is the best in the school.
> That student thinks; his teacher is the best in the school.

As you proofread your own composition, watch for mistakes you've made in previous papers. When you have an incomplete word at the end of a line, divide only between syllables. If you are not sure of the word's syllabication, check your dictionary.

And now for spelling. When you read for spelling, your lips should form sounds; you may even mispronounce words to stress spellings—for example, soph–O–more, pic–nic–King, vac–U–Um, at–ten–Dance, and in–dis–pen–SABLE. Think what the word is. The troublemakers are usually such pairs as *then/than, whose/who's, their/they're,* and *its/it's* rather than long words, but look up any words you are uncertain of. Use your pencil when you check a longer word, putting the pencil's point on each syllable. If you customarily misspell three words per page, search for four or five.

The Finished Paper

At last the job is done. You've traveled the "final inch." William James once complained that "everything comes out wrong with me at first, but I torture and poke and scrape and pat it until it offends me no more." When you go through this long process and watch bad writing become the good writing you perhaps saw glimmering up there ahead of you all through the ordeal, you feel a tremendous satisfaction and you have a sense of real accomplishment. This feeling, and the knowledge and skill in writing that you have gained, will encourage you to pay the same careful attention to detail when you revise your next paper—and the next and the next. Each time you will learn, and each time you will be impressed with the results.

Projects

1. Indicate the weak verbs in the following student theme and decide how they can be strengthened:

Each spring high school students all over the country are confronted with various college entrance examinations; the most often taken of these exams are the Scholastic Aptitude Tests. Of all the tests given to college students, I believe these are the least indicative of a student's ability.

Now you may ask, "How can she say these things?" and I'll say, "Easily!" The psychological effect that college board exams have on high school students is unbelievable. All of the students who are about to take these exams are well aware of the ultimate effect their scores will have on their immediate future. They are so nervous and so tense that they are just not able to function in their normal capacity. Speaking for myself, when the day came for me to take my final set of boards, I was so nervous that I was ill and naturally didn't do as well as I should have. I'm not using myself as an only example; what happened to me happened to thousands of others all over the country. . . .

2. As you work to improve your diction, don't forget to consult your dictionary or *Roget's Thesaurus*. To see how this technique works, replace each of the italicized words in the left-hand column with a word from the right-hand column; choose the one you feel is the *best*. Read the entire left-hand column first to see the continuity. Be sure you can explain why you rejected any word in the right-hand column. Then compare your effort with the version on page 207, which was written by E. M. Forster.

The people I *like* most	admire, respect, revere, enjoy, love, relish, favor, desire, fancy, crave, choose, take delight in, revel in, gloat over, appreciate, acknowledge, relate to, regard, esteem, venerate, idolize, honor
are those who are *sharp*	sensible, discriminating, touchy, subtle, refined, responsive, sensitive, receptive, sympathetic, delicate, demonstrative
and want to *make*	grow, generate, produce, create, breed, work, cause, form, manu- facture, fashion, forge, build, construct
something or *find*	learn, discover, master, bring to light, encounter, ascertain, absorb

something, and do not see life in
terms of power, and such people
get *more of an opportunity*

more time, more of a chance, more
of an occasion, more room, more
scope

under a democracy than elsewhere.
They *start*

begin, invent, establish, create, set
up, found, form, forge, build,
concoct

religions, great or small, or they
write literature

create, perform, produce, manufacture, originate, devise, hatch,
contrive

and art, or they do disinterested
scientific research, or they may be
what is called "ordinary people,"
who are *constructive*

productive, prolific, creative,
contriving, incentive, blastogenetic,
epigenetic, incubational, fruitful

in their *own* lives,

personal, secluded, private, con-
fidential, individual, intimate

rear their

bring up, produce, raise, grow,
garden, share crop

children decently, for instance, or
aid their

succor, assist, help, remedy, benefit,
subsidize, befriend, give a leg up
for, defend

neighbors. All these people need to
talk;

speak, express themselves, chatter,
converse, gab

they cannot do so unless society
permits
them to do so, and the society
which allows them most liberty is a
democracy.

allows, lets, sanctions, tolerates,
suffers, enables, authorizes

E. M. Forster almost always selected the simplest synonyms, avoiding
any expressions that were jocose or frivolous. He is speaking seriously. His
version:

> The people I admire most are those who are sensitive and want to
> create something or discover something, and do not see life in terms of
> power, and such people get more of a chance under a democracy than
> elsewhere. They found religions, great or small, or they produce literature
> and art, or they do disinterested scientific research, or they may be what is
> called "ordinary people," who are creative in their private lives, bring up
> their children decently, for instance, or help their neighbors. All these
> people need to express themselves; they cannot do so unless society allows
> them to do so, and the society which allows them most liberty is a
> democracy.—E. M. FORSTER, *Two Cheers for Democracy*

3. Take the best paper you have written thus far in this course and give it a full-scale rethinking and revision as described in the last two chapters. When you submit the paper, accompany it with a paragraph in which you describe and explain the steps that were most appropriate and most worthwhile for *your* writing.

Part  *Special Problems*

Chapter  The Research Report

There is more to college life than the routine of registration, paying
fees, and even a dutiful attendance of classes and fulfillment of
assignments. You do not really become a college student until you go,
alone and because of some question of your own, to the library.
. . . When days begin to pass in which you do not look up a new
word in the dictionary or you do not seek an answer to a new
question, then you are beginning to die. I reemphasize my point:
intellectual life begins and ends, if not in the library, at least in the
research impulse.—*Freshman Orientation, Boston University, 1967*

Research needs no defense. The most successful corporations today are
the ones that annually allocate large portions of their budgets to research
and development. In a recent study a large number of Americans indicated
that they honor research scientists second only to statesmen. Most of us are
aware that our material well-being is heavily dependent on the activities of
our researchers. We have heard the romantic and dramatic stories of how
penicillin and the polio vaccines were discovered. Besides scientific research,
we are aware of the research activities in social studies and of the polls that
predict which candidates are most apt to be successful in the next elections,
the market analyses that result each year in new automobile styles, foods,
fads, and fashions. When a community votes on whether funds should be
appropriated for a new school building, citizens turn almost automatically

to studies of population distribution, pupil counts, and transportation facilities. In short, research is an important and respected aspect of modern life.

The probability that a college student will at some time find himself doing research, professionally or nonprofessionally, is large enough to warrant his learning some basic techniques. Research is nothing more than a systematic method of problem solving. If a person decides to buy a new stereo system, he has a need for information. If he limits his information gathering to reading a few magazine advertisements and hearing a television commercial or two, his effort is not worthy of being called research, and he deserves the trimming he will probably get. If he talks to a number of his friends, visits a number of dealers, and tests a number of stereos, he is doing superficial research. If he goes to a library and studies the numerous consumers' services that have analyzed, compared, and evaluated stereos, he has done commendable research. He will probably save money and undoubtedly will get the system best for its sound, range, durability, price, and beauty.

High-school graduates want to know what colleges will best suit their needs. They want to know whether they can afford an automobile. They want to know how to get rid of acne. How can they control weight without starving? What is the best way to study? What is the shortest, cheapest, and most interesting way to Chicago or Santa Cruz?

Research can be one of the most exciting and rewarding of all occupations. The human organism has many wants, and one of the most driving is the impulse to know. That student is fortunate who has joined the large brotherhood whose members find research, one of the most important aspects of education, fun instead of work. The fun in this fraternity is a little like a mosquito bite: the feeling of not knowing is irritating, but it is sweet torment to scratch.

Types of Research

There are two ways to look at research. From one point of view, it is either pure or applied. From another, it is either primary or secondary.

The distinction between pure and applied research depends on why the researcher is asking his question. When Robert Boyle (1627–1691) experimented with the effect of pressure on a volume of gas, he observed that, temperature being constant, when pressure on a confined gas is increased, the volume of the gas decreases proportionally. A successor, Jacques Charles (1746–1823), was also interested in the effect of changed variables on gases. Charles discovered that when heat is applied to gas, its volume expands proportionally. Neither Boyle nor Charles had considered how to use this information. Driven simply by the impulse to know, they were doing *pure* research. When Charles put these discoveries to use by heating gas in a balloon and getting himself yanked two miles into the air in the hope of producing a method of transportation, he was doing *applied* research. Charles' contemporary, James Watt (1736–1819), also put research about gas to use and developed the steam engine by harnessing the energy of the expanded gas. This too was applied research.

Pure researchers often have great difficulty securing support for their work and acceptance of their discoveries. Galileo (1564–1642) earned the antagonism of his fellow scientists when his findings about the relative motion of bodies differed from the teachings of Aristotle, and the wrath of churchmen when his theory of the solar system seemed to support Copernicus and contradict Genesis. Pure research has made history, and it has made history possible. Adding to the work of Joseph Priestley (1733–1804), Antoine Lavoisier (1743–1794) isolated and named oxygen; Sir Isaac Newton (1642–1727) determined the laws of gravity; Michael Faraday (1791–1867) pioneered the transformation of mechanical energy to electrical energy; Marie Curie (1867–1934) isolated a radioactive substance; and James Van Allen, a professor at the University of Iowa, discovered a belt of radioactive material just outside the earth's atmosphere. All of these discoveries were the result of pure research, but every one of them was used in the applied research that transported man to the moon. The fuel used was liquid oxygen; the rocket was blasted out of the effect of earth's gravity; most of the controls were activated by electrical impulse transformed to physical activity; the astronauts avoided the effects of the radioactive materials in the Van Allen belt.

Besides the differentiation between pure and applied research, there is a distinction between primary and secondary research. The primary researcher takes the first look. He may work with manuscripts and published materials, but he will interpret them as no one else has or draw conclusions not reached by anyone before him. He may compare the prosody of Chaucer to that of Shakespeare, or he may observe the attention given by newspapers to sex (as measured in inches of column space in news and advertising). Another primary researcher may study the effect of various ammonia ions on carbohydrates. Still another, by means of a series of interviews, may make a sociological study of man's reliance on God, the automobile, advertising, or tranquilizers. All of them may use highly intricate statistical procedures. These are primary; they result in the first generalization.

The secondary researcher uses the primary reports for his own end. He uses encyclopedias, scholarly journals, diaries, and all manner of oral and published reports. If an archaeologist pulls on his boots and pokes around the Mohenjo-Daro ruins, he is doing primary research; if he goes to the library and scans scholarly journals about the diggings, he is doing secondary research. If a botanist takes notes on a diver's report about flora at forty fathoms, he's doing secondary research.

The techniques of pure, applied, and primary research will be discussed in chemistry, physics, biology, psychology, literature, and sociology courses. The instructors of such courses will assume that their students have mastered the techniques of library research.

We must emphasize the fact that college undergraduates can do primary research. Several years ago a sophomore at Stanford University did some primary research that set full professors at Harvard, in the Big Ten, and at Stanford itself back on their heels. At first they snorted with contempt at his discovery—and then they were humiliated. Henry James is the scholar's novelist. He is not popular with the average reader, but critics love him. Their favorite novel is probably *The Ambassadors,* and they have loved to write about little obscurities here and there that they think they can clarify. When the Stanford sophomore read *The Ambassadors,* he noticed that one sequence of incidents made no sense and wrote a paper insisting that the chapters were out of order. He suggested a rearrangement that made the incidents clear. When he read his paper to the class, his professor and his classmates smiled at his brashness. The general reaction was "Tut! tut!" When the persistent sophomore submitted his paper to a very scholarly journal, the editors sent back a printed rejection slip pointing out that the journal was for experienced scholars. But the sophomore persevered. Acting on a hunch, he arranged by interlibrary loan to get a copy of an edition that had been published in England. Sure enough, he found the chapters in the order he suggested. He then dug back into the autobiography of the novel's publisher and found that Henry James had sent one chapter at a time via steamship to the American publisher—and that several chapters had got out of order. The sophomore could now produce irrefutable evidence to support his conclusion that every American edition of the book was improperly edited. You can imagine the embarrassment of the distinguished professors who had never noticed the error before.

Nobel prizes tend to go to researchers in applied sciences, the standard of judgment being that their contributions must do something to help mankind, but such contributions are usually based on the earlier efforts of pure scientists, who rarely are known, except by other scientists. Great thinkers are, in part, great because they are able to use the work of men who have gone before them. A cardinal principle of research is, in fact, that no sound scholar embarks on a research project before he has located and studied the relevant research that has preceded his own efforts. The earlier research, when published, is called the "literature" of the particular subject or field.

Much undergraduate research—indeed, much of *all* research—results in a report. A researcher surveys the available literature on a subject and then selects, organizes, and presents the information in a report. Though this report is invaluable, it may have one shortcoming in the eyes of the college freshman. "Where," he may ask, "is my chance to be original?" The question is important, and the answer is complex. Before it is answered, however, the question must be put in the proper perspective.

By itself, originality is no virtue. If a man makes up some idea and presents it as a "fact," he is being original, but his effort is useless and dishonest. A writer may have an original thought, but unless he presents it very clearly, it will have little value. Thus an original idea must have worth in itself and be expressed clearly. Lacking significance and clarity, an original idea may be worth very little.

Of the famous team of Charles Darwin and Thomas Huxley there is little doubt about which was the more original and creative. Darwin, the collector, observer, and generalizer did the first work; Huxley was the expresser and popularizer. But the contribution of each is vitally important. Ironically, almost no one reads Darwin today, but Huxley is still read frequently. What Darwin created was science; what Huxley created was literature. Even Shakespeare profited from his predecessors. He often demonstrated his creative genius by reworking a secondhand story, especially bits of history from Plutarch's *Lives* and Raphael Holinshed's *Chronicles*. The answer to the question of where originality lies in a research paper is that originality plays a part during the whole process. The selection of relevant material and its orderly presentation produce a work that has never been seen before, and this work can have value and excellence. In the process of finding, selecting, organizing, and writing, there is opportunity to be highly critical.

The Library Tour

Of the many ways to become familiar with a research library, one of the best is the individual tour. Every student should read this section on the library and then, book in hand, make his own personal tour.

THE CARD CATALOG

Enter the library and look around. Make your way, first of all, to the card catalog. Follow the alphabet from A to Z to be sure you know where all the drawers are. Pull out a drawer. Does it come out so that you can take it to a desk where you can write? How will you know how to return it to the proper place? Is the drawer numbered?

To give yourself some valuable experience, try a few operations. Select a famous person for whom there may be an author card, a subject card, and a title card, for instance, Ernest Hemingway, Thomas Jefferson, Virginia Woolf, Adolf Hitler, Winston Churchill, Amelia Earhart, Frank Lloyd Wright, or John F. Kennedy. As you leaf through the cards on your subject, notice that some of the cards are obviously books written by your subject. This is an *author card*, an example of which is shown in Figure 11-1.

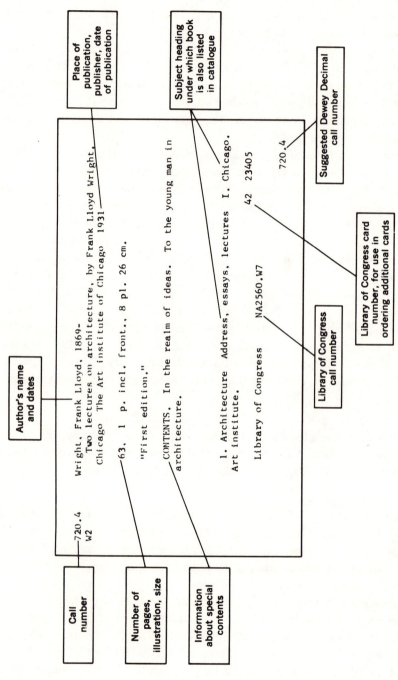

Call number

Author's name and dates

Place of publication, publisher, date of publication

Number of pages, illustration, size

Information about special contents

Subject heading under which book is also listed in catalogue

Suggested Dewey Decimal call number

Library of Congress card number, for use in ordering additional cards

Library of Congress call number

720.4
W2

Wright, Frank Lloyd, 1869-
    Two lectures on architecture, by Frank Lloyd Wright.
Chicago The Art institute of Chicago 1931

63, 1 p. incl. front., 8 pl. 26 cm.

"First edition."

CONTENTS. In the realm of ideas. To the young man in architecture.

    1. Architecture Address, essays, lectures I. Chicago.
Art institute.

Library of Congress   NA2560.W7

42   23405

720.4

Figure 11-1

The information that is found in the top left corner is the "call number." There are two systems of numbers used to provide the call numbers.

Dewey Decimal System

The sample card in Figure 11-1 has a number based on the Dewey Decimal System, still the system most frequently used, although more and more libraries are changing to the Library of Congress system because it has more divisions and more accurately covers the breadth of modern knowledge. The Dewey Decimal System has the following divisions:

000–009   General Works (encyclopedias, periodicals, bibliographies)
100–199   Philosophy, Psychology, Ethics
200–299   Religion and Mythology
300–399   Sociology (economics, civics, education, vocations)
400–499   Philology (language, dictionaries, grammar)
500–599   Pure Science (mathematics, physics, chemistry, biology, zoology, botany)
600–699   Technology (applied science, medicine, engineering, agriculture, radio, aviation)
700–799   Fine Arts (painting, music, photography, recreation)
800–899   Literature (novels, poetry, plays, criticism)
900–999   History, Geography, Biography, Travel

Each of the main classes is subdivided into the subjects appearing within the parentheses, and the smaller divisions are again divided. For instance, the numbers 630–639 represent agriculture, which is subdivided into field crops, garden crops, and dairy products. When the classes become very fine, decimals are used: books on insects useful to agriculture are grouped under 638; if a library has many books on useful insects, those on honeybees are kept under 638.1 and those on silkworms under 638.2.

Library of Congress System

The Library of Congress system is divided as follows:

A	General Works	L	Education
B	Philosophy and Religion	M	Music
C	History	N	Fine Arts
D	World History	P	Languages and Literature
E	U.S. History	Q	Science
F	Local History	R	Medicine
G	Geography and Anthropology	S	Agriculture
H	Social Sciences (economics and sociology)	T	Technology
		U	Military Science
J	Political Science	V	Naval Science
K	Law	Z	Library Science and Bibliography

Card Information

The number underneath the classification, or call, number is the one by which the library stores the book within its class. Very often it begins with the first letter of an author's last name. On the specimen card (Figure 11-1), the Dewey number 720 stands for architecture, and the number 720.4 W2 indicates that the exact work is Wright's *Two Lectures on Architecture*.

Notice that the author's name, last name first, is on the top line. The dates after his name are his birth and death dates. Is your man alive or dead? Or was he alive when the card was entered in the catalog? (Some libraries never catch up after the author dies, so don't rely on catalog cards for such information.) Just under the author is the complete title of the book followed by the pertinent publication information: place, publisher, and date. The next line, "63, 1 p. incl. front. 8 pl., 26 cm.," indicates the number of pages of text (63), which, in this case, includes an illustration, a frontispiece, and eight plates. The final entry on this line, "26 cm.," tells the height of the book. One centimenter equals about four-tenths of an inch.

The next line usually indicates whether there is a bibliography in the book; if there is, its page numbers will be indicated, as "Bibliography: p. 222–238." Next comes a list of subject headings under which a book may be found. The phrases "1. Architecture Address, essays, lectures" and "I. Chicago Art Institute" mean that the book's card will be found under those two entries. Occasionally, this list will also indicate that a card is found under the name of a joint author or collaborator.

The next line is for librarians. The left number, "NA2560.W7," is the number under which the book is classified if the library uses the Library of Congress system. The number on the right indicates the catalog number of the card itself; it is the number by which the card is ordered from the Library of Congress. The number at the bottom right provides the suggested number for libraries that use the Dewey Decimal system.

Now look for a *title card*, that is, a card alphabetized in the card catalog according to the book's title. The card is exactly like an author card except that the title is typed or printed above the author's name. Look next for a *subject card*, also exactly like the author card except that the subject of the publication—for instance, "English language—Phonetics"—is typed or printed at the top of the card, often in red ink. As you thumb through the cards, you will notice that subject-card headings are often "inverted"—for instance, "Photography, Aerial" and "Photography, Commercial." Subdivided subject headings are also inverted; you may notice something like the following.

Dancing
Dancing—Children's dances

Dancing—England
Dancing—Mexico

Another card you will find in the card catalog is the *cross-reference card*. Such cards suggest synonyms for subjects; for instance, under "Aviation" you will find a list indicating that cards are also filed under "Flight," "Aeronautics," "Air Force," and "Flying." When an author has a pseudonym, there will be a cross-reference for him. In the case of Mark Twain, for instance, reference to "Clemens, Samuel Langhorne, 1835–1910" is given.

UNION CATALOG

Now that you know your way around the section of the library where the card catalog is housed, check to see whether your library has a *Union Catalog*. Usually, the card catalog indicates only those books that the library has on its own shelves, but some libraries have either a shelving system with cards for all the books in the Library of Congress and more than seven hundred cooperating libraries, or a copy of the Library of Congress catalog (eighteen cards on each page, bound in a large volume). Using this catalog, you can ascertain what books exist, and then you can request that your library secure a book for you via interlibrary loan.

THE STACKS AND OTHER FACILITIES

If your library allows you to wander through its stacks—that is, the area in which books are stored—secure a floor plan of the stacks and follow the classification system in order. Where are the philosophy, social science, natural science, literature, and history books located? A trip through the stacks with an eye to the classification numbers will give you some sense of the strengths and weaknesses of your library. Your library may have an "open shelf list" which will help you tell what materials are found there.

INDEXES TO PERIODICALS

Now make your way to whatever facilities your library has to help you find the information contained in magazines, journals, microfilms, and other materials. Locate, first of all, the *Reader's Guide to Periodical Literature*. This multivolume guide indexes more than a hundred periodicals of a general nature, giving the author, title, source, and number of pages of information. It is indexed by subject, author, and title. To see how the entries work, look up several topics, for instance, *automation, existentialism, Winston Churchill,* and *Martin Luther King*. Near the bound volumes indexing periodicals of past years, you will find paperback indexes for the current year. In the front of the *Reader's Guide*, check what periodicals are indexed. The *Reader's Guide* begins with 1900. For periodical literature prior to 1900 locate *Poole's Index to Periodical Literature,* which indexes by subject about 470 English and American periodicals of a general nature. It differs from the *Reader's Guide* in that it is indexed by subject only, and it includes fiction, poetry, drama, and book reviews, all of which are indexed alphabetically according to the first important word of the title. The dates of its coverage are 1802–1907.

Most libraries now own collections of material on microfilm or microfiche form, usually with appropriate optical enlargers for whatever space-saving system is used. With such equipment libraries can put newspapers or such ephemeral materials onto microfilm and store in a small cabinet what would have occupied a huge room. Familiarize yourself with these resources, both by locating materials and by using the enlarger or reader.

Your library may subscribe to a service called Newsbank, which indexes many newspapers from all parts of the country. For relatively current events occurring a distance from you, such a resource may be invaluable. Find out whether your library is a subscriber.

While you are looking at the indexes to periodical literature, check to see what other indexes are obtainable in your library. In general, periodical literature is divided into two classes, *general* and *professional.* While you are looking at general indexes, see whether your library has the following:

1. *Biography Index.* Gives birth and death dates, occupation of persons indexed, and shows where more complete biographies can be found.
2. *Book Review Digest.* Indexes and condenses reviews of current books. A plus or minus sign indicates whether reviews are favorable or not. Author, title, pages, price, publisher, and dates for books reviewed are included.

Now turn to indexes of professional literature:

1. *International Index to Periodicals.* Indexes "scholarly and highly specialized periodicals in many countries."
2. *Education Index.* Begun in 1929; "a selected list of educational periodicals, books and pamphlets," including publications from the U.S. Office of Education.

Almost every discipline has its own extensive bibliographic reference works, as is shown by these examples:

1. Fine Arts: *Art Index, The Literature of Jazz, Music Index.*
2. Literature: *Cambridge Bibliography of English Literature* (cited as CBEL), *Abstracts of English Studies* (annotated fully), *Literary History of the United States.*
3. Philosophy and Psychology: *Dictionary of Philosophy and Psychology.*
4. Religion: *Index to Religious Periodical Literature.*
5. Science: *Guide to the Literature of Mathematics and Physics, Guide to the Literature of the Zoological Sciences, Industrial Arts Index.*

6. Social Sciences: *Guide to Historical Literature, Public Affairs Information Service.*

Obviously, you cannot master all the information about bibliographic reference books, nor would you wish to do so, because they become obsolete very quickly. What you are learning on this trip is that, no matter what subject you have in mind, there is undoubtedly a reference work for it. There are even guides to guides, such as Constance M. Winchell's *Guide to Reference Books* and Robert Murphey's *How and Where To Look It Up.*

One of the tribulations of a researcher is that, after he finds the title of an article that is exactly on his subject, he learns that his library does not subscribe to the periodical containing it. To help out in such a predicament, almost all libraries have what is called a union list of periodicals, a book that tells in what libraries your periodical can be found. There is now a union list for microfilms, newspapers, motion-picture films, pamphlets, and even advertising materials. If you happen to be doing your research in a large city, you may be able to go across town and find your article in another library.

DICTIONARIES AND ENCYCLOPEDIAS

You can now move on to the rest of the reference section, notably the dictionaries and encyclopedias. Since you are probably familiar with the second and third editions of Webster's *New International Dictionary,* look for the so-called *OED,* the thirteen-volume *Oxford English Dictionary,* which provides a history of English words introduced since 1150, giving the date each was first used and selective uses since then. Each use is illustrated with a quotation. Look up *bleed, nature, college, uncouth,* and *sanguine* to see how meanings change. Your library may have the two-volume shorter edition.

Your next stop may be in front of the encyclopedias. Take out a volume of the *Encyclopaedia Britannica* and note what edition it is. Note that most articles have a bibliography. Note also that the initials at the end of each article are decoded in a list at the beginning of Volume I, "Initials and Names of Contributors." Your library may have other general encyclopedias such as the *Americana* or *Collier's.* There is an encyclopedia for almost every subject; for example, your library may have:

Cyclopedia of American Agriculture
Consumer Reports Buying Guide
Crowell's Dictionary of Business and Finance
Encyclopedia of Educational Research
Grove's Dictionary of Music and Musicians
Facts on File

A Literary History of England
Literary History of the United States
Encyclopedia of Religion and Ethics
Encyclopedia of the Social Sciences
Dictionary of American History
New Dictionary of American Politics
New Encyclopedia of Sports
The Golden Bough: A Study of Magic and Religion (by Sir James G. Frazer)

Most encyclopedias are dependable, but if you think of them as repositories of absolute fact, you may disabuse yourself by comparing the entries under "Luther, Martin" in the *Catholic Encyclopedia,* the *Universal Jewish Encyclopedia,* and the *Encyclopaedia Britannica.* Also see the entries under "Abelard, Peter" for differences in interests and viewpoint.

HANDBOOKS, ATLASES, GAZETTEERS, BIOGRAPHICAL REFERENCES, AND OTHER TOOLS

By now you are probably mentally saturated, so take time for a cup of coffee, for there are many more important reference publications to become acquainted with. Besides the encyclopedias we have discussed, there is an absolute myriad of works that condense a wealth of specialized information. In fact, there is a condensed reference work about almost every subject you can think of, the following list naming only a few:

American Universities and Colleges
Lovejoy's College Guide
American Library Directory
Oxford Companion to American Literature
Oxford Companion to English Literature
Familiar Quotations (John Bartlett)

A particularly important class of handbook is the *yearbook,* an annual compilation of general and special information. Many encyclopedias are kept up to date with an annual supplement, but the following annual publications provide information that is less fully covered elsewhere:

Famous First Facts (J. N. Kane)
International Motion Picture Almanac
Statistical Abstract of the United States
World Almanac and Book of Facts
University Debaters' Annual

You should look around also for atlases and gazetteers, especially:

University World Atlas
Commercial Atlas and Marketing Guide
Atlas of American History

There are numerous biographical reference works, including:

1. *Dictionary of National Biography.* (Dead British celebrities. Cited as *DNB.*)
2. *Dictionary of American Biography.* (Dead American celebrities. Cited as *DAB.*)
3. *Twentieth Century Authors.*
4. *Webster's Biographical Dictionary.*
5. *Who's Who, 1848——.* (Principally living British celebrities. The space after the dash indicates that the series is continuing to the present; if your library's holdings are incomplete, the actual dates held will be in parentheses.)
6. *Who's Who in America, 1899——.* (Biennial biographies of living Americans. Also regional editions.)
7. *Dictionary of American Scholars.* (Now divided into several fields.)
8. *Who's Who in American Education.*
9. *Biography Index: A Cumulative Index to Biographical Material in Books and Magazines.*
10. *Current Biography: Who's News and Why, 1940——.* (Monthly with cumulative index to previous issues; discusses authors, foreign leaders, scientists, entertainment stars, and others.)

A last form of reference book you should know about and perhaps locate during your trip is a *concordance,* which explains allusions and terms in one particular book. A concordance of the Bible, for instance, lists important words used in it and tells where each word is used and what it means. Concordances have been prepared for the works of most important British authors, including Chaucer, Shakespeare, Milton, and later writers, and for the works of such American writers as Emerson and Poe. Besides using the concordance to locate quotations, you can find where characteristics appear and also find explanations of confusing incidents and allusions.

Projects—Library Usage

Your instructor may assign some of the following projects to individual students who will report on them in class; if appropriate, the instructor may assign certain of these projects for discussion by all members of the class.

1. Indicate the meaning of all the information published on the library cards reproduced in Figures 11-2 and 11-3.

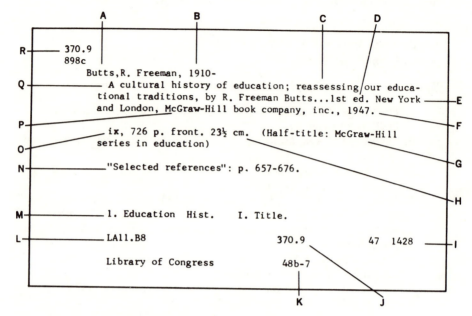

Figure 11–2

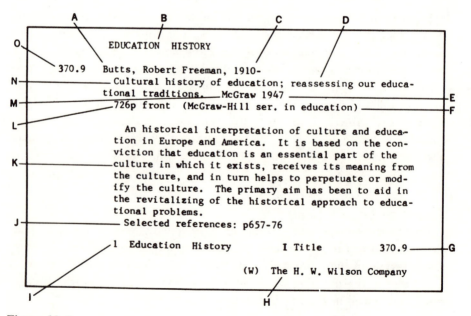

Figure 11–3

2. Your topic is "The Popularity of Charles Augustus Lindbergh." Find five newspaper articles that indicate what the public thought of him after his solo flight to Paris in 1927.

3. Your topic is "The Teaching of Rhetoric in American Colleges, 1850–1900," and you wish to find a summary statement about the effectiveness of instruction in that period. Report what Albert Kitzhaber said about the period in his Ph.D. dissertation, University of Washington, 1953.

4. What part did Pete Martin play in the preparation of Bing Crosby's autobiography, *Call Me Lucky*?

5. What is the home address of the linguist Mario Pei?

6. Is an organ a percussion instrument like the piano, a wind instrument like the flute, or a reed instrument like the clarinet?

7. Where did Arthur Mizener get his Ph.D. and when?

8. Your topic is "The State of the Stock Market Just Before the Crash of 1929." Check to see whether there was much evidence of fraud involving the New York Stock Exchange.

9. In a review of *Go Down, Moses* (New York, 1942), what critic wrote the following? "This is Faulkner at his best and worst—perhaps not quite his worst, for no loonies, degenerates, or gentlemen who fall in love with cows are major characters in these stories."

10. What anthology, published in 1962, contained Mortimer Adler's essay "The Democratic Revolution?"

11. In the late 1930s and early 1940s there was some educational experimentation with a device called a "student interferometer." In what issues of what journal can you find a description of such experiments?

12. Where can you find a reproduction of Andrew Wyeth's "Lobster Pots"?

13. When was Dwight D. Eisenhower first commissioned as an officer?

14. You are writing an article about the part played by Italians during World War II. Where can you find an article, written during the war, about the Italian-American fighter pilot Don Salvatore Gentile?

15. What is the name of the article Malcolm Cowley wrote in 1944 about George Santayana? In what periodical was it published and in what issue?

16. Who invented the first fountain pen and when?

17. What was the name and occupation of the wife of the British economist John Maynard Keynes? What organization did Keynes establish and what building did he build as a result of his interest in her occupation?

18. On March 11, 1954, the Secretary of the Army charged that Senator Joseph R. McCarthy had tried to get "preferred treatment" for an army private who had earlier been the Senator's aide. What was the complete name of the soldier?

19. You have been asked to secure a prominent lumberman to give a

speech and you have been informed that the "CRA" could recommend a speaker for you. What is the full name of the "CRA" and what is its address?

20. The editor of *American Heritage* has regretted that Clarence King is "the least known famous American in the 19th Century." Compare the coverage given King in the *Encyclopaedia Britannica,* the *Encyclopedia Americana,* and the *Columbia Encyclopedia* for completeness, interest, and recency of information.

21. In one of Blackstone's famous legal tomes, there is the sentence "No man should be permitted to stultify himself." What did Blackstone mean?

22. What was the name, author, and publication information of an article written in 1960 defending crying?

23. Some readers of Matthew 3:13-15 wonder why Jesus had to be baptized. He was already pure, they say, and He had no sins to wash away. What explanation can you find?

24. How many Negro men were there in the United States in 1860? How many were slaves? How has the increase in the number of Negroes compared to the increase in the number of Caucasians since 1860?

25. Who is the author of the entry on "Grammar" in the *Encyclopaedia Britannica?*

26. The Lenin State Library is the largest in the U.S.S.R. and probably in the world. How has it come to be so large?

27. Where and when did the first tong war in America take place?

28. What did Edward Everett, the other speaker that day at Gettysburg, think of Lincoln's Gettysburg Address?

29. Have pajamas always been night wear? How was the word originally spelled?

30. In the *Encyclopaedia Britannica* several articles about money are attributed to "N.T.R." What are the name and qualifications of this authority?

31. In *Vanity Fair* (1848) Thackeray writes, "The little woman parried and reposted. . . ." What did Thackeray probably mean? Is the expression a metaphor? How would *reposted* be spelled now?

32. In Matthew 6:25 Christ admonishes his audience, "Be not anxious about your life," which is hard advice to take and difficult to understand. What did Christ mean?

33. When and where was the first church for Indians in New England, and who established it?

34. What was the particular contribution of "Mother Mary" Jones to labor agitation?

35. (A project for all students). Prepare a one-page checklist of information about the reference works in your library: where each kind is (floor

plan), the name of the work, how to use it, and what it contains. Your instructor may wish to see this list.

A College Student Prepares a Library Research Paper

To be able to use a library efficiently requires a great deal of study. Graduate students usually take a course called, say, "Bibliography and Methods," and ten years later admit they are still improving their technique. In the life of a working scholar–researcher, hardly a month goes by without his discovering some new reference facility or technique to make his work more thorough and efficient. Since some college freshmen have already used a library for elementary research, some of the suggestions in this section will be old hat. However, even the most experienced researcher–adventurer can learn something new.

Obviously, there are many ways to prepare a research paper. One hundred scholars have one hundred different techniques. But we believe that the best techniques have a similar origin. A tyro may blunder along and slowly patch a technique together, but it will rarely be a good one. The most efficient researcher can profit by the experiences of those who have preceded him. He will follow almost slavishly the technique devised by first one master researcher and then another. Having experimented with two or three systems, he will then devise his own system. Many learned men began their careers while writing their freshmen research papers; many even kept their notes and began a system of filing information that was to play an important part in their lives.

We suggest, therefore, that you go along with the routines outlined in the next few sections of this textbook. They may be the systems best for you—and you will not know whether to reject them or use them until you have tried them. On your next papers you may try other procedures, and eventually you will develop your own system.

STEP 1. PLANNING

In this project your ally will be the library; your enemy will be the shortage of time. No matter how much time you have, it will not be enough. It will be disastrously short if you do not, at the very beginning, do the planning that will ensure the essential steps. The allocation of time varies with the nature of the project, of course, but a good rule of thumb is that you devote about one-sixth of the time to preliminary steps, one-third to research, one-third to blocking out and writing the first draft, and one-third to revision. Yes, that is more than 100 percent of the time you have been assigned, but we hope you will know about the assignment well in advance and will be able to find an extra weekend. The first step is to sit down and prepare a schedule and resolve to follow it, or you will get no sleep during the last three days of the assignment. The following model schedule is based on an assignment for which students were given three weeks plus a preceding weekend. At the risk of sounding a little too dramatic, we have used the military field order system to accentuate the passage of time.

1. The preliminary weekend: Select subject, preliminary bibliography, do general reading in encyclopedia, prepare a prospectus.
2. First week (research), D-day minus 20–14 days: Do the research— find books, periodicals, and other literature; start note taking; determine issues or topics ("slugs"); begin slug outline; complete note taking.
3. Second week (writing): Complete outline, strengthen weak sections—or eliminate them; write first draft; insert footnotes and rudimentary transitions.
4. Third week (revision), D-day minus 6–1 days: Verify all facts, quotations, and sources; tighten the organization; smooth out the prose; check for grammar, spelling, punctuation, and manuscript conventions. Type. Proofread, proofread, proofread.
5. D-day: Submit paper, making sure that all requirements have been fulfilled.

STEP 2. WORKING OUT THE TOPIC

Selecting your subject may be your simplest problem, if your instructor makes the choice. Very often—perhaps because he knows what subjects are well provided for in your college library, or because he knows from past experience that some subjects yield good research papers and others do not —the instructor will pass out a packet of three-by-five-inch cards, each with a topic on it, and let his students take their pick. There is much to commend in this procedure. The function of the assignment is primarily to teach the student how to use the library and how to do research, and selecting a topic is a skill that is secondary to this assignment. If a student spends two-thirds of his time on false starts, he will fail to accomplish the most important part of the problem.

Ironically, when an instructor selects the topic, unexpected benefits sometimes result. Often a person does not like ripe olives until he forces himself to eat them, and then he loves them. Often an instructor introduces a student to an intellectual discipline that strongly influences him during the rest of his life. Various students of ours, because of research papers we assigned, have entered geology, speech therapy, play production, psychology, primary-school teaching, linguistics, football coaching, Canadian professional football, research in military ordnance, and physical therapy. Others have been converted to Roman Catholicism, to existentialism, to pragmatism, or to the religious position of John Dewey. One person was in a class where the teacher dealt out subjects like a deck of cards. How he groaned when he drew "Notre Dame at Chartres." He wasn't sure whether his subject was a football game or a book by Henry Adams. By the time he finished his study of the famous French cathedral, however, he was fascinated by church architecture. During two trips to Europe, he began a collection of color slides and a library about beautiful churches. Wherever he goes he visits famous churches and takes pictures of them. Thus a lifetime hobby developed from an assigned topic for a freshman research theme.

Suggested Topics

Some instructors, hoping for greater interest and motivation, prefer to leave the responsibility of selecting the subject to the student. A student who is given an utterly free choice will, in general, select his topic from the following groups.

1. Vocations. Subjects related to his prospective major in college or his prospective vocation: the prelaw student may study the contributions of Oliver Wendell Holmes or Sir William Blackstone, for example.

2. Current Affairs. Some students will look about them and see some topic currently of interest, and they may want to know how the present situation came to exist. They may wish to study the roots of materialism, the background of pragmatism, existentialism, the history of bluegrass music, hotrodding, dianetics, cybernetics, cryogenics, or ulcers.

3. My Hometown. Very often students have lived all their lives in one place and yet know very little about it. These students are often eager to fill in the vacuum. Students of ours have written on "the history of the western trail leading to Bozeman, Montana"; "where Odebolt, Iowa, got its name"; "why Jasper and Newton appear so close on so many maps"; "the Chinese names in Illinois (Pekin and Canton)"; "the three Oskaloosas"; and "social structure in Enid, Oklahoma, from 1910–1929."

4. Hobbies. Having dabbled in stamp or coin collecting, jazz or some other pastime, some students decide that since they have to do some kind of research, they might just as well do it in a field in which they have an amateur interest.

5. College Subjects. Often an instructor will encourage students to deepen their perceptions of materials they are currently studying. Students may select concepts (utopianism, states' rights, symbolism, time and motion economy, double-entry bookkeeping), important figures (Iqbal, Sun Yat-sen, John Maynard Keynes, a local politician, Enrico Caruso), a process (fractionation, modern math, silk screening, or dacron manufacturing).

6. Language and Rhetoric. Many instructors prefer to have students select subjects relevant to the study of writing, for instance, famous linguists, logicians, or rhetoricians; aspects of the new linguistics, dialects, slang, jargon; public speaking; topics about mass communication, such as television programming or the power of the press.

The Assumed Audience

Fortunate is the writer who knows his audience. Unless your instructor specifies otherwise, you should assume that your readers will be the entire generally educated community, the people who read, say, *The Atlantic Monthly, Harper's Magazine,* or *Psychology Today.* Some instructors suggest that your class be your audience and that each student defend his topic orally before it. Each student must explain why he thinks the class will find the topic important and interesting. During this report he can get some idea of how informed the class is on his subject; he will thus know how much specialized vocabulary to use and how much development is necessary. As we have mentioned many times, the nature of the audience is one of the strongest generative influences on writing; the writer who is writing for his class can be very exact. He can even read portions of his paper to his classmates to see how he is doing. The questions they ask will provide him with a guide to the topics he should cover in his paper, if he has not already covered them.

Preliminary Bibliography

An essential part of selecting a subject is the preparation of a preliminary bibliography. You cannot write about something if you cannot find any material on it. When you have a subject in mind, go to the library and read about your subject and its related fields in the encyclopedia. You will want to know the history and background of your subjects, and you will want to know something about the key people involved in it. You will want to know the issues that are important in order to begin the process of narrowing from subject to topic. You will also want to know the issues and questions that will help you begin your organization. And finally, you will want to look at the entries in the encyclopedia to get your first bibliographic material.

Go to the card catalog in your library to find whether books are available on your subject. We use the word *available* advisedly. It is not enough to find your library owns the books, for all too often you will find that books you need are out, on interlibrary loan, or at the bindery—and with only a few weeks for your project, you will be stymied. Take out the books you need as soon as you find them; if you wait a day or two, you may find that someone else has them.

The next step is to go to the general index works, especially the *Reader's Guide,* Poole's (if your subject is pre-twentieth century), the *Education Index,* and the general encyclopedia index related to your subject. Check the list of reference works discussed in this textbook and refer to your own college library guide.

Once you have your subject, some idea of the direction you will take, and a bibliography of several books and a number of periodical articles, you can prepare your preliminary prospectus and, if required, submit it to your teacher. This part of your project is extremely important. If you have a false start here, you are in trouble. You will be behind schedule, and your work will suffer. Worse, you may be tempted to take some shortcuts, the worst being "borrowing" of a paper prepared by someone else. Remember the Lord's Prayer not only says, "Deliver us from evil"; it says, "Lead us not into temptation." If your preliminary prospectus is adequate, you will not be tempted.

Narrowing

After you have selected a broad subject, continue to the process of narrowing, which, as Jacques Barzun writes in *The Modern Researcher,* "begins with the first steps of research and ends only when the last word has been rewritten and revised." He defines *topic* as "that group of associated facts and ideas which, when clearly presented in a prescribed amount of space, leave no question unanswered *within the presentation,* even though many questions could be asked outside it."

From the very beginning a researcher should avoid the kind of topic that he can phrase as "I am going to prove that. . . ." This mind-set leads to bad research. The student may slant his work, happily absorbing information that supports his contention and ignoring any that contradicts it. If the student is working on a controversial subject, he may profit from setting up a hypothesis which he plans to prove or disprove. He should not make his decision until he has surveyed all the relevant evidence he can accumulate. Even then he may decide that, at this time and place and considering his own competence, he cannot make a decision. Instead he will elect to present both sides of the question.

STEP 3. NOTE TAKING, PRELIMINARY ORGANIZATION, AND BIBLIOGRAPHY REFINING

The next step requires two simultaneous approaches. Since the accumulation of notes gives you the illusion of real, tangible progress in "doing" research, note taking offers you the temptation to waste your time on interesting but useless information. You must constantly keep in the back of your mind the nagging question: "How will I use this material?" Try to compartmentalize your attention during this part of your research. One part of your mind will keep thinking about the final thesis and the organization of the final paper. At the beginning of your efforts, you will have in mind a statement of purpose: "I am writing a report about cryogenics." As you take notes, you may begin to develop a hypothesis combining cryogenics with some aspect of industry or society; this hypothesis may or may not become part of your final paper. Another part of your mind will focus on the particular source at hand and attempt to identify the essential elements for your thesis. The constant double awareness of the possible implications of what you are discovering will cause you—at first—to take many notes; then, as you come to understand more about your subject matter and about the possible focus for your paper, you will take fewer, but more useful and usable notes.

Note-taking Systems

Almost all college professors recommend that research notes be taken on three-by-five-inch index cards. Almost all college freshmen object that they have notebooks, that notebooks are looseleaf, that they are easy to carry around, and that the pages don't slip away. Okay. We are not going to press the question of cards versus notebooks. *But,* whenever students have stubbornly insisted on using notebooks, despite our urging them to use cards, we have had the almost unanimous response, after the exercise was over, of somewhat embarrassed students coming to us and saying, "Ya know? You were right about those damned cards; I had an awful time finding my notes, especially since I used both sides of the page to save space." I'm afraid we have not resisted the mean impulse of saying, "I told you!" on such occasions. However, if you wish to learn the same lesson the hard way, go right ahead and use a notebook. You might well listen to these few points:

1. Leave a W I D E margin on the left side of the page.
2. Write on *one* side of the page only.
3. Take *only* two or three notes per page. Leave two spaces between notes.
4. Identify *each* note as fully as possible.
5. When you have finished taking all the notes you can conceive of needing, *separate your notes:* take pages from the notebook, cut each note from the page, and group related notes. Now the wide margin on the left permits you to staple or paper clip related notes together and still be able to read them, as in a little book.

(Of course, you *could* buy a twenty-five-cent package of blank index cards and a few rubber bands, and save yourself some extra work.) For cards, the instructions are much simpler:

1. Write on one side of the card only.
2. Write one note per card.
3. Identify the source of the note as fully as you need to.
4. When you have completed your note taking, put the cards into stacks of related material, and place a rubber band around each pile.

Whichever system of note taking you use, be *sure* to include certain elements on *every* note you take:

1. The author, title, and publishing information for every book, article, or essay you are quoting from, either directly or in paraphrase. Make a bibliography card, and you can use a brief reference or abbreviation on your notes.
2. The page or pages, by number, on which the quote appears; the column if the quote is from a newspaper; the date of the quote or some other identification if the source is an unpaged or undivided pamphlet.
3. An indication, for your own use, as to whether the note is a direct quotation or a paraphrase.

The Slug Outline

A helpful technique at this point is the use of the "slug." In the parlance of the researcher, a slug is a temporary heading for a subtopic in the final paper. As a result of your preliminary reading, you begin to think of your topic in sections. Like so many aspects of writing, the topic itself is generative. By its very nature, it suggests certain headings. Almost any topic has certain stock subtopics, such as background, definition of terms, personalities involved, and current, timely developments. Keep your eyes open and notice how many researched articles, especially those in popular magazines, cover these subtopics. As you do your research, the current, timely developments will become evident, and very soon you will have at least a feel for the major organization of your paper. As you take notes, you will begin to classify your cards under these headings.

The Bibliography Card

You will have two kinds of cards, the bibliography card and the note card. Probably, you will keep your bibliographic information on a three-by-five-inch card, and it will exactly duplicate the entry that will eventually appear on the bibliography page of your paper.

You may, with wisdom, decide to keep the call number of the work on the bibliography card, perhaps putting it in the top left corner of the card, as in Figure 11-4. A bibliography card for a book is shown in Figure 11-5, and one for a magazine is shown in Figure 11-6.

901
S413
 Schweitzer, Albert. _The_
  Philosophy of _Civilization_.
 New York: Macmillan.
 1949.

Figure 11–4

 Gilbert, John. _Scientific_
  Experiment. New York:
  Harcourt, Brace, and
  Company. 1963.

Figure 11–5

> Bloom, Terence. "Science
> or Culture?" _Saturday_
> _Review_ LxII (May 31, 1962),
> pp. 27 - 28.

Figure 11–6

You may wish to indicate a "short title" at the top right corner of your bibliography card. This short title may be the author's name or a key word from the title, for instance, either "Adams" or "Education" representing *The Education of Henry Adams,* by Henry Adams. Some students, in their zeal to cut down on motion, number their bibliography cards and use the number in place of a short title; but more often than not the number is forgotten or confused, and the system does not work. Use the short title during your note taking. Instead of laboriously writing out the complete bibliographic information to indicate the source of each note, use just the short title, thus, "Adams, p. 311."

The Note Card

Basically, your note cards will contain three bits of information: (1) the source of the note, condensed to short title and page number, (2) a hint as to the section in which the information will be used, condensed to a slug, (3) and the information itself. Any direct quotation will be in quotation marks. All other information will be assumed to be a paraphrase. Some researchers put their paraphrases and editorial insertions in brackets or double parentheses to be sure to avoid accidental plagiarism.

Bibliography Refining

Besides adding to your bibliography, you should refine it by *evaluation.* Primary laboratory or field research is checked by caution and replication;

that is, the experiments are repeated under controlled conditions to corroborate all findings. Secondary research is corroborated by checking with other authorities and by checking on the authorities themselves. If a number of authorities agree, you can have some faith that they are right, but even when agreement exists, and always when you are depending on one authority, check your references. There are several ways of evaluating authorities:

1. Check to see which authorities are listed in encyclopedias. Reputable encyclopedias list in their bibliographies the best and definitive sources for each subject. A definitive work is one that is generally accepted by authorities, because it is complete, dependable, and recent and thus assumed to make use of the best of all preceding studies.

2. Check to see how many other books refer to an authority. If a book listed in the card catalog has a bibliography, the fact will be given on the card. Take the book out and check quickly to see which authors the author of that book has depended on. Often the bibliography will be annotated; that is, the author of the book will comment on the contents, dependability, and shortcomings of each entry in his bibliography.

3. Until now your evaluation of your authorities has been rather tenuous. Your hypothesis is that the author of an encyclopedia entry or of a book respected the sources he listed or he would not have included them. For greater confidence, check to see if the books you are using have been reviewed by competent authorities. If you are writing about Ernest Hemingway, for instance, and have come across *Hemingway* by Phil Young, you can look in the *Book Review Digest* to see what competent critics thought of Young's book. Most scholarly journals have a number of reviews in each edition, and the reviews are indexed yearly. Thus if the book you are concerned about is literary criticism, you can probably examine the reviews in *College English* or find a review listed in the bibliography issue of *The Publication of the Modern Language Association* (*PMLA*).

4. You can also evaluate an authority by reviewing his background yourself. By looking in the appropriate volume of *Who's Who* or the *Directory of American Scholars*, you can find his education, his training, and his experience. If your authority is listed in *Twentieth Century Authors*, you can find personal details about the author there.

You will be forced to make judgments about the value and objectivity of your authorities. A free-lance writer who contributes "medical" articles to a popular magazine may or may not be dependable; the late Dr. Paul Dudley White writing on heart disease in the *Journal of the American Medical Association* would obviously be more so. The fact that your author possesses a Ph.D. means little in itself, for he may be competent in Greek literature, but not necessarily so in international affairs. If you are reading an article by him on the political vicissitudes of the United Arab Republic, evaluate it not by his reputation but by the force of his logic, the worth of his evidence, and the dependability and value of his sources.

Do not accept statistics uncritically. Check the qualifications of the compiler, but more importantly, check the meaning of his statistics. Statistics about the crime rate, for example, can be almost meaningless. Compilers classify crime into various categories like major and minor crimes, and almost every year the definitions change. In one year a fifty-dollar robbery might be considered a minor crime, but in the next year, if the robber is carrying a gun—whether or not he uses it—the crime might be recorded as major. Then, too, crime rates are based on reported crimes. Only in very recent years have adequate reporting systems been developed, and even now many villages and rural areas do not use them. A sound researcher learns to determine how statistics were compiled, whether they are estimates, like future wheat yield, petroleum under the surface, and enemy armament, and whether they are sound. For instance, the small country of Kuwait has the highest per capita income in the Middle and Far East, but if you take away the income of a few families, the ones who own all the oil, the per capita income is among the lowest in the world.

When you finish step three (note taking, preliminary organization, and bibliography refining), you will have several piles of note cards, each headed by a slug that indicates approximately where the pile will be used in your paper.

At this point the process of synthesis takes place.

Earlier in this text we discussed the process of division, the process of breaking down the information and message that you propose to convey. This division was the basis of the structure of a paper. Now the reverse takes place. You will need to look at all the material you have accumulated and let it tell you what it says.

STEP 4. SYNTHESIS

In Chapter 6 we discussed putting your article together to form a unified whole. The following are examples of how synthesis took place during some student research papers.

Case History 1: "The Student Who Liked to Ride on Trains"

A student was asked to write a paper in which he was permitted to take any approach and use any tone, but he had to write on the merits of any one system of transportation. Since travel by air is modern and popular, the student began to do research on its advantages. He read about the speed, efficiency, and luxury of this form of travel, and he accumulated statistics about how air travel has boomed in the last three decades. The more he read, the less enthusiastic he became. He decided that he just was not personally enthusiastic about air travel, and he could not sincerely defend it. He preferred to travel by rail. He knew he would have a difficult time writing a convincing paper about the advantages of rail travel, but he decided that he would try. He felt that his honesty and sincerity might make up for the fact that his paper would oppose a majority viewpoint. As he began to plan his paper, he realized that he really did not know why he preferred the railroad. He thought for a while and decided that, if he was to be honest, he must confess that he preferred surface transportation because he was afraid to fly. He also realized that at this stage of his life he really did not care much whether a trip took four hours or twenty. What he did not like was all the trouble and expense of getting out to an airport, standing in line to select seats, gambling on the weather, and then, at the end of his flight, having to spend two more hours getting to his actual destination. If anything, instead of streaking through the air on a trip, he preferred each journey to be a "between-two-worlds" experience, a break in which he could talk to people, relax a bit, and enjoy doing nothing. He saw that his preference was made up of personal inclinations, and he doubted whether he could persuade anyone to accept his viewpoint. He came across a poem by Ogden Nash and an essay by E. B. White and learned that they too liked to travel by train, and he decided that his approach would be to write a personal essay about his own preference, the tone of which would be whimsical. He would jest at those hurried people who rush from airport to airport; he would ruefully admit to being a coward; he would show how rail travel gave him a chance to rest. In short, he would admit that he just felt a great deal more comfortable traveling by railroad.

Case History 2: "What Was Naturalism?"

A student who was taking a writing course for which the textbook was an anthology of selections by Thomas Malthus, Charles Lyell, Karl Marx, Herbert Spencer, Thomas Huxley, Hippolyte Taine, Emile Zola, Arthur Schopenhauer, Herman Melville, Hamlin Garland, Stephen Crane, Jack London, Frank Norris, and Theodore Dreiser was asked to write a paper explaining the philosophy uniting these writers. The instructor explained that these writers had a common philosophy that has come to be called naturalism. The student was not even sure what a "philosophy" was, but some inquiries to his instructor and a session with an encyclopedia informed him that a systematic philosophy tends to be based on notions about the nature of God, man, society, and the relationship among them. The student began to reread his anthology to secure an idea of how these authors viewed God, man, and society. He noticed that the writers varied widely in their views about the exact nature of God: Marx seemed to be an atheist and Huxley an agnostic; Spencer seemed to be a determinist, believing that God wound up the universe and let it go in directions that He was able to predict. All the writers agreed that God does not interfere in the day-to-day activities of man. They seemed to agree also that there are no events that take place in an inexplicable fashion, no miracles, no random developments. History is, for these writers, the result that can be expected from the laws of physical science and the laws, both legal and psychological, of man's institutions and innate nature. With these perceptions the student put together an extended definition of naturalism.

Case History 3: "The Manufacture of Penicillin"

In a science class a student was required to write a term paper on penicillin. This was strictly a research project; the student did not have a clue as to what he would write. He went through the appropriate steps to get a bibliography, and he began to read and take notes. He put his note cards into four piles that formed naturally because these were the directions taken by his sources: the chemical nature of penicillin, its properties, the story of its discovery, and its manufacture in large quantities for marketing. As the piles grew, he realized he must limit his subject; he rejected the first two piles because the structure and properties of the compound were rather more technical than he felt he could handle and because these two subjects were mechanical and routine. He could not see anything that he could contribute to them that would demonstrate any originality on his part. He rejected the third pile because the story of the discovery of penicillin has been told so many times in popular magazines. He preferred the fourth pile, about manufacturing procedures, because it was timely: pharmaceutical companies were still trying to refine their techniques. He examined the notes in the appropriate pile, and he shuffled them into new piles based on the headings: (a) the preparation of materials, (b) the process of manufacturing, and (c) the control of quality.

He now began to put the parts together, deciding that the obvious order would be sequential. He would write a report describing step-by-step the process of manufacturing penicillin. He wrote a rough draft and was dissatisfied with its lack of freshness. As he read over his paper, he decided that what really interested him was the care taken to ensure quality. His research told him that the dependability of penicillin depends on a meticulous selection of materials and a careful process of manufacture. Curious as to how this state of dependability developed, he decided that the story he wished to tell was that the integrity of the pharmaceutical industry.

working within the regulations based on the Pure Food and Drug Act, was the cause of this success. He now saw that a step-by-step description was not necessarily appropriate. He decided to describe the manufacturing process and then work backward to show how and why the procedure was developed. The student felt that now his thesis was rather significant; he was using the manufacture of penicillin to illustrate how industry, science, and government can work together for the common good.

These three case histories demonstrate how a writer can arrive at the central idea of a paper. By going over their experiences and the results of their research, the writers put together ideas that were new to them. They hurried the creative process by phrasing appropriate questions.

The process of synthesis illustrated by these three examples varies about as much as other examples of synthesis would vary. On some occasions almost no systematic, recordable synthesis would precede the writing of a paper. A free-lance writer might be commissioned by the editor of a semi-technical magazine to write an article about a new use of a laser. The editor might say frankly, "I'm not asking you to do anything creative. All I want is a straight, factual report." On another occasion the same writer might be asked to do an in-depth study of a new political luminary in the state of Oregon. "See what this guy has to offer," the editor might say. After a great deal of study and thought, the writer would come to a conclusion.

Synthesis, which classical writers called invention, can be thought of as the process *before* organization. When the writer begins to organize his paper, he is obviously influenced by the mental activity that caused him to believe in his own thesis. However, in none of the illustrations of synthesis would the writers cause the reader to follow the paths they took to reach their own conclusions. Each would look at his task and say, "Now what must I do to help my reader understand or accept my thesis?" Once the writer begins to organize, synthesis becomes part of the influential past. In organizing, he begins to seek a method of taking an idea apart in order to see how best to present it effectively to his audience.

STEP 5. REVISION
The processes of revision that are characteristic only of a research paper and are therefore not discussed in Chapter 10 are related to verification and to manuscript techniques. Jacques Barzun has estimated that 10 percent of all quotations in published works contain errors. In each new draft check your quotations and statistics against your verified notes or against the original source. Watch numbers and publication dates in particular. Every time

you verify a reference, put a small check mark in the margin to show what you have confirmed and what you have not. Check and recheck each and every footnote. (A suggested form for footnotes is given in Chapter 12.) Each capital letter, period, comma, quotation mark, abbreviation, and underlining must be exactly right. When you proofread, read the capitals and punctuation out loud, preferably to another person who is looking at the verified draft. By now you probably have several dozen hours invested in the paper, and it is simply foolhardy to skip this last-minute check, perhaps to lose full credit for careful, thorough research because of careless presentation. If a typist has done the final draft for you, assume that she knows nothing about manuscript form, typing, or your subject and check every mark on the paper.

STEP 6. THE FINISHED PRODUCT

Your instructor is not concerned only with the quality of the paper; he is also interested in knowing you accomplished every step of the research and writing process. Unless he specified otherwise, make sure you have all of the following items ready to submit:

1. Planning prospectus. (Schedule of personal deadlines, preliminary bibliography, preliminary estimate of questions to be researched.)
2. Packet of bibliography cards in alphabetical order. (Some of the cards will be for sources you checked but did not use. They will not be listed on your bibliography page.)
3. Note cards, one pile sorted under slugs used as subtopic headings, and another pile containing notes you did not use.
4. Rough or first draft. (Your instructor may require you also to submit the fair copy used by your typist.)
5. The final manuscript.

All cards should be right side up and secured with rubber bands. The rough draft should be paper-clipped together, as should the final draft. Never staple a manuscript.

Project—Research Paper

One of the problems in a fast-paced college course is that the student rarely gets the opportunity to repeat an exercise. Since a research paper takes so much time, too often a student tries hard but makes a number of mistakes—and has no chance to profit by what he has learned. We hope that in your perusal of the following student paper, you will see the deficiencies that creep into a research paper. The paper is a good one, but there is room for improvement. What suggestions would you make? What are the strengths of the paper? You can use the materials in the next chapter to check the manuscript form. You may find it helpful before you critique the paper to check the assignment to see just what the student was expected to accomplish:

Research Paper Assignment: "Since the Day of My Birth": This assignment has two functions. First, it introduces you to the realm of primary and secondary research and provides you with practice in synthesizing your research results into a thoughtful, creative paper and in presenting these results in a paper that follows conventional manuscript techniques, including footnotes and bibliographic entries.

Second, it requires you to make a judgment of whether history is progress or merely change. This aspect of the assignment is important, since it requires you to look at what you have found, consider it carefully, establish some criteria for your judgment, and then explain whether you are discussing progress or the lack of it. For instance if you decide to discuss medical care in your hometown, you will conclude by stating whether care has improved or regressed—but you must be very careful to show just what your basis for judgment is. Are you speaking of general availability, cost, completeness, effectiveness, or what? Thus this paper is not a "report," or a copying down and transmitting of raw material; it is original and creative. It is about *you*, because while writing the paper, you will formulate and expose your own judgments and values.

To begin to find the proper perspective, your first task will be to prepare a newscast which might have been given on the day you were born. Whether your research paper topic is national or international, or about sports or something more limited, you will limit your newscast. For instance, if you are going to be writing about fashions or business, you can limit the newscast accordingly. If you are going to discuss meteorology, you might give a weather forecast.

The period you are evaluating begins, approximately, with the day you were born; you may change the year somewhat but not before the year of your birth. The reason for this limitation is to make it clear that you are encouraged to do both library research from secondary sources and original research from your own memory, interviews with your parents and friends, and contemporary newspapers and magazines.

The final paper should be something like 1200–2500 words in length. You must follow the form book provided in the textbook. On the due date, you are required to submit a packet (in a large envelope) containing your rough draft, notes and final draft, complete with title page, text, notes, and bibliography page. In a paper this short, a table of contents is not recommended.

ROCK AND ROLL—1953-1973
FROM MONEY TO MEANING, AND THE WAILERS
BECOME ARTISTS

Nanette Lambert
Section R—Composition IA
April 16, 19 _ _

INTRODUCTION

Early in the '50's and even through the '60's, rock and roll was not considered music. It was loud noise, trash adolescents listened to. The stars were considered by many as fortune hunters milking youth of all their money and poisoning their time with records of nonsense and of little, if any value. The lyrics were meaningless and most often the music itself was tied together by scores of la la la's and doo da da's.

Since that time, rock has matured and developed into a valid addition and asset to the music world. The lyrics are now of social meaning and many of them are beautiful poetry with social and/or personal significance. The music is more intricate and complex with a use of various instruments and orchestral arrangements. The stars, though, still of fame and fortune, are artists having some guilt feelings of regret, sometimes for their excessive wealth. Yet they maintain elements of humanism such as love and understanding that heightens their consciousness above materialistic money concepts to living in a real world of emotion and experiences.

Rock and roll began in the '50's as a combination of rhythm and blues, country and western, folk and jazz.[1] Though influenced by these different types, or feelings of music, it lacked substance or any real heart. It was something youth could jive and dance to by jumping up and down, clapping their hands. But it was a new concept of dance, for the couple were far apart from one another which was something parents couldn't understand. Aside from the music, the lyrics had little meaning or depth.

". . . Up stepped a man
With a big cigar
He said, 'C'mere cat
I'm gonna make you a star'
So I picked my guitar
With a great big grin
And the money just kept pourin' in. . . ."[2]
　　　From 1959 hit song, "The All
　　　American Boy"

During the 50's, Elvis Presley was rock and roll's chief evangelist.[3] Presley's discoverer, Sam Phillips said Elvis sang Negro rhyths with a white voice, borrowing mood and emphasis by popular music.[4]

But during the time, rock was not considered music, and so many people were inclined to disagree with Phillips. One in particular was Jack Gould, a television critic for the New York Times, who attacked "The Pelvis" as a likely assignment for a sociologist and stated,

> "Presley has no discernible singing ability.
> His specialty is rhythm songs that he
> renders in an undistinctive whine. . . ."[5]

Gould expressed the opinion of the older generation with love manifested in Glenn Miller, Tommy Dorsey, Chopin and Bach.

In spite of the opposition, Elvis, for his time, was a different kind of idol, almost godlike.[6] Screaming, and pulling out their hair for a glimpse of him, young girls would get excited when he sang, "I Want You, I Need You" (Ah Wa-ha-hunt Yew-who Ah Ne- he-heed Yew -who).[7]

The craze of the age was to be close to the idol. There were contests in magazines, and prizes from Dick Clark's television show, "American Bandstand," to win a lock of Elvis' treasured hair, or from his trimmed sideburns. Lettered skirts were made with his name on them. Boys got their hair cut in the duck-tail style like Elvis.[3]

There were others at the time, trying to meet Elvis' fortune by creating their own through mimicry or competition. The closest facsimile of Elvis was Gene Vincent who recorded Be-Bop-A-Lula. And his strongest rival was Carl Perkins who recorded Blue Suede Shoes.[9]

During the early '60's, rock still rolled, but the stars were practically picked out of a hat. The most least likely to succeed did succeed in the world of rock music. Little Eva was a one time babysitter of Carole King and Gerald Goffin. While they were at the piano one fine morning trying to write a song, Eva told them it sounded like a locomotive and proceeded to imitate a train with her voice. King and Goffin thought she was great, got her on a record, and her single of the Loco Motion sold more than one million copies.

Chubby Checker, inventor of the dance, the Twist, once

plucked chickens in a poultry market. And Dion (Runaround Sue) was a door-to-door magazine salesman. Little Peggy March (I Will Follow Him) had training in a church choir which is more singing than a lot of other stars of the time probably ever did, even in the bath tub. Other top names and big hits of the early sixties were Allan Sherman (Hellow Muddah, Hellow Faddah), Peter Paul and Mary (Blowin' in the Wind), Stevie Wonder (Fingertips), and Surfaris (Wipe Out-the beginning of the surfing sound inspired by the California surfing craze). During the early 60's were quite a number of white all girl groups who tried to sound like Negroes. such as The Angels (My Boyfriend's Back), the Sirelles, Cookies, Crystals, Chiffons.

Lesley Gore (Judy's Turn To Cry) had in the 60's what is known as 'the dumb sound', that is having the adolescent identity with the record because it sounded like himself.[11] Many of Lesley Gore's songs were girl-gets-boy, girl-loses-boy, and she either pities herself or takes revenge.

The Beach Boys (Surfin' U.S.A.) were made stars in eighteen hours from the time they were discovered and taken to the studio, their record was an instant hit.

As the records climbed to the top of the chart, so did the star's ego. And usually, the ego didn't stay inflated very long, for a singer usually never lasted more than three years. In the pop record business, it seemed not everyone lived happily ever after. Some went bankrupt, some could never cope with the fall, and others tried desperately to get back on the top, but never made it.

Yet though this seemed to be true in most cases, one performer still fascinated the whole country, Elvis Presley. He seemed to have overcome obstacles of declination and was truly a phenomena.[12]

A new group emerged from England that set a whole new light in the field of rock music in 1963. The Beatles sold 2.5 million records of their own compositions (She Loves You, Love Me Do, Please Please Me). A new phenomena had been born that made Elvis seem more understandable, for it was happening a second time. Girls again would scream their hearts out and the same contests were run in all major teen magazines.

The Beatles worked their way up from sleazy clubs on the Liverpool waterfront where they originated, and made their

big break when they played a strip joint in Hamburg, Germany
where they were to present "The Liverpool Sound" also known
as the "Mersey Sound."

Many adults still thought of rock music as garbage, and the
Beatles were considered the eiptome of the trash pile. The
critics found their music 'high pitched, loud beyond reason, and stupefyingly repetitive.' Of their stage presence,
many adults said they 'prance skip, turn in circles, and are
even known to kiss their guitars!13

But the Beatles were the businessmen's singular delight,
and if they were strange because of their long hair and tight
fitting pants, it really didn't matter, for they were laugh-
ing all the way to the bank. Their American tour grossed
$1,000,000 and their first movie, "A Hard Day's Night," in
sex weeks made $5,800,000. By 1964, the Beatles received a
third gold disc (each one designating 1,000,000 sales for a
single release) surpassing Elvis' two.

As the Beatles fame grew, so did their talent, and they
were recognized as artists even by people who at one time
opposed them. Their lyrics developed from games,

"Oh yeah, I'll tell you something
I think you'll understand.
When I say that something,
I want to hold your hand . . ."
I Want To Hold Your Hand

to intensity and spiritualism,

"We were talking—about the love we all
could share- when we find it
To try our best to hold it there.
With our love- we could save the world
If they only knew.
Try to realize it's all within yourself
No one else can make you change.
And to see you're really only very small,
and life flows on within you and without you."
Within You, Without You

to drug experiences,

"Picture yourself in a boat on a river,
With tangerine trees and marmalade
skies

Somebody calls you, you answer quite slowly,
A girl with kaleidoscope eyes . . ."
    Lucy In the Sky With Diamonds

to societal and world matters.
"I don't know why
Nobody told you how to unfold your love
I don't know how
Someone controlled you
They bought and sold you . . ."
    While My Guitar Gently Weeps

Many critics are inclined to agree that the Beatles helped to introduce new instruments in the field of rock music such as the sitar, organ, and the use of a back up orchestra as used in "The Who"'s rock opera, "Tommy." Electronic music carried the expansion of rock music one step further. Electronic music was established as a legitimate and powerful development of western musical tradition. It greatly extended the sound resources available to composers and provided new means to organize these sounds into music. The tape recorder, oscillator, filter, contact microphone, computer and most popular, the moog syntesizer, became familiar in all areas of music, not only rock and roll.[15]

Also, by the late 1960's, many groups were influenced by the drug culture and the Haight Ashbury hippie cult in San Francisco. From this period, the San Francisco sound was born by groups such as the "Grateful Dead" and the "Jefferson Airplane."

One pill makes you larger,
And one pill makes you small,
And the one that Mother gives you
Don't do anything at all
Go ask Alice,
When she's ten feet tall . . ."
    White Rabbit

Youth along with rock music became neither silent nor invisible assuming the responsibility of tomorrow. Music and songs were/are youth's tools and means of expression. The young wrote/write about what they know, what they sense.[26]

Some artists of the time, John Lennon, John Sebastian, Paul Simon, and Janis Ian were/are all performers, troubadours, whose poetry was/is to be sung rather than read, whose work reflects popular speech and its rhythms.

Paul Simon's Sounds of Silence;
"Hello darkness my old friend
I've come to talk to you again.
Because a vision softly creeping
Left its seeds while I was sleeping
And the vision that was planted in my brain
Still remains
Within the sound of silence . . ."

Paul Simon (of Simon and Garfunkel) was said by one observer to be a cross between romance and realism grown out of the crush of city life. Simon, of his work says, "Elvis influenced me to play guitar, the Everly Brothers influenced our singing and Bob Dylan. . . . Later these things merge with your personality."[17]

The songs are of subject matter from sex to war to pleasure and the hypocricy of relationships.

"The goal is communication." says Janis Ian.[18]
". . . . . They called you boy
Instead of your name.
When she wouldn't let you inside,
When she turned and said, 'But honey,
He's not your kind.'
She said, I can't see you anymore . . ."
          Society's Child

Though rock and roll is a musical expression provoking the most violent conflict among adults generally and music educators in particular, it is communication, if only between the members of the younger generation. As Superintendent William Cornog of Winnetka, Illinois stated at the symposium (Tanglewood Symposium, conference on music),

"If you want to know what youth are thinking
and feeling today, you cannot find anyone who
speaks for them or to them more clearly than
the Beatles and you should listen closely to
the Rolling Stones Mammas and Papas, Jefferson
Airplane, Simon and Garfunkel and the Grateful
Dead."[19]

There were others that didn't catch the message. McLendon Corp. radio station chain in '67 wanted to convince the boss, Dallas based Gordon B. McLendon, to launch a morality campaign against "dirty lyrics" in pop music. Songs attacked were ; "Let's Spend the Night Together" by the Rolling Stones, "Penny Lane" by the Beatles for its earthiness, "Candy Man" by the Nitty Gritty Dirt Band for it's reference to God, and "Sock It To Me Baby" by Mitch Ryder and the Detroit Wheels. Luckily, the campaign didn't get very far or last very long.[20]

Yet there was dissatisfaction within the rock music field for on June 27, 1971, The Fillmore East and The Fillmore West closed down because of the "unreasonable and totally destructive inflation of the live concert scene.' These were centers like music halls, rock festivals or havens themselves, where rock artists performed their shows. In the earlier days, a sense of community and integrity was more apparent. Toward the end, there had been much packaging by booking agents.

Cornyn, Vice President of Warner Bros. Records, said, "If there is one message the Rock Generation wants us to hear it's this, 'Be a civilized man—a thinking, feeling, moral human being."[21]

Even though rock artists sometimes get caught up in their money, they are artists trying to run, escape, or hide away from the pressures of fame and the plasticity of society, valuing the deep rooted elements as opposed to surface materialism. In other words, they fight against this conformity, this mold society shapes them to become, sometimes and most often in their music, as Joni Michell did in "For Free."

". . . Now me, I play for fortune
And those velvet curtain calls.
I got a black limosine and two gentlemen
Escorting me to the halls.
And I'll play if you have the money,
Or if your a friend to me
But the one man band by the quick lunch stand
He was playing real good, for free. . . .
. . . . . . I meant to go over, and sing out a song
Maybe put on a harmony

I heard his refrain as the signal changed
He was playing real good, for free. ."

Having turned itself away from being a quick million single
to be played at pajama parties, rock has matured to a point
of sophistication and social awareness. This attitude is
expressed by the Bengla Desh Concert held at Madison Square
Garden in August 1971 presented by George Harrison, Bob
Dylan, Ringo Starr, Eric Clapton, Leon Russell and Ravi
Shankar which raised $250,000 for East Pakistani refugees
with money to be distributed by UNICEF.[22]

At the same time, a rage of street freaks or "buskers" as
they preferred to be called, formed bands consisting of
flute players and violinists playing in the streets of San
Francisco, performed their gigs more for love than money.
These musicians, earning usually less than $100 a week,
played pieces from Bach to the Beatles.[23]

The spirit still lives on. Go to the Boston [Public] Garden
on a warm, sunny day and see guitar players and singers en-
tertain for you, helping you to feel the nice day, helping
you to know the world you live in. All for free just because
you're alive too and we're all here together.

In the 1950's, rock music was new, underdeveloped, and a
money game. By 1973, rock has developed itself and grown
into an art. The singers are the composers, valuing life
for it's goodness, or it's simplicity, and have removed
themselves from materialistic concepts such as fame and
money filled with fortune. Going from a state of nonsense
into a work of art is definitely a case of progress.

Progress, itself is an art, that which entails becoming
more enriching and of usefulness, both entertaining and intellectually valuable. Paul Williams, (contemporary com-
poser) stated a case for rock as an art form with a history,
a future, and more important, a meaningful substance.[24]

The music itself is more stimulating with added instruments, orchestras and complex arrangements. The lyrics of
songs have gone from Be- Bop-a-lula and itsy bitsy teenie
weenie yellow polka dot bikini to Led Zepplen's Stairway
to Heaven;

"There's a feeling I get when I look
To the West.
And my spirit is crying for leaving.

In my thoughts I have seen rings of smoke
Through the trees.
And the voice of those who stand looking. . . .
And it's whispered that soon if we all
Call the tune.
Then the piper will lead us to reason.
And a new day will dawn for those
Who stand long.
And the forests will echo with laughter. . ."

It may be a matter of taste, but judging any art form or other abstraction tends to be an opinion. Yet, I believe I've shown enough examples and displayed a criteria that after reading, most anyone would agree rock music has progressed in the last twenty years and has definitely become a form of art.

FOOTNOTES

[1]Murphy, Music in American Society (Music Educators, 1968), p. 18.
[2]Alan Levy, Operation Elvis (New York: Henry Holt and Co., 1958), p. 25.
[3]Murphy, op. cit., p. 19.
[4]Levy, op. cit., p. 6.
[5]Ibid., p. 5.
[6]"Elvis—A Different King of Idol," Life (August 27, 1956), p. 101.
[7]Ibid., p. 102.
[8]Ibid., p. 103.
[9]Ibid., p. 105.
[10]Saturday Evening Post (October 5, 1963), p. 91.
[11]Ibid., p. 92.
[12]Ibid., p. 94.
[13]"Beatlemania," Newsweek (November 18, 1963), p. 104.
[14]"Businessman's Delight—the Beatles," Time (October 2, 1964), p. 112.
[15]"Electronic Music—Wiggy," Newsweek (May 22, 1967), p. 98.
[16]"Of Times that are Changing," Saturday Review (August 26, 1967), p. 76.
[17]New Yorker (September 2, 1967), p. 26.
[18]Saturday Review (August 26, 1967), op. cit., p. 77.
[19]Murphy, op. cit., p. 19.
[20]"Purge," Newsweek (May 8, 1967), p. 114.
[21]"The Future After the Fillmore," Saturday Review (May 29, 1971), p. 56.

[22]"Bengla Desh Concert" Newsweek (August 16, 1971), p. 46.
[23]Ibid., p. 48.
[24]Murphy, op. cit., p. 18.

BIBLIOGRAPHY

1. Levy, Alan Operation Elvis (New York: Henry Holt and Co. 1958), pp. 5, 6, 25.
2. Life (August 27, 1956), 101-105.
3. Murphy, Music in American Society (Music Educators, 1968), pp. 18-19.
4. Newsweek (November 18, 1963), p. 104.
5. Newsweek (May 22, 1967), p. 98.
6. Newsweek (August 16, 1971), pp. 46-48.
7. New Yorker (September 2, 1967), p. 26.
8. Saturday Evening Post (October 5, 1963), pp. 91-94.
9. Saturday Review (August 26, 1967), pp. 76-77.
10. Saturday Review (May 29, 1971), p. 56.
11. Time (October 2, 1964), p. 112.

Chapter 12 Manuscript Conventions

Only those who have the patience to do simple things perfectly will acquire the skill to do difficult things easily.—*Johann Christoph Friedrich von Schiller*

Human beings are so different in their natures that, inevitably, their activities are different. If a society is to succeed, it must often standardize group activity. When the wheel was invented, each man made his own wheels to fit the cart he constructed for himself. Several thousand years later, wheels came to be made by mass production, and a carriage maker in Springfield, Massachusetts, could make wheels for a wagon in Harp, Kansas. The wheel, at that time, had to fit only reasonably well; if it did not, the blacksmith could warp it to fit. After the invention of the automobile, labor costs and the speeds the vehicle was capable of demanded accuracies within a thousandth of an inch.

The population explosion has been accompanied by a knowledge explosion and a communications explosion that have made standardized presentation essential. Laws must be written in a special jargon; it is not enough for a law to order someone to "stop" doing something, because he could stop, thus complying with the law, and then start again. The law must say "cease and desist" to mean "stop and don't start again." A study of linguistics shows us that language is in part an attempt by society to standardize communication so it will be effective. Another aspect of communication that has been influenced by the need to standardize is manuscript form. When a military field order goes from headquarters to a regiment, there cannot be any possibility of misinterpretation. The field order therefore conforms with absolute rigidity to a prescribed form. A doctor's prescription, as illegibile as it seems to the layman, follows a form about which the pharmacist can make no mistake. The list of prescribed forms is endless, order blanks, routing memos, maintenance records, inspection charges, and applications for government grants being only a few.

Today almost every person needs to master manuscript techniques. Not everyone, of course, is a publishing scholar, but almost every college student is required to prepare various kinds of term papers for which footnotes and bibliographies are necessary. Even if he does not do research himself, almost every educated person today reads textbooks, technical manuals, scholarly periodicals, and other publications for which an understanding of the symbols and formats is necessary. Most important, everyone can profit from learning how to work with the ideas of other people, from being able to evaluate and coordinate the thoughts of others, and from the training in honesty and responsibility inherent in the proper use of manuscript techniques.

Plagiarism

There comes a time when plagiarism must be discussed. Almost all college students realize that, like other forms of property, ideas and expressions can be owned; to take them without authorization is, of course, to steal. But there is an indistinct line of demarcation. Taking an orange from a fruit stand is theft. That is clear enough. But if we *paraphrase* an idea we know to be commonly held, is that plagiarism?

It has been said that a college education is the only thing in the world that a person will pay for and then try not to get. There are some students who will submit a paper written for an assignment in another year, for another class, or another college. Setting aside the consideration of simple honesty, which is important in and of itself, such a practice defeats the whole purpose of a research assignment. The student is paying money and investing time to learn a skill; if he takes another student's paper, he is being more than dishonest; he is being stupid. Fortunately, such plagiarism is easy to avoid; the intelligent, honest student would never use an assignment prepared by another student.

Less obvious than "borrowing" another student's work, and more difficult to avoid, is a more complex kind of plagiarism: taking material without proper credit or authorization from published materials. Plagiarism is briefly defined by the *American College Dictionary* as "copying or imitating the language, ideas, and thoughts of another author and passing off the same as one's original work." Some colleges, in order to avoid any misunderstanding, say that any instance of a student's using five or more successive words in the same way as his source is beyond the probability of chance, and such sections should be put in quotation marks. If the student paraphrases some writing, that is, if he expresses another's thoughts in his own words, he is still using the author's ideas, and he should make an appropriate acknowledgment. Certain factual information is considered to be in the public domain and does not have to be credited: birth and death dates of well-known figures; dates of military, political, literary, and other historical events; and statistics about population, national economy, and agricultural productivity. You can safely assume that any factual information found in a standard reference book is part of the public domain, but if you quote it in the exact words of the source, you must acknowledge your source. As a rule, the speeches of important public figures tend to be treated as public papers, and no source need be cited (although the speaker and date should be given). All illustrations, charts, and tables must be credited.

Guiding Principles

Acknowledgments, which are made either in the text or in footnotes, are governed by two principles. The first one, as expressed in the *MLA Style Sheet,* is: "Perhaps the only unchangeable rule is that authors must be consistent in their own practice." The second principle is pragmatic: footnotes and acknowledgments must accomplish their specific purpose. For that reason, we must understand what footnotes are supposed to accomplish.

Some footnotes are for a purpose other than acknowledgment. In times past, when printing costs for changing from one type font to another were less, and when readers could be more leisurely, footnotes were used to define terms and advance other explanations. Such information giving is now usually held to a minimum, the necessary explanations being included in the regular text. In textbooks and technical periodicals, footnotes are used to show that the author has, for instance, surveyed all relevant or contradictory information on his subject and has deliberately decided not to discuss some of it in his article. Some textbooks use footnotes to suggest further reading material for the audience.

In a college paper, however, there are often two reasons for any kind of notation, whether it be in the text or in a footnote. A writer, in an argumentative paper, may want to impress his reader with the weight of an authority or with statistics. In this respect, a footnote may make evidence psychologically more impressive. The second reason for the notation is simply to fulfill the requirements of honesty and law, to give credit where credit is due. In this case the notation can often be accomplished in the text itself. A name can be mentioned or a book cited, and nothing more needs to be done. There are instances, however, when an article is so important that the reader may want to follow up the reference and see for sure that the original source, in the original context, was interpreted appropriately. Footnotes should be as easy to read as possible and as complete as necessary, but they need not repeat any information contained in the text.

From this pragmatic analysis of the function of footnotes, you can understand that, ordinarily, a writer who is being published tries to use footnotes as rarely as possible, if only because it is time-consuming for the reader to drop his eyes and adjust to the new type. If, on the other hand, and this is being very realistic, the writer is a student in freshman English, he has another purpose: he needs to show his instructor that he has mastered footnote conventions, and therefore when there is a question of whether he should footnote, he does footnote. A freshman research paper with two or three footnotes and two bibliographic entries may be an excellent, original paper, but it certainly frustrates the teacher who is trying to determine whether his student has mastered the research and footnote techniques.

A word about present trends: customs are changing. Whereas many periodicals once abounded in involved footnotes and Latin abbreviations, the movement is toward simplicity. The most recent *Style Sheet* of the Modern Language Association, the bible for most graduate papers and many undergraduate programs, opposes Latin terms. It recommends that the writer double space footnotes and place them at the end of the paper, rather than confront the typist with the difficult placement at the bottom of the page. It points out that the less information there is in the footnote the better, if there is a complete bibliography at the end of the paper. The guiding principles are consistency, brevity, and clarity.

The Tag

One of the numerous problems that students must solve is how to handle quotations effectively. The normal procedure is to put the information in quotation marks and to precede the quotation with a "tag," that is, an expression with a synonym of "say" in it, for instance, "Cardinal Richelieu responded," or "John Dewey wrote." Your reader must always know, without reference to a footnote, who is being quoted. Information given in your text need not be repeated in your footnote.

Long Quotations

The procedure for the handling of long quotations varies markedly from one form book to another. Until recently, all long quotations—variously described as anything over three lines, over ten lines, or something in between—were put in smaller type and indented five spaces from left and right margins. When typed, long quotations were single spaced to resemble smaller type. For example:

```
Gobbledygook has become one of the real irritants under the
intellectual's hide. George Orwell has led the fight against
tortuous, jargonistic, flaccid prose, but many others have
joined the fray. In a recent Harvard Alumni Bulletin, Rich-
ard D. Fay translated Abraham Lincoln's Gettysburg Address
into "Faculty English":
     Eight and seven-tenths decades ago the pioneer workers
     in this continental area implemented a new group based
     on an ideology of free boundaries and initial conditions
     of equality. . .
```

Form Books

The problem of form boils down to a matter of following directions. The goals of brevity, consistency, and clarity are easy to achieve if you almost slavishly pattern your notes and format after the rules and models in one of the many complete form books set up by scholars and publishers. Your selection of the appropriate form book will depend on your subject. If you were writing for a specific journal or publisher, you would select the form book prescribed; the first pages of most scholarly publications tell how to submit manuscripts and what form book is to be followed. The following are widely recommended.

General

Kate L. Turabian, *A Manual for Writers of Term Papers, Theses, and Dissertations* (Chicago: University of Chicago Press [Phoenix Books]). Revised frequently.

Literature, modern languages, and humanities
William Riley Parker, *The MLA Style Sheet* (New York: The Modern Language Association). Revised and reprinted almost yearly.

Science
American Institute of Biological Sciences, *Style Manual for Biological Journals* (Washington, D.C.)

Social sciences and education
A Manual of Style (12th ed.; Chicago: University of Chicago Press).
The College of Education Style Manual (Columbus, Ohio: Ohio State University Press).

Government
U.S. Government Printing Office Style Manual (Washington, D.C.: G.P.O.). Revised and reprinted frequently. An abridged version is available.

As you turn to more advanced and specialized research and reporting, you will want to secure the appropriate manual, but until then the conventions described in this chapter should suffice.

Manuscript Terminology

Although the use of special terms is decreasing, if you are using older works, you may need to understand some of these expressions.

anon.	Anonymous, no author shown.
c. or ca.	*Circa*, Latin for *about*. Thus "*c.* (or *ca.*) 1610" means "about 1610."
cf.	Compare or confer.
ed.	Editor, or edited by. Plural: eds.
e.g.	*Exempli gratia*, Latin for *for example*.
i.e.	*Id est*, Latin for *that is*.
f.	And following. Thus "p. 16 f." means "page sixteen and the following." Plural: ff.
ibid.	*Ibidem*, Latin for *the same as previously given*, or *ditto*. Thus "from the same source as the one just cited."
ms.	Manuscript, Plural: mss.
n.d.	No date shown.
n.p.	No page numbers shown.

op. cit.	*Opere citato*, Latin for *the work by this author already cited*. Thus "Hemingway, *op. cit.*" means "the book by Hemingway cited in an earlier footnote."
p.	Page. Plural: pp. Note: pp. 18–19 (not 18–9), and pp. 332–342 (not 332–42), but pp. 1127–31.
passim	Latin for *here and there*. Thus "p. 16 *passim*" means "on page sixteen specifically and also in several other places in the work cited."
q.v.	*Quod vide*, Latin for *which see*. Thus the encyclopedia sentence "Napoleon's greatest disaster came at the Battle of Waterloo (*q.v.*) and from it he never recovered" means that there is further relevant information under the "Battle of Waterloo" entry which the reader is advised to consult.
[sic]	Latin for *thus*. This bracketed expression, inserted in a quotation just after a spelling, grammar, factual, or logical error, indicates that the editor has noted the error but has decided to retain it in the quotation. He wants the reader to know that the error occurred in the original passage.
text	The main part of the manuscript; the term does not include the title, footnotes, bibliography, and so forth.
trans.	Translator, or translated by.
II; iv	About a play: "Act Two, Scene Four." About the Bible: Chapter Two, Verse Four.
(September, 1968), 6, XXXII.	The September, 1968, issue which when bound is Part Six of Volume Thirty-two.

How to Use a Form Book

The key to success in manuscript preparation is simply the ability to follow instructions. As you work on your essay or term paper, assume that you know absolutely nothing about footnote or bibliographic entries. Using the index or section headings, search through the form book you are using until you find an example that is exactly equivalent to the note you are preparing. If you wish to make a reference to a two-author essay in an anthology, scan the model footnotes until you find just such an entry. If you wish to make a reference to a pamphlet whose author is unknown, look for a model covering that instance. When you find the appropriate model, copy its form exactly, using a capital where indicated, a comma here, parentheses there. There must not be a single mark of punctuation out of place. This meticulous care guarantees consistency and completeness.

If someone other than yourself types the final manuscript, you and the typist should have a conference to discuss the format, and the typist should be provided with a copy of the form book to permit a check of questionable items. In case of error, you will get the blame, since you are responsible for the final proofreading.

A Manuscript Form Book for College Freshmen

TYPE OF PAPER

Use white 8½-by-11-inch bond paper with a weight of at least 16 pounds. Do not use onion-skin or second-sheet paper except for carbon copies.

FINAL SUBMISSION OF PAPER

Do *not* staple or bind the final paper. Your reader will want to keep the notes beside the text as he reads, and staples or other binding will serve only to inconvenience him.

TYPING

Any standard type is acceptable, but the type that resembles handwriting and the straight heavy Roman that has no lower-case letters are not recommended. Your typescript should be double spaced except for long quotations (four lines or more), which will be single spaced and indented five spaces from the left and right margins. Use black or very dark blue ribbon *only*.

HANDWRITING

Handwritten papers are considered acceptable by only a few college teachers. Handwriting must be legible; paper must be wide-lined. Long quotations should be indented as on typewritten papers; if your handwriting is sufficiently legible, you may elect to identify long quotations further by putting two lines of longhand between two ruled lines. Use only black or very dark blue ink.

CORRECTIONS

Erasures are less damaging than mistakes. Erase carefully or use correction tapes or fluids; insert corrections neatly. Do not use proofreaders' marks, and do not make marginal insertions; put the corrections at the place where the error was made. If corrections are extensive, redo the page.

MARGINS AND SPACING OF TEXT

Title Page (if required)

Type the title three or four inches from the top of the page, centered. Author's name should appear three line spaces below title, centered. Only the author's name is necessary; the word *by* is redundant. Center the assignment number, course identification, date, and other information required by the instructor four line spaces below author's name. If there is more than one line of information, double space.

First Page

If there is no title page, center the title four to six line spaces (about an inch and a half) from the top of the page. Triple space and start text. Leave margins of one inch on the bottom and both sides of the page. If using elite (small) type, you may triple space between paragraphs. Center page number at bottom of page or omit.

Subsequent Pages

Put page number four to six line spaces from top of page, consistently either centered or on right margin. Put no marks around the page numbers. Avoid (10), -10-, 10., or /10/. Simplicity and typist economy are virtues. Start typing the text three or four spaces below the page number.

FOOTNOTES

Footnotes may appear in any of three places.

1. At the foot of the page. Triple space after the text, and type the footnote double spaced (note the position of the raised figures):

Professor Turner seems to be in the mainstream of education when he comments upon the "uniqueness of literature in the student's experience." He writes,

The student discovers for himself that the sciences have no usable past; that the social sciences acknowledge only the present; but that literature encloses past and present and is the essence of prophecy. It is both timely and timeless, always timely because timeless. Alone among the major subjects in the curriculum, literature encompasses both the understanding and the imagination and at its best fuses them without joint or seam.[1]

He can hardly be included among the progressive, however, when he discusses techniques of teaching. The only visual aid he approves is the book.[2] He has no use for such casebocks which "barricade" novels or short stories with a "tangle of brambles," by including a collection of critical essays.[3]

---

[1]Arlin Turner, "Literature and the Student in the Space Age," College English, XXXVII (April, 1966), 520.
[2]Ibid., p. 521.
[3]Ibid., pp. 521-522.

---

2. Immediately after quoted material, wherever it occurs on the page. Use the same form for the note. This position is acceptable only if the manuscript is being prepared for publication *and* the editor or publisher requires this practice.

One of the primary findings of a study of comparative religions is the relationship between other religions and Christianity, particularly about how much of its teaching will be tolerated. About Hinduism, Stephen Neill writes,

> A Hindu, if he wishes, may accept in his heart all the tenets of the Christian faith; he may be regular in attendance at Christian worship and may contribute largely from his means to the support of the Christian Church. He may even openly profess himself to be a friend and follower of Jesus. If he stops short of baptism, and is careful not to offend against the rules of his caste, his position in the Hindu community is unendangered and unimpaired. But once let him take the fatal step, and all is altered. He is at once cut off from home and family, from all social ties, and from all the ancient roots in the life of his community. To his own people he is as one dead. It is baptism alone that makes the separation irrevocable.[7]

---

[7]Stephen Neill, Christian Faith Today (Baltimore: Penguin Books, 1955), p. 179.

The followers of Islam are permitted an even more sympathetic relationship. Most Muslims respect all religions which have a written record.

---

3. At the end of the chapter, part, book, or paper. This is now the recommended position unless your instructor directs that notes appear at the foot of the page. The form of the note is the same, no matter where it appears.

Footnote Form

If there is a full bibliography with the paper, your instructor may recommend "new style" notes, in which case all you need for first and subsequent notes is the name of the author and the page number. If there is more than one book by an author, you should include a short but clear indication of the work referred to, for instance, "Adams, *Education*" would indicate *The Education of Henry Adams* by Henry Adams.

To give you experience with the Latin expressions, your instructor may recommend "old style" notes. In this style "*ibid.*" is used to indicate that a reference is to the book cited in the immediately preceding note, and "Adams, *op. cit.*," is used for second and subsequent references to a work when other works are cited between the references to that work.

The following samples are "full style," which many teachers recommend to make sure the student has ample practice in providing all relevant information.

Books (two authors)
   [1]Charles Brown and Ronald Cole, *Understanding Science* (Boston: Houghton Mifflin Company, 1960), pp. 251–258.

Reference to one volume of a multivolume work
   [2]Thomas Mann, *Joseph in Egypt* (New York: Alfred A. Knopf, 1938), II, 383.

Edition indicated
   [3]Will Durant, *The Story of Philosophy* (rev. ed.; New York: Garden City Publishing Co., 1938), pp. 1–19.

Editor instead of author
   [4]Richard Ellmann and Charles Feidelson, Jr., eds., *The Modern Tradition: Backgrounds of Modern Literature* (New York: Oxford University Press, 1965), pp. 633–637.

Both author and editor
   [5]Thomas Jefferson, *Democracy*, ed. Saul K. Padover (New York: Appleton-Century, 1939), p. 65.

Periodicals
   [6]"Population Data on China Studied," *The New York Times* (October 2, 1966), p. 3, col. 1.

[7]"Larceny in Everyday Life," *Time* (September 9, 1966), pp. 26–27.

[8]Louis Seltzer, "Why I Went West—And Stayed There," *Saturday Review* (April 9, 1966), p. 68.

[9]Hanson W. Baldwin, "The Fall of Corregidor," *American Heritage,* 17 (August, 1966), 16.

Pamphlets

[10]*Newton Buyers' Guide* (Newton, Massachusetts: Chamber of Commerce, 1967–68), p. 18.

[11]*Who Is Eligible for Welfare Benefits?* (Washington, D.C.: Department of Health, Education, and Welfare, 1965), n.p.

[12]*Proscribed Commodities* (Bellington, Massachusetts: Committee Against Un-American Activities, n.d.), n.p.

Dictionaries and encyclopedias

[13]*Webster's Third New International Dictionary of the English Language* (1961).

[14]"Athens," *Encyclopaedia Britannica,* 14th ed. (1957) I, 678.

Selections from collections or anthologies

[15]Fyodor Dostoevsky, "The Legend of the Grand Inquisitor," *A Casebook on Existentialism,* ed. William V. Spanos (New York: Crowell Publishing Company, 1966), pp. 118–122.

[16]Emily Dickinson, "303," *American Poetry,* ed. Gay Wilson Allen, Walter B. Rideout, and James K. Robinson (New York: Harper & Row, 1965), pp. 532–533.

[17]Christopher Marlowe, *Tamburlaine the Great,* in *Elizabethan Plays,* ed. Hazelton Spencer (Boston: D. C. Heath and Company, 1933), II:v., 11. 1–6.

Bible references

If the reference is to the King James Authorized Version (1611), information can be very brief; if the reference is to a different version, more information is necessary.

[18]Luke, XXII: 1–8.

Stating the chapter in Arabic numbers is also correct and even preferable.

[19]II Kings, *Interpreter's Bible,* 4:i–iv.

References to unpublished information

You must provide your own form when you refer to pamphlets, microfilm, mimeographed messages, speeches, conversations, minutes of meetings, television and radio programs, or interviews. Be sure to include any names involved, the place of production or source, appropriate dates, and location where the materials may be secured or the information confirmed.

[20]Mitchell Marcus, "A Plan for Freshman English" (Paper delivered at the Convention for College Communication and Composition, St. Louis, April 6, 1973), p. 4. Copies may be secured from the National Council of Teachers of English, Champaign, Illinois.

[21]"Minutes of the Committee for Improving the Condition of Chicanos and Native Americans in California, 1970–74," Papers of the Committee, Archives, Santa Clara (California) Public Library.

[22]Douglas Hindley, "The Concept of Nature in Victorian Literature" (Ph.D. dissertation, Stanford University, 1952), p. 28.

[23]Abraham Flexnor's *Statistics on Higher Education,* (Ann Arbor, Michigan: University Microfilms, 1950).

[24]Interview with Norman Erbe, Attorney General, Iowa State House, Des Moines, Iowa, March 28, 1953.

[25]Alistair Cooke, "The Edwardians," produced for the Public Broadcasting Service by Masterpiece Theater, Station WGBH, Boston, Massachusetts, March 10, 1974.

Simplified Forms

There have been many attempts to simplify systems of footnoting, the most extreme being by educational and scientific journals that wish to convey the most possible information in the least space. *The Journal of Educational Research* requires its authors to number all entries in their bibliography, which is printed at the end of the article. In the text a number enclosed in parentheses refers to the appropriate source; usually, a second number indicates the page. In the example given (from the April, 1966, *Journal,* p. 366), "(6, 14)" indicates a reference to page 14 of the sixth entry in the bibliography.

> Using the California Test of Mental Maturity, Cook and Lanier found that the language IQ of dropouts was considerably below that of those who remained in school (6, 14).

The need for reduced costs and simplicity has caused many publishers to ask that all footnotes be omitted and references be indicated in the text itself. Another condensation has been made possible by the general acceptance of standard abbreviations for many periodicals, *C. E. (College English), PMLA (Publications of the Modern Language Association), Amer. Schol. (American Scholar), JHE (The Journal of Higher Education),* and *Sci. Amer. (Scientific American).* A code for these abbreviations can be found in most libraries, encyclopedias, and the publication using the symbols.

Subsequent References

To avoid the need for Latin terms such as *op. cit.* and *ibid.,* a simple form of citation has been devised. In subsequent references to a source already cited, only the author's last name and the page number of the article are given, no matter whether the repeated reference directly follows the previous reference to the same source or not. If there is no author for an article, the title is repeated. The footnotes below represent second references to the sources given in the footnotes on pages 265–266.

[1]Brown and Cole, p. 259.

[2]Mann, *Joseph in Egypt,* I, 30. (Repeating the title here suggests that another

work by Mann is cited; the volume number is given because this reference is to a different volume.)

[3]Durant, p. 67.

[4]Ellmann and Feidelson, p. 635.

[5]Jefferson, p. 52. (The use of Jefferson's name only indicates that his words or thoughts were referred to; if the editor's introduction had been quoted, his name would appear first in this footnote.)

[6]"Population Data . . ." p. 3. (If the title is long, a short form is used.)

[7]"Larceny in Everyday Life," p. 28.

Subsequent references to the remaining sample footnotes on pages 266–267 should be relatively easy to work out.

A form book, no matter how detailed, cannot list all possible types of footnotes, and there always will be problems that you must solve, using your own judgment. Just remember to be sure to fulfill the demands of honesty and completeness. Your reader must know who wrote the article or book and where to obtain it.

Explanatory Footnotes

Although, as we have stated, most writers try to avoid explanatory footnotes, preferring instead to work the explanation smoothly into the text, there comes a time, particularly in a scholarly work, when such footnotes cannot be avoided. A writer, discussing a controversial topic, may wish to demonstrate in an explanatory footnote that he has read all the material both for and against his point. Or he may want to explain a point to his reader when he doubts that the reader has the background information necessary to understand it. He thus presents the reader with an option: if the reader knows the necessary information or does not need the reference he ignores the footnote; otherwise, he reads it. The following appeared in an issue of *College Composition and Communication.*

> In order to be of more than peripheral interest to rhetoricians and literary scholars, linguistic research must move beyond the sentence, even though passing over this threshold vastly complicates linguistic theory. However, the initial steps toward a theory of language which explains both grammatical and rhetorical patterns can probably be made by extending grammatical theories now used in analyzing and describing sentence structure. The purpose of this paper is to illustrate how one such theory, tagmemics, can be extended to the description of paragraphs.[1]

> [1]This work is the result of my collaboration with Kenneth L. Pike and Richard Young in research on rhetoric, sponsored in part by the Center for Research on Language and Language Behavior, University of Michigan, under a grant from the Language Development Branch, U.S. Office of Education. Tagmemic theory is developed in Kenneth L. Pike, *Language in Relation to a Unified Theory of the Structure of Human Behavior* (Glen-

dale: Summer Institute of Linguistics, Part I, 1954; Part II, 1955; part III, 1960). See also Robert E. Longacre, *Grammar Discovery Procedure:* A Field Manual (The Hague: Mouton and Co., 1964), and, for a brief description using English examples, Robert E. Longacre, "String Constituent Analysis," *Language,* XXXVI (1960), 63–68.

Later in the article, when the author, Professor A. L. Becker, refers to a theory that is not well known, even to the usual readers of the journal, he adds the note:

[2]This three-part definition of a paragraph reflects the assumption in tagmemic theory that three perspectives are necessary to a complete description of behavior: a *particle* perspective, which views behavior as made up of discrete contrasting parts; a *wave* perspective, which emphasizes the unsegmentable continuum of behavior; and a *field* view, in which units are seen in context (sequence, class, or ordered set). This article focuses on paragraph tagmemes as particles in sequence. For a fuller explanation of tagmemic trimodalism, see Kenneth L. Pike, "Language As Particle, Wave, and Field," *The Texas Quarterly,* II (Summer, 1959), 37–54; and Pike, "Beyond the Sentence," *CCC,* XV (Oct., 1964), 129–135.

BIBLIOGRAPHY

Research papers customarily include a bibliography, that is, a list of all the sources that were referred to in the text and were, therefore, footnoted. On rare occasions—for instance, when a writer wishes to provide further reading on his subject—works appear in the bibliography that were not referred to in the text. The writer must always be scrupulously careful not to pad his bibliography to suggest that more work and learning were involved than actually were. Even when there is a reference to it, the Bible is not listed in a bibliography—unless the reference is to some nonstandard version. The bibliography is alphabetized according to the authors' last name; when there is no author, the item is listed according to the first major word in the title. If there are several items by one author, they are listed in alphabetical order according to their title, as demonstrated in the sample bibliography that follows. *The Fall of the House of Usher* would be alphabetized under *Fall,* not *The.*

A bibliographic entry resembles a footnote, with these differences:

1. The author's last name is placed first and is separated from the first name by a comma.
2. A period, not a comma, comes between the author's name and the book title and between the book title and publication information. (Article and periodical entries, however, use commas.)
3. Publication information is not placed in parentheses.
4. No page numbers are included for books.

5. Inclusive page numbers are indicated for articles and selections from anthologies, encyclopedias, and collected works. This means that, instead of listing only the pages to which your footnotes referred, you should list the page numbers for the complete article.

6. The indentation is the reverse of the indentation for a footnote: the first line of a bibliography item is flush with the left margin; the second and following lines are indented five or more spaces. This "hanging indention" makes the author's name and its place in the alphabetic order more noticeable.

7. Bibliography entries are usually not numbered.

8. Bibliography entries are double-spaced for term papers.

Here is a sample bibliography:

Anderson, David D. "Pakistan's Search for National Identity," *Yale Review*, 55 (June, 1966), 552–569.

"Athens," *Encyclopaedia Brittannica*, 14th ed., I, 677–679.

Becker, A. L. "A Tagmemic Approach to Paragraph Analysis," *College Composition and Communication*, 16 (December, 1965), 237–242.

Clark, Donald Lemen. *Rhetoric in Greco-Roman Education*. New York: Columbia University Press, 1957.

"The Crowded Left," *Time*, September 9, 1966, p. 46.

Ellmann, Richard, and Feidelson, Charles, Jr., eds. *The Modern Tradition: Backgrounds of Modern Literature*. New York: Oxford University Press, 1965.

Graff, Henry F. "The Wealth of Presidents," *American Heritage*, 17 (October, 1966), 4–5, 106–110.

Hartnett, Rodney T., and Steward, Clifford T. "Final Examination Grades of Independent Study Students Compared with Those of Students Taught by Traditional Methods," *Journal of Educational Research*, 59 (April, 1966), 354–357.

Jefferson, Thomas. *Democracy*, ed. Saul K. Padover, New York: Appleton-Century, 1939.

——. *Autobiography of Thomas Jefferson*, ed. Paul L. Ford. New York, 1914.

Marlowe, Christopher. *Tamburlaine the Great. Elizabethan Plays*, ed. Hazelton Spencer. Boston: D. C. Heath and Company, 1933.

Newton Buyers' Guide. Newton, Massachusetts: Chamber of Commerce, 1967.

"Population Data on China Studied," *The New York Times*, October 2, 1966, p. 3, col. 1.

"Quaid-i-Azam's Contribution to Political Thought," *Pakistan News Digest*, September 1, 1966, pp. 6–7.

Seltzer, Louis. "Why I Went West—and Stayed There," *Saturday Review*, April 9, 1966, pp. 68–69, 81.

Spanos, William V., ed. *A Casebook on Existentialism*. New York: Thomas Y. Crowell Company, 1966.

Webster's Third New International Dictionary of the English Language. Springfield, Mass.: G. & C. Merriam Company, 1961.

Wilson, Gay Allen, Rideout, Walter B., and Robinson, James K., eds. *American Poetry*. New York: Harper & Row, 1965.

Projects

1. For each of the following footnotes, explain the exact meaning of each item, that is, raised number, author, title, publication information, and page number:

[1]Philip Hone, *The Diary of Philip Hone*, ed. Bayard Tuckerman (New York: Dodd, Mead & Company, 1889), II, 163.
[2]*Ibid.*, p. 196.
[3]"Current Naval Court Proceedings," New York *Express* (December 17, 1842), p. 1.
[4]Hone, *op. cit.*, pp. 165–167.
[5]Alexander Slidell Mackenzie, quoted in *Proceedings of the Naval Court Martial in the Case of Alexander Slidell Mackenzie* (New York: Henry C. Langley, 1844), pp. 1198–99.
[6]*Ibid.;* cf. "Triton, The Mackenzie Affair," *New York Weekly Tribune* (December 24, 1842), p. 3, for another viewpoint on the mutiny.
[7]*Ibid.*
[8]*Proceedings of the Court of Inquiry* (New York: Greely & McElrath, 1843), p. 31 in *The Somers Mutiny Affair*, ed. C. K. McElroy (Boston: D. C. Heath and Company, 1954), p. 6.
[9]"Current Naval Court Proceedings," p. 1.
[10]William Shakespeare, *A Midsummer Night's Dream, Shakespeare: The Complete Works*, ed. G. B. Harrison (New York: Harcourt, Brace & World, 1952), III; ii, p. 519.
[11]*Ibid.*
[12]Robert Griscombe (ed.), *Great Disasters at Sea* (2d rev. ed.; Cambridge: Cambridge University Press, 1963), II, 19–21.
[13]Hone, *op. cit.*, p. 167.
[14]*Ibid.*, pp. 166–167.
[15]Griscombe, *op. cit.*, pp. 22–23.
[16]Arthur Vanderbilt, "New Light on the Somers Mutiny Affair," *American Naval Quarterly*, XLVI (Spring, 1949), 16–18.

2. The author who prepared the manuscript below obviously did not follow instructions carefully. Correct any errors you find.

According to foreigners traveling in England during the eighteenth century, the English had very simple foods which were not prepared very elaborately. Their main plain foods were in great abundance, however, and a variety of wines relieved the plainness of their fare.[1]

In spite of the opportunity to do so, the English did not really eat very much during the course of a day. For breakfast they had a few slices of bread with butter and tea, which meager nourishment had to last until tea at three or four in the afternoon.[2] "What would be scarce enough for a Frenchman of an ordinary appetite would suffice three hungry Englishmen.[3] The dinner meal was not heavy, but it was more varied than the breakfast. An eighteenth-century Englishman dining at home usually ate a dinner of half-broiled or half-roasted meat and cabbage leaves. The cabbage leaves were boiled in water and then served with a sauce made of flour and butter. In fact, most vegetables were served this way. The dinner meal was also accompanied by bread and butter and Cheshire cheese.[4] As for dinner in a tavern, the German Charles Moritz reported that in London for a shilling he got a meal consisting of roast meat and a salad. A half-shilling tip to his waiter caused Moritz to declare the whole meal too expensive,[5] and thereafter he dined at home on pickled salmon.[6]

[1]George Christoph Lichtenberg, *Lichtenberg's Visits to England, As Described in His Letters and Diaries*, trans. Margaret L. More and W. H. Quarrell (Oxford: The Clarendon Press, 1938), vol. I, p. 49.

[2]Pierre Jean Grosley. *A Tour To London; Or New Observations on England And Its Inhabitants*, ed. by Thomas Nugent (London: Lockyer Davis, 1772) vol. I, pp. 21–4.

[3]Grosley, *ibid.*, I, 69.

[4]Moritz, Charles P. *Travels, Chiefly On Foot, through Several Parts of England in 1782* (London: Robinson, 1795) pages 33–7.

[5]*Ibid.*, 27.

[6]*Ibid.*, 33.

3. The bibliography below is in need of editing. Revise it.

Aristotle, *On Man In The Universe.* Ed. Louise R. Loomis. New York: Classics Club, 1943.

Anderson, Wallace L. and Stageberg, Norman C. *Introductory Readings on Language.* (New York: Holt, Rinehart and Winston, 1966.

Allegro, John Marco. Untold Story of the Dead Sea Scrolls, The. Harper's Magazine, Vol. 233, No. 1394. August, 1966, p. 46.

Blackburn, Ruth H., *The Bronte Sisters: Selected Source Materials for College Research Papers.* Boston: D. C. Heath, and Company, 1964.)

Milton, John. "Areopagitica." in Josephine Miles' *Classic Essays in English*, Boston: Little, Brown, 1961.)

Horgan, Paul (Pulitzer Prize Winning Historian). *Conquistadors In North American History.* (Greenwich, Connecticut, Fawcett Publications, copyright, 1973.)

Sarton, George. *A History of Science.* (2 vols). Cambridge: Harvard University Press. (1959).

L. E. Steele. *Essays of Richard Steele.* London: Macmillan and Co., Ltd., 1937.

"The Meritocracy: Ability Testing and the American Spirit." Carnegie Quarterly, Volume XIV/Number 2, Spring, 1966. p. 5.

West, Robert J. "A Time of Exciting Ideas," *Stanford Today*, Palo Alto, California: Stanford University Press, 1940). pages 3–6.

Wright, Robt. "Education, Freedom, and the "Yes" Technique," *Education* vol. 72, no. 7 (March, 1952) p. 498.

Chapter 13

Technical Reports and Business Communications

Technical Reports
Business Communications

Every organization, regardless of size, needs information and communication to carry on whatever its purpose is. Small organizations often get along with a single secretary, a filing cabinet, and an informal allotment of duties among members of the organization to take care of, for example, responses to customers, ordering goods or services, and preparing bills. As organizations increase in size, they also increase in complexity, and their needs for acquiring and handling information grow with both these changes. At a certain point, probably different for each industry, a separate department will be developed in order to establish formal requirements for the treatment of all information relating to the work of the organization. These formal requirements differ from company to company and, within companies, from one year to the next. The new employee cannot expect to find the specific requirements of his company listed in the following discussion.

However, every company necessarily attempts to achieve roughly these specific goals in handling information: clarity, accuracy, accessibility, storage, and retrievability. Therefore, many companies have printed forms for information, and these forms often include similar blank spaces as a part of the first page of reports and memoranda. See Figure 13-1 for an illustration. This hypothetical form has some of the hallmarks of the ordinary memorandum: the addressee and the sender are identified in the left-hand top part of the form, as is the subject of the report. The date the report originated is also given a readily locatable position. Other parts of the form are those designed to aid the company (1) to make the information available to those people who *need* it, (2) to *store* the information, and (3) to *retrieve* the information from storage.

A classification, such as "secret" or "top secret," is used by some companies engaged in government-sponsored work: The contract number permits the company to assign the cost of preparing the report to the appro-

---

Classification:

WODGET ENGINEERING CORPORATION
Technical Report Form 11B73

TO: **Contract No.:**
FROM: **File No.:**
SUBJECT: **Distribution:**
                                           Date:

....

Enclosures:
   [Here any special drawings, charts, tables, or other documents that are not part of the report would be listed.]
References:
   [Here any relevant materials bearing on the report, its subject, its conclusions, or its procedures would be identified by an appropriate file number and, perhaps, by title.]

....

ABSTRACT
[This summary is included in order to permit recipients to determine *quickly* whether they need to read the report or send it to someone else.]

Figure 13-1

priate account, as well as aiding in storing and retrieving the report. The file number is probably related to the contract number, and the distribution code makes the report available to those people who need the information and keeps it away from those people who do not.

Technical Reports

Obviously, if a junior engineer prepares a technical report with direct application in one department, other departments should not receive the report; if they do receive it, they should be able to determine—without reading it—whether it applies to their responsibility. Companies cannot afford to have senior people using valuable and expensive time in work that is not productive or, to use an overworked term, relevant.

Beyond the purely formal matters of identifying the kind of information, to whom it is written, to whom it is distributed, and who originated it, many organizations expect the matter of the report to be presented in some version of one of the following two patterns. Technical or scientific organizations probably expect a variation of the second pattern.

I	II
Summary	Abstract
Conclusions	Statement of problem
Full statement of problem	History of problem
Hypotheses	Hypotheses
Work done	Work done
Full presentation of conclusions	Conclusions, evaluation,
Evaluations	recommendations
Future work	Future work

Any writer of reports must make a series of judgments and be careful to identify clearly the various parts of the report. C. L. Crowell, a staff engineer for the Raytheon Company, tells the report writers in his department: "Always keep the reader in mind." To Mr. Crowell, this injunction means, among other matters, that paragraphs should be numbered and titled or that clear transitions should be provided to lead the reader carefully from one step to the next. Any diagrams, charts, tables, or mathematical derivations included in the report should be clearly titled and numbered for easy reference.

Individual supervisors spend a good deal of time trying to keep the flow of information within a company moving smoothly and swiftly. Other members of management are concerned with the flow of information between companies: the general contractor for a product must ensure that the subcontractors have all of the correct information so that the smaller elements fit exactly into the final product, whether that product is a Cadillac or a guided missile, a Massey-Ferguson harvester or a Frigidaire freezer.

Technical reports in many fields of technology, science, and medicine often have broader use than just to the individual company that did the initial research. Such reports are usually offered for publication to any of several specialized journals. These publications now specify the form they require for articles and reports.

When a chemist sends a report of an experiment to *Carbohydrate Review* in Brussels, he has no choice but to follow a prescribed form—not only insofar as the organization and style of the paper are concerned, but also in footnote and bibliographic information. In the early years of the information explosion, scholars could submit manuscripts in almost any form. Then, as time passed, each periodical began to establish its own rules, and an author had to get directions from each journal before he submitted an article. As related journals began to quote each other, it was only a matter of time before groups of journals cooperated to create form books, or style manuals, for several disciplines. A number of journals officially adopted *A Manual of Style,* published by the University of Chicago Press. This manual is now in its twelfth edition. It was not appropriate, however, for all branches of learning, and so the American Psychological Association, for instance, created its own form book, and the Modern Language Association prepared the *Style Sheet,* whose conventions have been adopted by *American Quarterly, Comparative Literature, Far Eastern Quarterly, French Review, German Quarterly, Journal of American Folklore, Library Bulletin, Princeton University Library Chronicle, Romantic Review, Quarterly Journal of Speech, Studies in Philology, Yale French Studies,* and about seventy other journals. The thoroughness exercised by its distinguished author, William R. Parker, and the enormous prestige of the parent organization have made the *Style Sheet* the most influential in the field of humanities. Social scientists and scholars of educational disciplines are gradually agreeing on form books; recently, biologists prepared a *Style Manual for Biological Journals,* and British chemists agreed upon a *Handbook for Chemical Societies.* Other professional groups have developed their own manuals.

Business Communications

All organizations, whether technical, commercial, or educational, deal with information. The preceding section dealt with some of the general requirements of handling technical information. This section considers some of the general requirements of other information. No matter what your occupation, if you are part of an organization, you are also part of the information system, either as a recipient of directives and policies or as a part of the process that produces information. (A sales clerk, for instance, must account not only for the sums of money received and disbursed, but also for the number and perhaps sizes of the items sold, either by recording these matters on a sales slip at the time of the sale, or by physically counting—inventorying—the goods, sometimes both.) Much information within any organization is recorded numerically on printed forms by means of codes and special symbols peculiar to the particular company or industry. (See any Sears catalog for illustrations of such coding.)

There is still room, however, for the writer as something beyond a recorder of quantitative data. A number of "business" occasions require that the writer be something other than a mere recorder or reporter of data, no matter how the data are acquired.

APPLICATION LETTERS

The first such occasion may well be the time when the writer decides he wishes to be employed by a particular employer. While almost all jobs are filled only after an interview or a series of interviews, the applicant must, in general, apply in writing before the employer will be sufficiently interested to interview him. In developing an application letter, the writer *must* keep in mind the specific audience he is writing for. At the time the writer begins writing, the prospective employer has *no* knowledge of the writer; further, the employer knows that he has something of value—a job that various people, including the writer, want very much.

What should the writer know before he writes? How should he write? What should he say—and what should he not say? Some of what follows may sound terribly obvious and naïve to you. We agree, but the following "dos" and "don'ts" are based on actual letters we have seen. Perhaps even those who believe this list to be obvious should use it to refresh their memories and test their judgments.

1. The writer should know what job is open and its general qualifications. (If you are qualified for a chemist's position, you probably should not waste your time—and the prospective employer's—applying for a typist's job, especially if you can't type.) Of course, an inquiry letter written to find out whether there are any positions open is different from an application letter.
2. The writer should remember that, usually, *he* is asking for some consideration from the employer; the writer is not in the position of conferring a favor on the employer. We are not urging humility or servility in tone here—merely a careful avoidance of any appearance of arrogance or contempt for the prospective employer, (To strain a point: if you are fervently supporting the ecological reexamination of an

industry's practices, perhaps you should not announce your intention to change the company's evil practices in its use of resources.)
3. The writer should:
   a. Identify the position sought and indicate where he learned of it.
   b. Give a *brief* indication of his qualifications, indicating why he would be the best possible candidate for the position. Many people attach, on a separate sheet, a résumé, which provides a chronological history of schooling, employment, and other activities or data that could relate to the position, such as honor awards, special recognition, or special training not recorded in the usual degree information.
   c. Request an interview. The writer may request the interview at the employer's convenience, or if he is planning to be in the employer's city only on specified dates, he can indicate the dates and times he will be available.

In general, other information should not be in the letter, unless there are special circumstances: for instance, the writer may want to mention a mutual acquaintance, make a specific reference to something the employer or his company has recently done *that is relevant to the position,* or tell about a particular handicap he has that is relevant and could be disqualifying if it were not explained early.

WRITING AS AN EMPLOYEE

Once the writer is an employee, he will have to learn a particular system of internal communications. As we have already said, much of this is obvious and numerical, and the systems used by different businesses are often similar to each other. Since each organization tends to develop its own forms, its own standard formulas, and its own system for routing of material, we will say little beyond the obvious: Know *what* you want to say, know *who* you want to say it to, know *why* you want to say it, and know what you will do after your message has been acted on, either favorably or unfavorably. (This set of recommendations merely restates the rhetoric situation schema that we refer to in Chapter 1 of this text.)

As a writer, you will have little difficulty in the small organization. As organizations increase in size and complexity, managment becomes more and more conscious of the problems their employees encounter in communication. In a number of companies this set of problems is taken so seriously that the company has what is in effect a small college within the company; often the employees can qualify for promotion by attending formal classes during working hours. These are advanced courses, not "skills courses" dealing with typing, shorthand, office machine operation, computer-related machine operation, or basic English.

One corporation offers a complete catalog of free courses, at three different levels (presupervisory, supervisory, and management). We have listed the courses related to aspects of communication:

Course name	Hours (60 minutes)
Spelling/Word Study	15
Business English I & II	25/40
Effective Writing	15
Effective Communication	6
Effective Listening	4
Effective Speaking I & II	15/15
Communications (upward within corporation)	12
Report Writing	10
Interview Techniques	12

You might meditate upon the implications of this list. To us it is clear that the management of this particular company and of others with equally elaborate educational programs have found a need among the employees that is not satisfied by the education or training these employees receive before beginning work. Since few corporations willingly spend money unless management can see a benefit to the company and its stockholders, there must be certain problems in prejob education. Now obviously the courses in the preceding list would not, in themselves, qualify the people passing them to be management- or supervisory-level employees. But the company's management believes that these courses help to provide the company with "promotable" people. What does this kind of thinking tells us about the efforts expended in the public schools and colleges to prepare people either to work or to advance in their work once they are employed? Some of the implications are disheartening.

Further, it is disheartening to hear from Marvin R. Brookes, associate controller of the John Hancock Mutual Life Insurance Company, that he is often surprised by the inability of effective employees to restate, in writing, a clear and significant idea that they can discuss effectively and cogently in a face-to-face conference. The implication of that fact we leave for you to draw.

CONSUMER WRITING

As a consumer, or customer, you have other relationships with business that require you to write business communications. When you discover that the article or service you purchased is, in some way, defective, you need to make your concern known. Further, you wish to make sure that corrective action is taken so that you will suffer no monetary loss or the service problem will be made as nearly right as possible. We do not speak here of those problems that can be settled only by recourse to law, but of those that arise in the ordinary affairs of American consumers, who purchase stereo systems, automobiles, air travel, and other items on an interminable list of goods and services. Every once in a while some goods will be delivered and turn out not to be what they were said to be, or some airline will lose your luggage or schedule you for a flight that is already full.

When you complain about such matters, there are, as usual, some principles to consider *before* you begin to write. First, do you have all of the necessary facts: proof of purchase, accurate references to the people involved or to the kinds of goods or services you in fact were purchasing, accurate dates and times (if relevant), and accurate statements about the events as they occurred? Then, you must know what *you* want: To have the entire article replaced? The entire sum refunded? Part of the sum refunded? (If you want "damages" of any kind, think about consulting a lawyer.) Or, as sometimes happens in these computerized times, do you want a service to stop—as a book or record club you may have been trying to get out of? When you are sure you know what you want and what actually occurred, then you should find out how to get what you want.

In any problem arising between you and an industry that is directly regulated by the federal government, you should write your letter to the appropriate officers of the company concerned, but prepare copies of your letter and send those to the appropriate regulating agencies. Indicate this fact on your letter to the company by noting it at the bottom, below your signature and to the left: for example, "cc: Federal Aeronautics Board." You thus indirectly apply pressure to the company, which may therefore react more swiftly than it would to a complaint that simply came in from a consumer. You need not refer to the copies you are sending elsewhere; just noting their existence will add some pressure to your own justifiable complaint.

Of course, many companies are eager to correct customers' problems and would do so without the external pressure. Small, local companies, however, may be reluctant to make good on a defective item. In such instances more than one letter may need to be written. The strategy of the complaining customer needs to be adapted to the specific company and the specific problem, but in all instances your letters should be directed, successively, to people who can correct the problem. For instance, if the local manager cannot or will not provide satisfaction, you should next write to his superior, whether it be a district, regional, or national manager. At each stage of the process, keep careful records of your letters and of any replies, either written or oral, that you manage to pry out of the company's employees. These will be invaluable as references, and they also indicate that you take the matter you complain about seriously—so seriously that the problem maker should also take it seriously.

THE APPEAL TO POWER

In all business communications, except those that deal exclusively with information, the writer of the memorandum or letter invariably wants to cause a change of some kind. In addition to the ordinary rhetorical principles of solid preparation, knowledge of the subject, careful analysis of the audience, and clear and effective presentation of the case, there is often an underlying principle that is *not* stated. This is an appeal to power. When you complain to an airline about the service, or failure of service, *and* send a copy of your complaint to a federal agency regulating the airline, you appeal, rather directly, to the power of the government. Similarly, when you address your complaining letter first to a local manager, then to a supervisor, and finally to the president of the company, you are directly appealing to higher and higher sources of power.

When you send a memorandum to your superior suggesting a change, you may discover that your argument, by itself, is not sufficient to carry the change. At this point you need to take a lesson from national and local politics: you need to know who has the power you need to get your change accomplished. Sometimes, the hierarchies of a company really indicate the levels of power. Equally often, they do not. But since this subject—the structure of power in institutions and organizations—is so complex, we will merely identify it here and let you, as you begin to function within the organization, watch carefully in order to locate the power.

Part V A Handbook of Style

14 *Grammar, Spelling, Punctuation, and Writing Conventions*

Chapter  Grammar, Spelling, Punctuation, and Writing Conventions

Rather than living in a world of "everything goes," we are living in a world in which language is an arbitrary system of symbols understood and practiced by people who need to communicate with one another. The so-called language conventions—grammar, spelling, punctuation, and manuscript practices—are justified only when they help a writer make his message clear without offending his reader. When they become elitist, inflexible, and stuffy, they are not justified.

The Soundness of Conventional Usage

We are apparently living in a world of "anything goes." Permissive education, the "hang-loose ethic," nondirective guidance, and the belief that the Church is dead are all around us. Marshall McLuhan insists that the day of the lineal-sequential book is gone, that it has been replaced by impressionistic sense-numbing multi-media WOW! and POW! communication. Linguists argue that common usage, not grammar rules, should be our standard for correct speech. One might indeed believe we are in a world of total social and linguistic chaos.

But we are not. Language, like society, has conventions and rules.

Language is an arbitrary system of symbols which men use in order to communicate. Without agreement on the symbols there is no communication. One man cannot make up his own set of symbols and expect to be able to talk with his neighbors. On the other hand, no language is static. As societies grow, their languages change. Groups of people get together and develop their own specialized jargon or dialect. Such change is good when it reflects the growth and needs of society; it is bad when it means that dwellers in one apartment house or on one mountaintop cannot communicate with their neighbors in the next street or valley. The ideal language would be one that would grow when necessary, but would mean tomorrow what it means today and would be understood by all people.

There is more to language than communication, however. Whether we like it or not, conventional language patterns have come to have social, educational, and economic overtones. Precise grammar has become an instant mark of status. Too many times a student applicant has been denied admission to a school, too many times an applicant has been denied a job, too many times a salesman has missed a sale, and too many times a politician has lost a vote, not because of a deficiency in what he had to offer, but because he said, "he don't" or confused the spelling of *to* and *too*. Call it snobbery or elitism if you wish, but many people look down on those who make such "errors," often believing that such mistakes reflect an absence of courtesy, concern, ability, or self-discipline.

As part of an experiment, a group of college teachers was given a set of themes to grade. Most of the teachers were trained in linguistics and were fully aware that language patterns are unrelated to mental ability. Although they did not know it, there were actually two sets of papers, identical except for the fact that one set contained grammatical and spelling errors. As might be expected, the error-ridden set received much lower grades on grammar and spelling. But, in addition, these papers were also given lower grades for content, organization, and style. The teachers subconsciously felt that a writer who can't spell or write grammatically can't organize or develop a thought either.

Since most writers seek understanding and acceptance by the largest audience possible, it is not surprising that they usually adopt the conventional language followed and found pleasing by most of their readers. They write sentences that begin with capital letters, end with periods, and have a thought in between. They spell carefully, making sure not to confuse *too many* with *to many*. Their verbs agree with their subjects; they avoid *he don't* and *they was*. They remember the total spectrum of rhetoric, and they know that while *they was* may communicate clearly enough, using it may cause a reader to think that a writer is uneducated, and therefore not a trustworthy authority, with the result that what he has written will lack effectiveness. Careful writers give their modifiers words to modify, and their pronouns clearly refer to specific words. They may choose a construction or a word for clarity, or they may choose it because it is the usual choice under the circumstances. In either case the reader can cope with it, and the result is communication.

There are some stuffy and old-fashioned conventions of grammar that can well be ignored and forgotten. And fortunately, very few composition teachers unreservedly demand grammar-book English, with *who* and *whom*, and *shall* and *will* used exactly as the rules dictate. They defend only those conventions that permit and guarantee clarity.

The instruction in this handbook, which attempts to help students clear up difficulties with grammar, spelling, and punctuation, is based on an acceptance of these mechanical underpinnings of writing as a product of logic and as an aid to effectiveness. A bit grudgingly, we accept, too, the need for certain conventions if we are to communicate with ease and clarity. Our guiding principles are:

1. If a deviation from convention in grammar, spelling, or punctuation causes confusion, it should be corrected. The sentence "John told Bill he had to go home" is indefensible, for the reader is left unsure as to whether it was Bill or John himself who had to go home. Prose must be clear. The reaction desired from the reader is "I understand," not "What's that again?"

2. Any deviation identified with slovenliness should be rejected. Nothing is gained by "He swum to shore," "You was robbed," "He flang the ball." The reaction desired from the reader is, again, "I understand"; we don't want him to chuckle at supposedly serious writing.

Admittedly, these two principles may lead a writer to adopt an essentially conservative posture about punctuation, spelling, and grammar. Lord Chesterfield once advised his son never to be the first nor the last to adopt a fad, and a writer might well consider this advice. The writer's desired posture need not be one of conservatism, but it should be one of discrimination. He must develop a "feel" for the mechanics of writing. About spelling, he has very little choice. There are almost no acceptable variations. He can use *centre* and *theatre* when they are parts of proper nouns; a resident of Newton, Massachusetts, for instance, might walk down the *center* of *Centre* Street. A writer may use phonetic spellings in trade names or highway signs, such as "Nu-Lite," "Thru Street," or "Hi-Way 101," and he may take his choice when it comes to some words about which there is as yet little agreement; for instance, he may choose either *programmed learning* or *programed learning*. With punctuation, he has a great deal of choice, so much so that he depends as much on the sound of his communication as he does on arbitrary rules.

When he confronts a problem of grammar, however, the writer's choices are limited. When two possible constructions occur to him and one is as clear as the other—and both are commonly used—he may turn to the one that is the more traditional. He will run into such problems rarely, but they do occur. Take these sentences, for instance:

1. All the students are here, but none of them are very happy.
2. I must say that he done good!
3. You will go!
4. The policeman said I should drive slow.
5. Ask him who he wants to see.
6. You are the person that I want.
7. I feel badly about this matter.
8. The document, hopefully, will provide the answer.

If we were to enter the mind of a writer confronted with these sentences, we might encounter responses such as these:

ABOUT 1.   Hm-m-m! Do you say "none is" or "none are"? Old grammar books tell you to use "none is," but most writers use *none* as a plural. There is a perverse kind of logic that supports using the plural: after all, *zero* is neither singular nor plural, and the sentence does have a plural ring, as though we are saying, "All are unhappy," and are merely rewording the sentence as, "None are happy." I guess either *is* or *are* would be satisfactory.

ABOUT 2.   This joking misuse of grammar adds force and may be tolerable in conversation, but strictly speaking, an adverb should be used with the proper verb: ". . . he did well."

ABOUT 3.   Almost no one knows the distinction between *shall* and *will*. Whether it is grammatically correct or not, I will use *will*.

ABOUT 4.   If I were quoting the policeman directly, I would use quotation marks, but since I'm not, I will use the strict form, "drive slowly," since I gain nothing if I don't.

ABOUT 5 AND 6.   The *who* and *whom* dilemma! This is a real "gray area" in usage questions. *Whom* often sounds prissy, even when it is correct. Some "correct" uses of *whom* sound downright silly—for instance, "Whom's he seeking?" Even "For whom is he calling?" sounds a bit stilted. Settling the matter by using *that* is not very good, because this often makes a split construction necessary: you cannot say, "You are the person for that I am looking"; you must say, "You are the person that I am looking for." In this dilemma I guess I will stick to *whom* when it is appropriate. I may be able to avoid using the construction altogether:

Ask him whom he wants to see.
You are the person I want.

ABOUT 7. Hm-m-m! There comes a time when a person has to draw the line. Ironically, "I feel badly" is used often by the semieducated, rarely by the uneducated. Half-knowledge tells us that we should use an adverb after a verb, and adverbs have *-ly* endings. Ergo: shouldn't I use *badly*? But there is also some rule about verbs of sense (*taste, smell, hear, look, feel*) taking adjective forms. If a fish smells badly, it means something is wrong with his nose. If he smells bad, he stinks. I should use adjective forms, as I do when I use the forms of the verb *be*.

> The fish smells bad.
> The fish is bad.
> I feel bad.
> I am bad.
> The meat tastes bad.
> The meat is bad.

Thus "I felt badly" is a ridiculous affectation. I do not care who uses it. *I* won't.

ABOUT 8. If I use *hopefully*, I should indicate who is doing the hoping. A document can't hope, as the construction seems to suggest. I will write, "We hope that the document will provide the answer."

A student often comes to a kind of reluctant truce in the battle with grammar. He says to himself, "Okay, I will be pragmatic and go along. I will wear a tie at dinner. I will not pick my teeth in a restaurant. I will try to write grammatically correct prose. I want my reader to think of me as an educated, stable, mannerly person, and I am more likely to create this impression if I follow the conventions than if I violate them." An experienced writer, on the other hand, often uses conventional grammar out of respect for it. He knows that although his style may be the mark of his own personality, grammar is something refined by society in order to achieve the best possible representation of a thought. He looks upon grammar not as a discipline, but as a part of freedom. Freedom, he reflects, is really only the privilege of exercising one's self-discipline. The discipline of grammar makes it possible for him to exercise real freedom in thought and style.

When college students approach the conventions of writing, they often ask certain basic questions. The rest of this chapter is an attempt to answer those questions and to provide the foundation for an understanding of the mechanics of writing. The categories of questions are listed in alphabetical order, and where an instructor is likely to use an abbreviation or symbol for a particular category, the appropriate symbol or abbreviation is given directly after the heading.

Answers to Common Questions

ABBREVIATIONS (abbr.)

Except for abbreviated titles, such as *Mr., Mrs., Dr.,* and *Lt. Col.,* and abbreviations for academic degrees and military honors, abbreviations are avoided in most writing.

> Eugene Yarrington, Ph.D., is one of the poets mentioned in the book.
> Sir Colin Richardson, O.B.E., has just approached the podium.

Such abbreviations as *C.O.D., TV, JV, stereo,* and *hi-fi* are currently so common that they are found in almost all publications, but they still have a slightly colloquial tinge and should be avoided for strictly formal writing. *Etc.* is not used in formal or semiformal prose. It often indicates sloppy, inconclusive thinking, and therefore should be avoided even where an abbreviation would be appropriate. The ampersand (&) is used only when it is part of a corporate name, for instance, *Harper & Row. UN, USA,* and *USSR,* without periods, are now considered short titles and are used almost everywhere. Otherwise, abbreviations should be restricted to legal documents, form books, footnotes, bibliographies, informal letters, and other writing in which saving space is essential or desirable.

AGREEMENT (agr.)

Verbs and pronouns both must agree in number with a preceding noun or pronoun. A verb must agree with its subject, and a pronoun must agree with its antecedent. Usually an error in agreement results from muddled thinking or slovenly writing, for instance:

> If a rookie has any ability at all, the coach will help *them* develop.

There are occasions when educated writers are puzzled about how to guarantee agreement. The following suggestions may help:

1. Indefinite expressions. Another, anybody, each, each one, either, everybody, everyone, neither, nobody, and *no one* take singular verbs and pronouns:

> *Everybody* wants *his* own way.
> If *anyone* objects, *he* must speak up.

Especially for informal audiences, writers increasingly are following *none* with plurals, as:

> None of the candidates *were* satisfied with *their* showing.

Discriminating readers, however, may still prefer traditional usage, and the careful writer may therefore use the singular after *none,* making sure that a plural modifier does not confuse the issue:

> None of the candidates *was* satisfied with *his* showing.

2. *Compound subject joined by* and. A compound subject joined by *and* takes plural verbs and pronouns:

> Babe Ruth and Gene Tunney *were* at the peaks of *their* careers in 1927.

3. *Compound subject joined by* or *or* nor. After a compound expression joined by *or* or *nor,* the number of the verb and of any pronouns is determined by the nearer subject or antecedent:

> The President or the Secretary of State is to give his verdict soon.
> The President or the members of the committee are to give their approval soon.

4. *Collective nouns.* Collective nouns take either singulars or plurals, depending on the writer's intent. If the writer is thinking of an action by a unit, such as a committee, army, group, number, or class, singular verbs and pronouns follow:

> The committee *has* finished *its* work.
> The group *is* much smaller than *it* was.
> Three-fourths of the land *is* in good shape.

If the writer is thinking of members of the group—that one, and that one, and that one—he will use plural verbs and pronouns:

> Until the family settled the quarrel, *they* all *were* shouting at the tops of their voices.
> When a *number* of the protesters arrived, *they* broke through the police lines.
> After he gave his explanation, *three-fourths* of the audience *were* satisfied.

Pronouns provide an additional problem in that they must agree with their antecedents in gender as well as in number. This is usually simple enough, but a problem is occasionally raised when the antecedent is both masculine and feminine. The inexperienced writer is tempted to use a double pronoun:

> The teacher asked that either the boy or the girl indicate his or her preference.

This is a stilted, unnecessary practice; in such cases a masculine pronoun is usually satisfactory, except to proponents of women's liberation.

Care in agreement is one way in which a writer shows precise thought. If his sentences grow long, he still remembers what his subject is and uses the proper verb. When he has used a construction that leads to loose agreement, he rephrases it. Even a purist would hardly object to the use of *them* in the following newspaper account:

> When the President got off Air Force One, everyone in the crowd cheered. He waved to *them.*

Nevertheless, the careful reporter would have been uncomfortable with these sentences and probably would have condensed the first one to "When the President got off Air Force One, the crowd cheered." He would then not have felt ill at ease using *them.*

In almost no other aspect of grammar is simple common sense a better guide than it is in respect to agreement. A writer can solve almost all problems of agreement by keeping pronouns relatively close to their antecedents and verbs close to their subjects.

Projects—Agreement

1. Check your mastery of agreement by improving the following sentences. Compare your versions with the ones we have suggested.

> **a.** Each did his or her part.
> **b.** Everyone did their jobs.
> **c.** When the team finished the season, they were in fifth place.
> **d.** The number of people in the club are quite inadequate for raising funds.

Our versions:

> **a.** Each did his part.
> **b.** Everyone did his job.
> **c.** When the team finished, it was in fifth place. (Plural verb would be contested only in strict usage.)
> **d.** There are too few people in the club to raise sufficient funds.

Submit the following exercises to your instructor and title them "Agreement." If you have had difficulty with this particular point of grammar, indicate on your exercise paper the particular theme or assignment where you encountered this difficulty.

2. Make the necessary improvements in the following sentences:

> **a.** The family were tired of one another.
> **b.** Everyone was waiting their turn.
> **c.** Two-thirds of the grapes has been placed in the first vat.

3. Write a sentence demonstrating an error in agreement between subject

and verb. Put one line under the subject and two under the verb. Then rephrase the sentence to correct the error.

4. Write a sentence demonstrating faulty agreement between a pronoun and its antecedent. Put one line under the antecedent and two under the pronoun. Then rephrase the sentence to correct the error.

BRACKETS [ ]

Brackets are used almost exclusively to indicate insertions by an editor in direct quotations.

> It is his [the writer's] privilege to help man endure by lifting his heart, by reminding him of the courage and honor and hope and praise and compassion and pity and sacrifice which have been the glory of his past.
> —WILLIAM FAULKNER

Occasionally, a writer comes across an error in a quotation he is using. If it is a typographical error, he may simply correct it, but occasionally, especially if he is preserving old spellings or regional peculiarities, he inserts [*sic*] at the point of the mistake: "Recently I received a letter that said, 'When a studnet [*sic*] has been enroddled [*sic*] for four years, he graduats [*sic*]. . . .' By the time I finished the letter, I was as 'enroddled' [*sic*] as the writer."

CAPITALIZATION (caps.)

The following are customarily capitalized:

1. The first letter of a sentence or direct quotation.
2. The pronoun *I*.
3. Interjections (*Oh! Ouch!*).
4. The first letter in each word of a salutatory phrase (*My Dear Sir*).

In addition, the first letter of each word in traditional or official titles is capitalized. Do *not* capitalize directions unless they refer to recognized regions or cultures. Thus you would write, "Aunt Martha told me that the Senior Class of North Mason City High School officially cited the Dean of Men of Tulane University, one of the finest institutions in the South. For many years he has taught his famous course, 'Introduction to Eastern Philosophy.'" But you would not capitalize similar words if they were not parts of titles, for instance, "When I was a senior in a high school on the north side of the city, my aunt introduced me to a dean from a nearby southern university. Before he was promoted, he taught a course in Eastern philosophy." Note that Eastern remains capitalized. While most directional adjectives (eastern, western, southern) are not capitalized, hemisphere directional adjectives (Western world, Eastern philosophy) are always capitalized.

In titles of three or more words, it is not customary to capitalize articles (*a, an, the*), conjunctions, and short prepositions (three letters or less) unless they are the first or last word: *Pride and Prejudice, The World We Live In, Man Against Destiny, Once Upon a Dream, League of Women Voters, Tales of My Landlord,* and *God, the Redeemer.* Some titles have traditional short forms, for instance, the *UN,* the *Met* (the Metropolitan Opera Company in New York City), and the *Y,* and they are capitalized. One oddity is that although names of planets, stars, and galaxies are capitalized, *earth, sun,* and *moon* are not—except when they appear in a list, as *Mars, Earth, Saturn, Sun, Dubhe,* and *Moon.* Capitalize the titles or names of towns, cities, counties, provinces, states, countries, regions, officials, peoples, races, tribes, languages, books, poems, short stories, essays, months, days of the week, holidays, congresses, unions, clubs, political parties, treaties, laws, historical periods, literary eras, geographical epochs, and celebrated events; also capitalize humorous, legendary, intellectual, sports-page, and honorific labels (*Iron Duke, Thin Red Line, The Four Horsemen,* the *Crusades,* the *Middle Ages, Willie the Wisp, the Sultan of Swat*). Almost any reference to the Deity and organized religion or to any of its special teachings or traditions is capitalized: *Apostles' Creed, Holy Communion, God,* the *Church,* the *Prophet,* the *Lamb,* the *Koran,* the *Talmud.* Generic and directional terms are capitalized when they are distinctly part of the title: *Mahaska County, Commonwealth of Massachusetts, Gulf Stream, Labor Department, Atlantic Ocean* (but the *Atlantic coast* and the *West coast*), *South Carolina* (but *northern Kansas*). Capitalize Latin names of classes, families, and genera, but not of species; for example, *Homo sapiens.*

When in doubt, the writer should ask himself, "Have I seen this concept given a proper name by a previous writer? Is it likely that it is an official name?" Thus he would write about the Italian Renaissance, but "The University of Chicago is having a football renaissance." Occasionally, he will come across a word that was once a proper noun but is now in general usage. Reference to a dictionary will indicate whether it should still be capitalized; for instance, *English horn, French fries, Salk vaccine,* but *china tea pot, venetian blinds, pasteurized milk.* Individual letters, when they are grades on an examination, part of a title (*Model A Ford*), or parts of abbreviations, are often capitalized, as, for instance, in *R.A.F., G.N.P., A.W.O.L., MA.,* and *Ph.D.,* but a dictionary often will indicate exceptions, such as *i.e., mph,* and *f.,* or *ff.* (and following).

COMMA SPLICE (c.s.)

The comma splice, joining two complete sentences with a comma, is a punctuation error that often obscures meaning.

I like studying but also pretty girls, strange to say, the pretty girls always win.

Does *strange to say* go with the first or second word group? The skilled writer avoids the comma splice and instead takes advantage of the proper mark of punctuation (in this case he might place a semicolon before *strange*) to make his meaning clear.

Take the expression "The sidewalk was slippery, I fell." It contains two complete sentences spliced together by a comma. Figuratively, the comma is the little brother of the semicolon and the period, and it cannot do their work. If the writer wants to show his reader that he thinks of "The sidewalk was slippery" and "I fell" as two complete thoughts, he separates them with a period:

The sidewalk was slippery. I fell.

These sentences are now grammatically correct, but they do not show the relationship that the writer apparently tried to express by handling them as one sentence. To show a relationship, he can join them in either of these balanced constructions:

The sidewalk was slippery; I fell.
The sidewalk was slippery, and I fell.

From this we can deduce that the semicolon is equivalent to a comma plus a coordinating conjunction such as *and, but,* or *or*. The semicolon is used to indicate either balanced ideas or markedly balanced structures. In revising a sentence with a comma splice, the writer will want to ask himself, "Just what is the relationship between these two thoughts?" If the total idea is that the one caused the other, a word must be inserted that says more than *and:*

Because the sidewalk was slippery, I fell.

The writer may have intended something else; for instance:

The sidewalk was slippery when I fell.

This sentence might be used in a court case when a plaintiff is suing for damages. He is primarily concerned with the ice on the walk, a fault, perhaps, of a property owner. Notice the meanings that are possible when one idea is subordinated to the other:

When the sidewalk was slippery, I fell. (Indicates point in time)

The sidewalk being slippery, I fell. (Acceptable grammar, but possibly a little stilted; indicates that slipperiness caused the fall)

The sidewalk was slippery, since I fell. (A way of suggesting that we can assume the sidewalk was slippery because the writer fell)

Julius Caesar's "I came, I saw, I conquered" has two characteristics: the clauses are short, and there is a rhythm to the parallel elements. There is little justification, however, for the sentences:

> I heaved a sigh, I wept, I nearly expired.

Often the intentional comma splice has a noticeable rhyme. The comma forces the units together, which enhances the effect of the rhyme:

> I sighed, I cried, I almost died.

Projects—Punctuation

1. Test yourself on the following sentences. Not all are incorrect. If more than one correction is possible, choose the best one. Then compare your versions with ours, which follow the exercise sentences.

> **a.** I will be at Field's at three, wait for me.
> **b.** Exercise is good, especially weight lifting, although it is quite strenuous, it builds the physique spectacularly.
> **c.** Katie chose the red one, Edie selected the pink, Irma picked the rose number with the flounce.
> **d.** I need you, I love you, I want you.
> **e.** The light flashed red, I jammed on the brakes.
> **f.** The batter gave a mighty swing, the ball went sailing over the fence.

Suggested acceptable versions:

> **a.** I will be at Field's at three; wait for me.
> Or: Since I will be at Field's at three, wait for me.
> **b.** Exercise is good, especially weight lifting; although it is quite strenuous, it builds the physique spectacularly.
> **c.** Katie chose the red one, Edie selected the pink, and Irma picked the rose number with the flounce.
> **d.** This sentence is all right as is.
> **e.** When the light flashed red, I jammed on the brakes.
> **f.** The batter gave a mighty swing, and the ball went sailing over the fence.

2. Correct the following sentences, and submit the corrected versions to your instructor.

> **a.** I will take the bus, you will drive, he will fly down.
> **b.** John came to school in shorts, everyone laughed.
> **c.** I knew the book forward and backward, I passed the test.

3. On the paper you submit to your instructor, write a sentence with a comma splice. Then rewrite it with an appropriate correction.

ELLIPSIS (. . .)

The ellipsis (three periods; if typed, with a space between each) is used to indicate places where material has been omitted, usually in a quotation. If the omitted material contains the end of a sentence, a fourth period is included.

> Jack Kerouac wrote, "At lilac evening I walked with every muscle aching among the lights of 27th and Welton in the Denver colored section, wishing I were a Negro. . . . a Denver Mexican, or even a poor overworked Jap . . ."

The two omitted sections are ", feeling that the best the white world had offered was not enough ecstasy for me, not enough life, joy, kicks, darkness, music, not enough night. I wished I were . . ." and ", anything but what I so drearily was, a 'white man' disillusioned." Note that commas and any other punctuation in the omissions are also dropped.

FRAGMENTARY SENTENCES (frag.)

The sentence fragment is an incomplete thought mistakenly punctuated as though it were complete. It usually results from an inadvertent substitution for an essential word, often a finite (limited in time) verb:

> Colin and Mary, being too old.

Such a construction is generally the result of haste, not ignorance, and the correction is simple: substitute a verb and punctuate appropriately. For example:

> Colin and Mary are too old.

If the error occurred because the idea was not completed on paper (although it may have been completed in the writer's mind), then the writer merely finishes his thought:

> Colin and Mary, being too old, were not included in the party.

A similar fragment—the afterthought fragment—occurs when the writer "tacks on" a qualifying clause without appropriate punctuation:

> John rushed to the ticket window. Although he had no money.

Logically, the last clause cannot stand without the preceding sentence, and its thought was apparently intended to be closely linked with that of the first sentence; remove *although*, and the meaning of the pair of sentences changes. The writer must have meant:

> John rushed to the ticket window, although he had no money.

He might revise this sentence to:

> John, although he had no money, rushed to the ticket window.
> Or: Although he had no money, John rushed to the ticket window.

Projects—Fragmentary Sentences

1. Carefully reread your papers to eliminate sentence fragments. If you discover that your current method of rereading does not catch these and other structural problems, try placing the index finger of one hand at the capital letter and the index finger of the other hand at the period; then read slowly all the material in between. Is this a sentence with a subject and a finite verb form? Does it depend grammatically or logically on a preceding or following sentence? Is it merely a clause with a subordinate relationship to another sentence?

2. Improve the following constructions, if a sentence fragment occurs. Then compare your versions with the versions suggested below.

   a. The Red Sox now have a left-handed starting pitcher. Thus improving their chances of winning the pennant.
   b. The Eagles need another quarterback. Although Gabriel does his best.
   c. He would not get up for class. Because he preferred to sleep.
   d. The current world situation sees two forces struggling for dominance. American democracy, characteristically free and individualistic, being opposed by communism, characteristically rigid and collective.

Better versions:

   a. Now that the Red Sox have a left-handed starting pitcher, their chances of winning the pennant have been improved.
   Or: Now that the Red Sox have a left-handed starting pitcher, they have a better chance of winning the pennant.
   b. The Eagles need another quarterback, although Gabriel does his best.
   c. He would not get up for class because he preferred to sleep;
   Or: Because he preferred to sleep, he would not get up for class.
   d. The current world situation sees two forces struggling for dominance: American democracy, characteristically free and individualistic, and communism, characteristically rigid and collective.

3. Spoken English often includes incomplete or fragmentary sentences, for the standard sentence order is so firmly fixed in our minds that we readily supply the missing elements. In written English, however, we cannot rely on vocal inflection, facial movements, and other such aids. We may occasionally use an incomplete sentence for a special effect, but generally we must make our sentences grammatically and logically complete if we are to be sure they will be understood.

Correct any deficiencies in the following examples and submit the corrected versions to your instructor. Title the exercise "Fragments."

    a. American literature, now recognized as a major influence on world literature, was long thought to be merely a provincial echo of English literature. Melville, being ignored even in the United States, serves today as a warning to critics.

    b. The "novel of manners" is a dying form. Society itself having withdrawn from public attention.

    c. The two reasons for the Packers' decline in recent years are quite obvious. Both their increasing average age and the absence of Vince Lombardi.

    d. Political history in the twentieth century shows increasing governmental control. Both in democratic and in socialistic countries.

    e. He could remember his first view of the city. How impressive the skyline and the smog.

4. On the same paper that you used for the exercise above, write three different kinds of sentence fragments and correct them.

HYPHENS (-)

Probably no other mark of punctuation is as slippery as the hyphen. Its use varies widely from writer to writer and from formal to informal style. The following suggestions will help:

1. For word breaks. Use a hyphen at the end of a line when there is not sufficient space for the entire word. Break between syllables; avoid breaking before a single-letter syllable:

    He goes on to dream of lying in the jungle, with great drums throbbing through the air, of dancing a lover's dance naked in the glistening moonlight.

2. For clarity. Use a hyphen to avoid confusion.

    She recovered the sofa.
    She re-covered the sofa.

    I have a great grandfather.
    I have a great-grandfather.

3. For compound words. When creating two-word adjectival modifiers, hyphenate them only if they precede the noun:

    The rebellion was short lived.
    It was a short-lived rebellion.

If the modifier begins with an adverb ending in -*ly*, it is not hyphenated:

    He was an overly enthusiastic person.

Compound words, especially compound nouns, seem to have their own evolution. First they are written separately, then hyphenated, and then joined. *Drug store* became *drug-store* and is now *drugstore*. When in doubt, check your dictionary.

The following examples will help you acquire a "feel" for hyphenation:

1. *ultra-ambitious, re-entry, bell-like, re-elected, pre-eminent, pre-existent.* Hyphens, in other words, are usually used to separate double letters at syllable breaks. Although some writers drop the hyphens, many tend to prefer the form which separates double letters at syllable breaks.
2. In the case of *co-*, some writers use *co-operate* and *co-ordinate*, or even *coöperate* and *coördinate*, while most simply write *cooperate* and *coordinate*.
3. *anti-American, ex-President Johnson, non-Birchite conservatives.* Use a hyphen to separate a prefix from a proper noun or adjective.
4. *thirty-five, one hundred twenty-five, three-sixteenths.* (Usage varies greatly in regard to fractions.)
5. *president-elect, all-state, ex-singer, self-importance.* These four affixes (*-elect, all-, ex-,* and *self-*) are rarely joined to a noun without a hyphen.

Occasionally, the hyphen will avoid confusion. Do you perceive the difference between "two-minute eggs" and "two minute eggs"? The context would be something like this:

> He has found that two-minute eggs have been boiled just enough to please his friend.
> In the robin's nest were two minute eggs.

IDIOMATIC CONSTRUCTIONS (id.)

All languages develop characteristic usages that seem, to the non-native speaker, illogical and/or ungrammatical. In English the idiomatic constructions that most frequently cause difficulty or uncertainty are those in which verbs require particular prepositions. Consider:

> He is capable to do anything.
> He is able to do anything.

The two sentences might look equally grammatical to a speaker of a language *other* than English. However, native speakers recognize that *capable* requires *of*, followed by a participle. Thus, the sentence must be:

> He is capable of doing anything.

Since there are hundreds of idioms involving verbs and their attendant prepositions (some verbs take several prepositions—and change meanings as they change prepositions), we make no attempt to list them. As a native speaker, you will automatically select the correct combinations most of the time—if you think through what you mean. When you are stumped, *Roget's International Thesaurus* may help you.

INCOMPLETE CONSTRUCTIONS (inc. const.)

Sometimes a writer hastily or carelessly leaves out essential parts of sentences because he expects the reader to provide a preposition, or verb, or subordinating word, from a previously established pattern. In both pairs of sentences below, the second version is more acceptable than the first:

> Dr. King long ago showed his concern and interest in civil rights.
> Dr. King long ago showed his concern for and interest in civil rights.

> You should assume your readers are the entire educated community.
> You should assume that your readers are the entire educated community.

ITALICS (ital.)

Italic is the name of a typeface used in contrast to roman type; the words you are now reading are in roman type, while the word *italic* has been written in italics. Italics are represented in a manuscript by underlining and are used for the following:

1. Emphasis.   I will *not* go!

2. Titles.   Italicize titles of books, periodicals, theatrical productions, works of art, and names of specific naval and air vessels: *Guard of Honor, Saturday Review, The Sound of Music, Guernica, Titanic.*

3. Foreign expressions used in English.   *Coup d'état, nouveau riche, Realpolitik, Weltschmerz, Weltanschauung.* Dictionaries indicate by such methods as a double cross (‡) or parallel lines (||) those words that have not become part of the standard English vocabulary and would therefore be underlined.

4. Words used as words.   "I dislike *oxygen, cheese,* and *pastiche* because they are such harsh words." (The writer is speaking of the words themselves, not what they represent. If he had said "I dislike oxygen, cheese, and pastiche," he would have conveyed a different meaning.) This use is appropriate also for single letters and numbers:

> There are four *s*'s in *Mississippi.*

> *Pago Pago* has been mispelled ever since the first cartographer to put it on a map did not have an *n* in his type case. It is pronounced *Pango Pango.*

5. Clarity.   Confusing sentences can be clarified by judicious underlining, as in the following example, where *had* appears eleven times:

> "Peter, where John had had *had,* had had *had had; had had* had had the teacher's approval."

MISPLACED AND DANGLING MODIFIERS (mod.)

Misplaced and dangling modifiers inevitably confuse the reader. Notice how modifying words, phrases, and clauses make the following sentences ambiguous:

D'Artagnan only challenged two people to a fight.	Does he mean "All he did was challenge. . . ." or "He challenged only two people"?
I like the painting that I told you about at your house.	Sounds as though the conversation took place at your house, but we suspect that it was the painting that was at your house.
They went for a ride in a convertible with a dual exhaust that was flaming red.	Or was it the convertible that was "flaming red"?

Occasionally, a modifier placed between two elements may modify either of them: "Students who make good decisions without a doubt will succeed." The sentence could mean either "Without a doubt, students who make good decisions will succeed" or "Students who make firm decisions will succeed." This error is called a "misplaced modifier."

To avoid this confusion, careful writers place modifiers as close as possible to the words being modified. They also make sure that there is a word for the modifier to modify. This sentence is not sound: "Pleased, his words rolled forth as from a bubbling fountain." Phrased as it is, this sentence says that the words were pleased. It should read, "He was pleased, and his words rolled forth . . ." This error is called a "dangling modifier" because the expression, in this case at the beginning of the sentence, modifies nothing. Other examples are:

Walking down the hall, my eye was caught by the sign.
While painting the house, my brush dropped into the bushes.

Projects—Construction

1. To demonstrate your ability to avoid such mistakes, rephrase any of the following sentences that contain errors; then compare your versions with the suggested rephrasings, which follow.

    a. Blast toothpaste has been effective against cavities in homes like yours.
    b. Looking from the bridge, a yacht was the first thing seen.
    c. The band having finished that number, another piece was played.
    d. Upon entering the museum, my eyes fell upon a small statue.

Better versions:

    a. Tested in homes like yours, Blast toothpaste has been found effective against cavities.

b. The first thing we saw, on looking from the bridge, was a yacht.
c. Although awkward, sentence 3 is acceptable. The following rephrasing is smoother: Having finished that number, the band played another piece.
d. Upon entering the museum, I saw a small statue.

2. Rephrase the following sentences and submit them to your instructor. Title the exercise "Modifiers."

a. While strolling through the park one day, my purse was stolen.
b. I delivered the message to the house where I was born this morning.
c. A person who is pleasant all his life will have friends.

3. Write a sentence containing a misplaced modifier. Correct it. Do the same for a sentence with a dangling modifier.

NUMBERS

Whether to write out a number or use figures is now largely an arbitrary matter, but conventions do exist that help the writer provide the information in a consistent, clear manner. Informal periodicals, for instance, tend to write out the numbers one through ten and to use arabic numerals for the rest. More formal publications often write out round numbers (one hundred, one thousand, one million) and use figures for other amounts over one hundred—for example, 101,342, 4,555, and 1,002,897. Almost all publications and form books require figures for the following:

1. Mixed numbers: $6\frac{7}{8}$; $4.32.
2. Dates: August 17, 1945. (Do not add suffixes to dates; say "17," not "17th.")
3. Percentages: 23 percent.
4. Addresses: 59 Hedges Avenue; Apartment 307-1.
5. Page numbers and similar references: page 49; pp. 423–444; and Act IV, sc. iv, 1. 22.
6. Statistical information, especially if a series of numbers occurs: "The state legislature now contains 38 Republicans, 143 Democrats, and 7 Independents."

It is conventional to write page numbers this way: pp. 18–19 (not 18–9), 332–342 (not 332–42), but 1127–31.

Do not use numerals at the beginning of a sentence.

Poor: 123 new officials went on duty today.
Acceptable: One hundred twenty-three new officials went on duty today.
Better: Today 123 new officials went on duty today.

PARALLELISM (‖)

Parallelism is a rhetorical device that demonstrates the equivalence of two or more concepts or grammatical elements. If the parallel units are expressed in dissimilar structures, the result is "faulty parallelism," which may confuse the reader or offend his sense of propriety and of rhythm, as in the sentence, "I like hunting, fishing, and to swim." Caesar's "I came, I saw, I conquered" would have been forgotten centuries ago had he written, "I came, observation was made, and conquest resulted." To make your parallel expressions effective:

1. Avoid a shift of voice within the sentences: "The exercises were done by the student, and then he handed them to the teacher." Write, instead, "The student did his exercises and handed them to the teacher."
2. Avoid a shift in person: "First the eyes close and then you shake your head." Better: "Close your eyes and shake your head."
3. Avoid a shift in tense: "I came in and there is a teacher writing on the blackboard." Better: "I came in, and there was a teacher writing on the blackboard," or, "When I came in, a teacher was writing on the blackboard."
4. Avoid a shift in construction for items appearing in a series: "The horse was swaybacked, uncomfortable to ride, and practically fell at every bump in the road." Better: "The horse, swaybacked and uncomfortable to ride, practically fell at every bump in the road."
5. Be sure that constructions following such paired connectives as "not only . . . but also" and "either . . . or" are parallel. Avoid "She not only made us punctuate better, but also our style improved"; instead, say, "She improved not only our punctuation but also our style."
6. Avoid using *and who* in an effort to make elements appear parallel: not "The prize goes to a boy worthy of the honor and who shows true humility," but "The prize goes to a worthy and humble boy" or "The prize goes to a boy who is worthy of the honor and humble in receiving it."
7. Be sure that articles and prepositions govern either all the elements in a series, or none. "I saw bell, book, and a candle" should be phrased "I saw a bell, book, and candle" or "I saw a bell, a book, and a candle."

Projects—Parallelism

1. To demonstrate your mastery of parallelism, construct at least one improved version of the following sentences. Compare your results with the suggested improvements.

a. They don't know whether to try harder or if they should give up right now.
b. The pamphlet describes the habits of rabbits, how to make them reproduce, and how to stop them.
c. Tom's grades in science have not progressed as well as he has in psychology.
d. This is for God, country, and for Yale.

Possible improvements:

    a. They don't know whether to try harder or to give up right now.
    b. The pamphlet describes the habits of rabbits, methods of making them reproduce, and ways to stop them. (A parallel construction with *how*'s is also possible.)
    c. Tom has not improved as much in science as in psychology.
    d. This is for God, for country, and for Yale.

2. Prepare improved versions of the following sentences and submit the results to your instructor. Title the page "Parallelism."

    a. Ask not what your country can do for you, but ask yourself what can be done by you for your country.
    b. He is a man above all others and who deserves promotion.
    c. The papers were collected by the Brownies, and they stored them in the church basement.

3. Write a sentence with an error in parallelism. Correct it.

PUNCTUATION (pn.)

The punctuation of a sentence communicates through written symbols the pauses, stresses, and intonation of vocal conversation. Punctuation thus has the responsibility of communicating meaning and preventing confusion. The so-called rules of punctuation were compiled after the fact; they are an attempt to represent in writing certain vocal circumstances. The best way to punctuate effectively is to have a general sense not only of the logical and grammatical function of each mark but also of the oral quality it attempts to represent.

The period. The period ends an utterance that is complete in structure and thought; it represents the end of what we traditionally call a sentence. It reflects a drop in the voice. Usually it is followed by a slight pause.

The period is used:

    1. To indicate the end of a declarative sentence.
    2. With abbreviations: Mr., Dr., lb., etc.

The semicolon. The semicolon is placed between units related in thought and noticeably equivalent in meaning and structure. The voice would reflect this relation not only by a shorter pause than is indicated by the period but also by an emphasis on the structures that are parallel.

    John is going home; *Mary* will remain.
    John is going to the *football game; Mary* is going to the *play.*

The semicolon stands between the comma and the period in ability to relate units.

The semicolon is used between independent clauses of a compound sentence when the independent clauses are not joined by a coordinating conjunction:

> After a year or two he ran out of money; she left him.
> At first I decided to go; later, however, I changed my mind.

A semicolon is used also when the independent clauses are joined by a coordinating conjunction, provided the clauses are long and complicated, and have internal punctuation:

> Propagators of the right-wing menace sensationalize, fantasize, and romanticize; but they only exaggerate our myth, deceive the liberals, and become our theatrical directors.

Use a semicolon to sharpen the distinction between long independent clauses, even though they are joined by a coordinating conjunction and contain little or no internal punctuation:

> Several misconceptions should be scotched here: in the plan there was no intention of restricting the enrollment of black and Puerto Rican students only; the students planning to major in these programs would have had to complete the core curriculum courses required of every student in the College of Liberal Arts and Sciences; and the curriculum would not have been composed of "soul courses" or "other unfortunate, insensitive, and foolish" responses to black and Puerto Rican cultural aspirations.

Use a semicolon as a kind of "supercomma" whenever the comma has already been used and a stronger mark of punctuation is required to show a larger unit of thought:

> His creed was simple: to believe in the Constitution, the Republican party, and the Methodist Church; to work on six days and fish on the seventh; and to love, honor, and ignore his wife.

The comma. The comma should be used to separate independent clauses joined by a coordinating conjunction (*and, but, or, nor, for*):

> I know he was there at two, and I am told he was still there at four.
> The symptoms grew more formidable every day, for medical supplies were lacking.

There are two exceptions to this rule: (1) If the independent clauses are very short, no comma is necessary. (2) If the independent clauses are long or complicated, a semicolon, instead of a comma, is used (see above).

Commas are used to set off *all* nonrestrictive modifiers, whether clauses or phrases. A nonrestrictive modifier adds information about the word being modified while a restrictive modifier defines or limits the word it modifies and cannot be changed without changing the meaning of the sentence. A nonrestrictive clause, as you can see in the examples below, can be omitted without affecting the meaning of the rest of the sentence:

The messenger, who had been five hours on the road, arrived shortly after dark.

His first contention, that the penalty is too severe, is surely reasonable.

The wolf, backtracking quickly, shook off the pack.

The committee, on going into the matter thoroughly, decided that the charge was unfounded.

We stopped there for the night, the hour being late.

The house, old and deserted, stood at the intersection of the roads.

Tom, my brother, was married yesterday. [But: My brother Tom was married yesterday.]

The class, naturally enough, felt bewildered.

Use a comma to set off such introductory elements as verbal phrases and clauses. Transitional words or phrases (*but, however, therefore*) and single introductory words (*finally, naturally*) are sometimes excepted.

Accordingly, the agreement was signed.

Taken aback, he fell silent.

If I come, I'll bring it.

If he refuses to obey orders, he will surely get into trouble.

Use commas to set off transposed elements occurring within the body of a sentence:

The narrative, as it progressed, became more and more incoherent.

Commas are used for direct address, mild interjections, dates, and geographical expressions:

For once, Tom, you are right.

Come here, you little devil.

Oh, what's the use!

The letter, dated March 1, 1889, bore his own signature.

He went first to Portland, Oregon, and then to Pullman, Washington.

Commas are used between coordinate modifiers, that is, modifiers which could be connected by *and:*

He lived in a cool, air-conditioned apartment.

The new models come in blue, red, green, and cocoa.

Contrasting coordinate elements in a sentence (elements that could be connected by *but*) require a comma between them:

I called him, not you.

Place a comma after a word or words that might otherwise be ambiguous:

Below, the trail was no less difficult.

The colon. The colon is used before a formal statement that is pointedly explanatory of a statement immediately preceding:

> I can but note the respect perhaps unconsciously paid to this great man by his biographers: every house in which he resided is historically mentioned, as if it were an injury to neglect any place that he had honored by his presence.

Colons are occasionally used before a quotation, especially in formal writing:

> The speaker began as follows: "I feel honored to have been asked to address you."

A colon is used before a series that the writer wishes to emphasize. Often the colon is preceded by *the following* or a rather legalistic expression like *viz., namely,* or *to wit:*

> The three reasons for his dismissal were the following: laziness, incompetence, and dishonesty.

The dash. The dash is used to indicate a break in sentence structure, especially in informal writing:

> She's like—well, I won't be so catty as to say.

Dashes are used also to set off strongly parenthetical expressions:

> Editorial writers have severely criticized our policy—or the lack of it—in this regard.
>
> Love—which has been called a "Many Splendored Thing" (whatever that means!)—can also cause one big headache.

Parentheses. Parentheses are used:

1. To enclose material inserted in a construction.

> The thought process is important, not because the poet thinks and then seeks poetic expression for his thought (which is the recipe for bad poetry), but because the good poet is a thinker, a philosopher whose thought naturally takes poetic form during expression.

2. To enclose cross-references.

> (see p. 29)
> (*cf. Luke* IV:1–6)
> (see *Encyclopedia Americana*)

3. To enclose letters or numbers in a list.

> There is an import tax on (1) handcrafted silver, (2) wines, (3) liquors, and (4) cigarettes.

In general, you should avoid the complication of a parenthetical expression within another parenthetical expression; but if it is unavoidable, place parentheses around the internal expression and dashes around the external one.

Quotation marks. Quotation marks are used to indicate titles of poems, essays, short stories, magazine articles, acts of plays, and any literary compositions not long enough to be published as a book:

> In "How to Tell a Story," Mark Twain tells about a soldier who has been asked to carry an injured companion back to the field hospital. On the way a cannonball decapitates his friend.

Use quotation marks to indicate an exact quotation or dialogue, as in the same story by Mark Twain:

> "Where are you going with that carcass?"
> "The rear, sir—he's lost his leg!"
> "His leg, forsooth?" responded the astonished officer; "you mean his head, you booby."
> Whereupon the soldier dispossessed himself of his burden, and stood looking down upon it in great perplexity. At length he said:
> "It is true, sir, just as you have said." Then, after a pause he added, "But he *told* me it was his leg!"

Use quotation marks to enclose expressions that are not your own. Note the way Thoreau's descriptions of weather are presented in the following student theme:

> Henry David Thoreau wrote, "There is no more Herculean task than to think a thought about this life and then get it expressed." This thought probably explains the effort he must have taken to devise such precious expressions as those he used to describe the weather: "fingering cold," "whitening snows," "moistening snows," and "remaining snows."

A writer may use quotation marks to surround an unfamiliar expression, a common word or phrase that he is specially defining, or an expression he has coined for the occasion:

> There are two types of reasons for doing anything. We have "good reasons," as when we tell a friend we did not attend a lecture because we disapprove of the speaker's conservative views. We also have "real reasons," which we often do not admit even to ourselves. We may actually have stayed home because we did not have money for the ticket or because we wanted to watch some dumb television program. Good reasons are what we report to society, expecting its approval. Real reasons are often the product of our emotions and our prejudices.

> I have observed that America is beset by a "paradox of opportunity": our economic system has given us enough money to buy almost anything good—but we can waste it on mere conspicuous consumption; our young people have so much entertainment available from so early an age that they are bored by the time they are teen-agers; science has given us the tools for a perfect life—and the tool to blow us all up. This is our paradox of opportunity.

Note that the writers use quotation marks only once for each expression. They do not have to repeat them when the same phrase reappears.

Slang and colloquial expressions require quotation marks in formal writing:

> Although the Mayor condemned the professor in most of his remarks, he praised him for "sounding off" every time American supremacy was mentioned.

H. L. Mencken referred to such quotation marks as "hygienic" because the writer seems to be holding his nose while sneaking slang into his writing. Very often such colloquial expressions, when out of place, make the writer sound too clubby and self-conscious; consequently, he may prefer to stick to a consistent level of usage. The masterful writer can either avoid slang altogether or use it without the necessity of quotation marks.

A quotation within a quotation is indicated by single quotation marks:

> In "How People Change," Allen Wheelis observes that "we have then a sense of identity that has existed all along, and in a blaze of frankness say, 'My God! I really am a crook!' or 'I really am a homosexual!' and then we conclude that this identity is our 'nature.' "

The notification that identifies a quotation, or the tag, is variously punctuated. Ordinarily, if the quotation is going to be included in the text (and not set off), the tag is separated from the quotation with a comma, or with two commas if it interrupts the quotation. When the tag is a short introductory phrase or when the quotation is closely built into the structure of the sentence, no comma is necessary:

> In *Democracy*, Henry Adams had one of his characters say, "You are all alike. You will grow six inches high and then stop. Why will not somebody grow up to be a tree and cast a shadow?"
>
> "I have always said," wrote Pascal, "that all of the troubles of man come from his not knowing how to sit still."
>
> My book says, "Periods of war do not yield great literature."
>
> Our priest, surprisingly enough, agrees with Jerry Rubin's belief that "we need some kind of a revolution every ten years."

How do you handle the quotation marks that appear with other marks of punctuation? To achieve uniformity, most writers follow these rules:

1. Periods and commas go inside quotation marks.

> Montaigne wrote, "The most manifest sign of wisdom is a continued cheerfulness."
>
> "Life is action and passion," observed Catherine Drinker Bowen, "and it is therefore required that a man should share the action and passion of his time."

2. Semicolons and colons go outside quotation marks.

An article in the Sierra Club publication invites us to consider "this bit of news":

In the U.S. alone, oxygen-producing greenery is being paved over at a rate of one million acres per year and the rate is increasing. Also, paving is contagious. Other countries are following suit.

The writer also notes "the oceans have become dumping grounds for as many as a half million substances"; he concludes by commenting that almost none of the substances has been tested to see whether the plankton we need can survive them.

3. The meaning of the sentence determines where question marks and exclamation points go. When the marks are part of the quotation, they are put inside the quotation marks; when they belong to the main sentence, they go outside the quotation marks:

Oliver Wendell Holmes wrote, "How good to hurl oneself against these magnificent heights, to put out all one's effort and feel body and soul respond!"

Who was it who said, "The Right Honorable gentleman is indebted to his memory for his jests and to his imagination for his facts"?

REFERENCE (ref.)

Pronouns are handy words that can be substituted for nouns to give variety and to tighten coherence. Since pronouns are substitute words, the reader must be certain of their antecedents. The following sentence is ambiguous, because the reader cannot be sure about the antecedent for the pronoun:

Tom told John that he was overweight.

According to the traditional rules of grammar, every pronoun should have a single noun or another pronoun for an antecedent, but recently many writers have let a pronoun refer to an entire sentence or paragraph; for instance:

The Board of Aldermen has recently acted on a simple voice vote. This is illegal.

The casual grammarian would be satisfied; the stricter one would rephrase the second sentence as, "This practice is illegal."

RUN-ON SENTENCES (r.o.)

A run-on or fused sentence is a construction in which two complete sentences are punctuated as one. Here is an example from a student's paper:

We must watch the Red Dragon of China during this period of the Cold War he would love to carve up the United States and devour it with relish.

The writer must decide where the middle modifier ("during this period of the Cold War") belongs:

We must watch the Red Dragon of China during this period of the Cold War. He would love to carve up the . . .

> We must watch the Red Dragon of China. During this period of the Cold War, he would love . . .

The writer cannot separate the two units with a comma. He might, however, wish to subordinate one of them:

> Since the Red Dragon of China would like to carve up and devour the United States, we must watch him during this period of the Cold War.

SPELLING (sp.)

What do you think of this sentence?

> A girl must watch her waste if she has a big appetite.

When such a sentence occurs, the writer causes either momentary confusion or a disruptive chuckle, and neither is his objective as a writer.

Everyone should and can learn to spell correctly. Fairly or not, poor spelling has come to be a mark of the uneducated, the careless, or the ignorant. Some people go through their lives ashamed to write letters to their friends because they have not mastered this simple skill.

Since many professors automatically give failing grades to all papers that have more than a very few misspellings, some students greatly harm their academic careers merely because they can't spell. And the ability to spell is just as important beyond college. When a number of business leaders were asked to list the types of instruction that they wished were given to all college students, spelling led all the suggestions. As one respondent wrote, "Why in the hell don't you teach them to spell?"

Spelling can be mastered. About 98 percent of the words in the English language follow simple phonic principles that a fourth grader can learn. Better than 85 percent of student spelling difficulty is based on carelessness and can be remedied if the student learns to proofread. For this reason, you might read or reread the section in this textbook on proofreading (p. 204). Studies have revealed that the words most frequently misspelled are not the multisyllabic terrors some students have come to fear, but rather, words like *an, and, then, than, its, it's, have, to,* and *too.* Many experienced teachers claim that students spell as badly as they are permitted to spell. After students are informed that any paper with more than three spelling errors will be failed summarily, misspellings occur much less frequently.

Two other factors also contribute to poor spelling. Some students like to think of themselves as having some peculiar kind of mind that simply cannot spell. Also, some students just do not take the time to learn the routine rules that clear up the spelling of some orthographic monstrosities.

Fortunately, the human mind can be trained in many ways. Some people do not have minds that remember pictorially. Some cannot remember people's faces, word configurations, and symbols on maps. They just cannot remember how a word should look; it looks as good spelled one way as another. There are, however, many ways to learn to spell, each based on a different ability of the mind.

One approach is through sense perceptions. The eye "takes pictures" and stores them in the brain for future use. This is the facility used by a witness to identify a suspect in a police lineup. The ear also has a memory; we might say that it makes a tape recording and stores it in the brain ready for "playback" when needed. This is the memory that helps you recognize a tune you knew years ago. The muscles can "remember" too; they remind you how to skate each winter and how to ride a bicycle when you have not ridden one in years.

Besides these memory banks, we have a rational memory, which we use more consciously than we do the sense memories. The student of spelling can use all four memories.

Using your eye's memory. When you confront a word for the first time or when you look it up in the dictionary, use your eye's memory. Look at the word intently for an instant; then close your eyes and envision it as you spell it silently. Write the word, and, closing your eyes again, envision how it looks in your own handwriting.

Using your ear's memory. While you are training your eye, you also help your ear remember. Many years ago, in spelling bees, experts often adopted a singsong way of spelling such words as *Constantinople* and *Mississippi* without thinking at all: they just sang out the spelling. "Em-eye-double-ess-eye-double-ess-eye-pee-pee-eye," they would chant in rhythm. Or sometimes they might use a syllabic approach: "Em-eye-ess-ess, *Miss,* eye-ess-ess, *Mississ,* eye-pee-pee-eye, *Mississippi.*" You can adapt this technique to your needs by audibly hissing out the spelling and getting your ear accustomed to how the spelling should sound. This technique is especially helpful when you are working on words that have an unaccented initial or medial vowel, represented by the *schwa* (ə) in dictionaries—words like *sophomore, telephone,* and *attendance,* in which the pronunciation does not identify the vowels. You can deliberately overaccent or even mispronounce the words to help your ear remind you that the letters are there: soph-O-more, tel-E-phone, atten-DANCE, con-fi-DENCE, cur-RIC-u-LUM, exist-ENCE, evi-DENCE, exper-I-ence, appear-ANCE, goverN-ment, main-TEN-ANCE, prim-I-tive, def-I-nIte, fem-I-NINE, DE-spair, sep-A-rate, priv-I-lege, univers-I-ty, and DI-vide.

Using your muscles' memory. Some writers use their kinesthetic memory bank by writing the word five or ten times, all the while saying it and looking at it intently. Just as the muscles learn to swing a golf club, so can they learn to spell a word. This system is particularly helpful for the student who has the sloppy habit of writing *more then* or *would of.* Train your muscle grooves by repeatedly writing *more than* and *would have.* If you have the careless handwriting habit of omitting the final letter of *and* or *they,* or if you have trouble with *its* and *it's,* write these words repeatedly in a context with other words; for instance, *more and more, it's raining,* and *its fur.*

Using your rational memory. As a writer develops sensitivity to language, he comes to value the host of spelling tips that appear in the fine print of his dictionary. One reminder you get from a dictionary entry is that the meaning of a word is the product of its parts, and the meaning is usually discernible from those parts. The following nonwords occur frequently in student themes: *perfessor, preform, definate, revelant,* and *irregardless.* A glance at the dictionary should cause you to forget these forms and never use them—even though you have just seen them in print. A professor PRO-fesses. *PRE-form* means "formed before"; the words *performance* and *per-form* are related and pronounced with the beginning *PER. Definite* is related to *finite* and *finish,* and the spelling shows that relation. *Relevant* is related to *relieve.* The opposite of *regard* is *regardless;* adding *ir* to the word cancels out your meaning by forming a double negative.

Your mind is a wondrous thing, and part of it can be constantly policing your spelling. As you write a word, let this question pop up in the back of your mind: "What does this word really mean?" The more you ask the question, the more carefully you will spell. This attention to word meaning will also prevent such howlers as "At four I was a toe-headed boy" and "He was a man of many faucets."

Listen to information about spelling. Often when you learn to spell a word, you pick up some information about a Greek or Latin root or affix. *Manu-* means "hand," *auto-* means "self," and *trans-* means "across," for instance; and these prefixes appear often in English words. Knowing *fini* means "end" or "limit" will clarify the spelling of *definite* and *infinite. Helios* is Greek for "sun," and *graph* is Greek by way of Latin for "writing"; thus, a *heliograph* is a mirrorlike instrument for sending messages using the reflection of the sun. Knowing these word units will help you spell their English derivatives. There are hundreds of such word sources, and you should be able to remember most of them.

A writer also must be able to distinguish between *homonyms,* words with the same sounds but different meanings and spellings (*meat, meet; affect, effect; led, lead; accept, except; capital, capitol; compliments, complements;*

council, counsel; stationery, stationary; principle, principal; they're, their, there; to, two, too). Most college students know these differences when they stop to think. What they need as they write is an imaginary warning light that will flash when one of these words appears. If any of the pairs listed confuse you, look them up *now*.

There are some spelling rules that most people find helpful:

Rule one.

> Use *i* before *e*
> Except after *c,*
> Or when sounded like *a*
> As in *neighbor* or *weigh.*

This old chestnut is surprisingly dependable. It indicates the proper spelling of *believe, retrieve, achieve, shriek, shield, siege, yield,* and *ceiling, conceit, deceit, receipt, freight, veil, reign.* There are a very few exceptions; some of them are *foreign, forfeit, either, leisure, neither, seize,* and *weird.* You may wish to check these words in your dictionary and, by studying their derivations, firm up your understanding of why they are spelled as they are.

Rule two.
Drop the final *e* before a suffix beginning with a vowel; retain the final *e* before a suffix beginning with a consonant. The words *accusing, aggravating, appreciative, commercial, conceivable, imaginary, medicinal, ridiculous, scenic,* and *usual* have lost the *e.* The words *accurately, achievement, adequately, advertisement, announcement, careless, likeness, suspenseful, useful, useless* retain their *e.* An exception is *judgment,* although *judgement,* more common in England, is generally considered acceptable in the United States.

Rule three.
The words *jet, tip, put, drop,* and *nap* all have a short vowel sound and end with a consonant. To keep the vowel sound short when you add a suffix beginning with a vowel (*ed, ing,* and *ance,* for instance), double the final consonant. Longer words whose last syllables have a short sound and are accented (*admit, permit, deter, propel*) follow the same rule. If you do not double the consonant, the vowel sound becomes long. Compare the following: *slopping, sloping; tapping, taping; bitter, biter; tubbing, tubing; ridding, riding; planned, planed; cured, occurred.*

The mnemonic system. Occasionally, you will encounter words whose spelling you just cannot master. In these cases, you may wish to devise your own remembering (mnemonic) system to fix the spellings in your mind. For example:

cemetery	You get to the cEmEtEry with E's.
dispensable	Some girls consider SABLE indispenSABLE.
friend	Be a friEND till the END.
stationery, stationary	You get *stationEry* by going to a *stationER;* you cannot get it by *stAnding stationARY.*

Your own self-help program. Learning to spell the words used in these examples is not enough. You should start on your own program toward accurate spelling. We recommend the following steps:

1. Keep a list of words you misspell or whose spelling you find difficult to remember.
2. Analyze the list to see why you misspell the words. We predict that over 80 percent of your mistakes will be the result of carelessness or deficient proofreading. As we mentioned earlier, follow the suggestions for proofreading on pages 204–205 to eliminate this cause.
3. If any of the misspellings fall into a pattern, memorize the appropriate spelling principle. Rules of spelling can be found in almost any grammar book.
4. Use the various approaches recommended for exploiting the memory bank of your ears, eyes, muscles, and conscious mind. In particular, pronounce the word carefully as you write it, and then close your eyes and try to spell it and envision it at the same time.
5. Resolve to make yourself a perfect speller. Why waste all your effort on a writing project because of a last-minute failure to be sure your words are spelled properly? Do not try to escape responsibility by claiming that some great men spell badly. We know that Abraham Lincoln misspelled *beginning, very, conferring, business,* and *privilege,* but we also know that he spent a great deal of time trying to improve his spelling. And don't wait for the day when you will have a secretary to correct your spelling. Forget it. Chances are you will have to correct hers.

SPELLING CONFUSION CAUSED BY THE APOSTROPHE (apost.)

The apostrophe is a frequent source of spelling difficulty. It is used to form some possessive and plural words, and it is used to form contractions, however, contractions are often confused with other word forms containing the apostrophe.

Possessives. The possessive case for most singular nouns is formed by adding *'s* (*Miami's* skyline, a *dog's* paw, her *mother-in-law's* ire). Usage varies, but if the singular noun ends with an *s* or *z* sound and the *'s* added for the possessive would not be sounded, the possessive may be formed with an apostrophe alone (*Achilles'* heel; but *box's* top and *boss's* salary).

The possessive case for plural nouns is formed by adding only the apostrophe (two *dogs'* collars, many *boys'* ideas) unless the plural is an irregular noun, in which case the possessive is formed with *'s* (*men's* possessions, the *alumnae's* program at Vassar, several *oxen's* paths).

Possessives for indefinite pronouns are formed by adding *'s* (*one's* ambition, *everybody's* needs, *another's* money, *everybody's* love, *anybody's* attention). Other possessive pronouns require no apostrophe (*yours, his, hers, its, ours, theirs*).

Plurals.   Although the practice is disappearing, plurals of numbers, letters, symbols, abbreviations, dates, and words referred to as words may be formed with an *'s* (*p's* and *q's,* the *50's,* 33 *rpm's;* too many *hell's* and *damn's* in his language).

Contractions.   The apostrophe is also used to indicate the omission of a letter or letters when words are joined in contractions: I've/I have, you're/you are, he's/he is, she'll/she will, it's/it is, we've/we have, they're/they are; also, 'tis/it is, Br'er Rabbit/Brother Rabbit.

TITLES

There are definite conventions about how to treat titles. The title at the top of the first page of your essay should have only the first letter of each major word capitalized. See page 293 for conventions regarding capitalization of words in titles. Do not put the title in quotation marks unless you mean to show your reader that your title is a quotation from someone else. You need not underline it either, unless your title could be confused with your name or some other nearby material. Its position on the page normally indicates that it is your title.

When you refer to a title in your text, you should show the nature of the work you are citing. Underlining in a manuscript, as was mentioned in the section on italics, is comparable to italics in print; it is usually used to indicate the title or name of a book, periodical, theatrical production, work of art, or vehicle. Quotation marks around a title indicate a poem, an essay, a short story, one chapter of a book, a magazine article, or an act in a play.

> The *Queen Mary* is not the setting of *Ship of Fools.*
> "Treasury of Words" is found in Margaret Schlauch's *The Gift of Tongues.*

VERBALS

A verbal is a form of the verb used as a noun or as a modifier. Three parts of a verb may be used as verbals: participles, gerunds, and infinitives. Participles can be in the past or the present tense and are used as adjectives:

> They came *running* from the barn.
> The *burned* house collapsed.

Gerunds are present participles used as nouns:

> *Walking* is a health-giving exercise.
> John likes *swimming* more than Joe does.

Infinitives, forms of verbs combined with *to*, are used as nouns, adjectives, or adverbs:

To climb Everest was his sole ambition.　　As a noun
He wanted *to climb*.

We have much *to give* to others.　　As an adjective
He is our best choice *to win*.

She is too smart *to lose*.　　As an adverb

VERBS

The verb in many ways is *the* word in the sentence. It can convey not only action and time, but also the tone, the pace, in effect, the "flavor" of the sentence. Verbs, when used in all their various forms, can add verve, effectiveness, and variety to a piece of writing.

In modern English there are only two classes of verbs: regular and irregular. (Our remote ancestors dealt with seven classes of "strong" verbs and three of "weak" verbs; the process of simplification has aided us considerably.)

Regular (formerly "weak") verbs are those—and they constitute the vast majority—that form their past and past participial forms by *adding* a suffix (pronounced *d* or t) to their present tense forms:

Present	*Past*	*Past Participle*
drop	dropped	dropped
carry	carried	carried
walk	walked	walked

Irregular verbs are those that form their past and past participial forms sometimes by *changing* the vowel sound *within* the verb, sometimes by making other changes, and sometimes by making no changes at all:

Present	*Past*	*Past Participle*
bear	bore	borne
begin	began	begun
bite	bit	bitten
choose	chose	chosen
do	did	done
run	ran	run
ride	rode	ridden
rise	rose	risen

There are about a hundred such verbs. If you have any doubts about a verb form, see your dictionary. Avoid sounding like the child, who proudly proclaims: "I *drinked* it all up."

Grammatical properties. Verbs possess the following grammatical properties.

Voice: active and passive
Mood: indicative, subjunctive, imperative
Tense: present, past, future, and perfect tenses of each

The active voice is used when the subject performs the action:

John hit the ball.

When the action is received by or performed on the subject, the passive voice is used:

The ball was hit by John.

You will probably discover that you write better papers by relying on the active voice. If you use the passive voice at all, use it sparingly. Do not inattentively alternate active- and passive-voice passages.

Most modern, informal expository writing relies exclusively on the indicative mood. Spoken English finds considerable use for the imperative, as in "Look out," "Watch out for the overhang," "Duck!" and so on. The subjunctive mood, illustrated in the next sentences, is seldom used today except in a very limited number of constructions, such as, for example, a statement that is contrary to fact.

If I were you, I would go.
If he were well, he might be a superb choice.

Colloquially, the second sentence would probably appear as "If he was well . . ." For the first sentence, "If I were you . . . ," there is no acceptable colloquial form other than the form shown here. "If I *was* you" is widely recognized as a barbarism.

Again, try not to mix your moods randomly or to shift inadvertently from one mood to another.

English verbs identify, by means of tense, the *time* at which the action of the verb is said to take place. Of the six tenses usually recognized, the three simple tenses—past, present, and future—are most often used. The following paradigm shows the full conjugation of the simple tenses of a regular verb:

Principal parts

Present	*Past*	*Past Participle*
walk	walked	walked

Present tense, active voice, indicative mood

	Singular	*Plural*
First person	I walk	we walk
Second person	you walk	you walk
Third person	he (she, it) walks	they walk

Past tense, active voice, indicative mood

	Singular	Plural
First person	I walked	we walked
Second person	you walked	you walked
Third person	he (she, it) walked	they walked

Future tense, active voice, indicative mood

	Singular	Plural
First person	I shall walk	we shall walk
Second person	you will walk	you will walk
Third person	he (she, it) will walk	they will walk

The final *s* in the third person singular of the present indicative is the ancient remnant of a complex system of endings. All other endings vanished around the year 1500. In the subjunctive mood, this *s* does not occur.

The future tense has been simplified over the past few decades. It used to be that the forms shown here indicated simple future; reversing them (I *will* and you *shall*) showed determination. Now such distinctions are ignored, and *will* is used in almost all cases.

The *perfect tenses* use the present, past, and future forms of the auxiliary verb *have* with the appropriate participle: *I have walked, I had walked, I shall have walked,* and so on.

Imperative:	walk
Subjunctives:	if he walk; if he be walked
Infinitives:	to walk, to have walked, to be walked, to have been walked
Gerunds:	walking, having walked, being walked, having been walked
Participles:	walking, walked, having walked, being walked, having been walked
Emphatic form:	I do walk
Progressive form:	I am walking

Indexes

Index of Names

Adams, Henry, 166, 229
Addison, Joseph, 8
Adler, Mortimer, *quoted,* 49
Aesop, *quoted,* 134
Agee, James, 129
Albee, Edward, 193
Aristotle, 77, 213; *quoted,* 105, 106
Arnold, Matthew, *quoted,* 10
Arnold, Tom, *quoted,* 9
Auden, W. H., *quoted,* 106

Babel, Isaac, 156
Bacon, Francis, *quoted,* 9, 115, 145
Bacon, Leonard, *quoted,* 130
Baker, Carlos, 156
Baldwin, James, 129; *quoted,* 202
Barzun, Jacques, *quoted,* 83, 231
Bauer, Raymond, 171
Berger, Bridgette, *quoted,* 76
Berger, Peter, *quoted,* 76
Black, Max, 145; *quoted,* 145–147
Blackstone, Sir William, 229
Blaine, James, G., 167
Boyle, Robert, 212
Brooks, Cleanth, 156
Brooks, Marvin R., 279
Buckley, William F., Jr., 130
Burke, Kenneth, 140

Camus, Albert, 93; *quoted,* 92–93
Carmichael, Stokely, 93; *quoted,* 94, 195
Carnegie, Dale, 192
Carson, Rachel, 129
Carter, Burnham, Jr., 136
Caruso, Enrico, 229
Caspi, E. et al, *quoted,* 69
Charles, Jacques, 212
Chase, Stuart, *quoted,* 134
Chaucer, 144, 213
Churchill, Winston, 215, 219
Cleaver, Eldridge, *quoted,* 127, 129
Clemens, Samuel Langhorne, 219
Coleridge, Samuel Taylor, *quoted,* 202
Coolidge, Calvin, 168; *quoted,* 178
Copernicus, 213
Cozzens, James Gould, 140
Crane, Stephen, 238
Croce, Arlene, 130
Croesus, 166
Crowell, C. L., *quoted,* 275
Curie, Marie, 213
Curtis, George William, *quoted,* 69

Cyrus, 166

Darwin, Charles, 215
Davidson, Sara, 129
Decter, Midge, 130
Democritus, *quoted,* 134
DeVoto, Bernard, *quoted,* 135
Dewey, John, 157, 229
Dickens, Charles, 126
Didion, Joan, 129
Disraeli, Benjamin, *quoted,* 115
Dreiser, Theodore, 238
Drinan, Robert F., *quoted,* 65

Earhart, Amelia, 215
Eisenhower, Dwight, 140
Ellison, Ralph, 156
Emerson, Ralph Waldo, *quoted,* 71, 133
Erskine, John, *quoted,* 134

Faraday, Michael, 213
Faulkner, William, 140, 156, 193; *quoted,* 135, 203
Fischer, John, 129
Fisher, Dorothy Canfield, 173
Fixx, James F., *quoted,* 79
Flaubert, Gustave, *quoted,* 143
Flesch, Rudolf, *quoted,* 100
Fletcher, Joseph, 11
Forster, E. M., 129, 206; *quoted,* 93, 207
Franklin, Benjamin, 8, 129
Freeman, Leonard, 35; *quoted,* 35–37
Freud, Sigmund, 157, 185, 192
Friedenberg, Edgar Z., *quoted,* 73

Galileo, 213
Gallico, Paul, 129
Garland, Hamlin, 238
Gibran, Kahlil, *quoted,* 133
Gordon, George, Lord Byron, 172

Hamilton, Alexander, *quoted,* 70
Handel, George, 157
Hansberry, Lorraine, 118; *quoted,* 119
Harding, Warren G., 140
Hawthorne, Nathaniel, 9
Hayakawa, S. I., *quoted,* 87
Hemingway, Ernest, 132, 140, 144, 156, 199, 215; *quoted,* 134
Henry, Patrick, 88; *quoted,* 88–89
Hitler, Adolf, 215
Hoggart, Richard, *quoted,* 32

Index of Subjects

75 76 77 9 8 7 6 5 4 3 2 1

A NOTE TO STUDENTS:

When your instructor critiques your papers, lack of space and time dictate that he use a kind of shorthand. To be sure you understand these marks and the vocabulary of theme marginalia, you should become familiar with these symbols. When you find them on your papers, study the appropriate entries in your text.

JUN 2 9 1979

ABBREVIATIONS

ms.   Manuscript

¶   Paragraph

cl.   Your meaning is not clear.

⌒   Delete

awk.   Words do not go together smoothly.

Id   This is not idiomatic usage.

coh or coherence   Continuity is not clear.

GENERAL CONCEPTS

Your instructor may write, for instance, "See Transitions," or just the word or abbreviation.

Précis p. 10

Description pp. 22–24

Narration pp. 24–26

¶ Struc. pp. 31–32

Org. pp. 49–63

Intro. pp. 67–74

Fallacy pp. 159–171

Source? pp. 256–259

Concl. Conclusions pp. 74–77

Trans. Transitions pp. 63–67

Dev. Development pp. 88–102

Vivid Vivid style pp. 106–110

Efficient Efficient style pp. 112–119

Style Personal style pp. 119–129

d Proper diction pp. 178–183

Biblio form? Appropriate bibliographic entry? pp. 269–270